UK on a G-String

Adventures of the World's First and Worst Door-to-Door Busker

Justin Brown

THIS BOOK HAS BEEN WITHDRAWN FROM LIBRARY STOCK

PRICE: 50p

summersdale

First published by Random House New Zealand Ltd in 2002.

This edition published in 2004 by Summersdale Publishers Ltd.

This edition copyright © Justin Brown, 2004

All rights reserved.

The right of Justin Brown to be identified as the author of this work has been asserted in accordance with sections 77 and 78 of the Copyright, Designs and Patents Act 1988.

No part of this book may be reproduced by any means, nor transmitted, nor translated into a machine language, without the written permission of the publisher.

Summersdale Publishers Ltd
46 West Street
Chichester
West Sussex
PO19 1RP
UK

www.summersdale.com

Printed and bound in Great Britain.

ISBN 1 84024 379 1

MILTON KEYNES LIBRARIES	
H J	286163
914.204BRO	£7.99

Acknowledgements

To all those who fed me, watered me
and humoured me: thank you.
It was a hell of a ride, but so many people's
generosity made it all worthwhile.
Feel free to sing on my doorstep anytime.
Special thanks to Barnaby Bocock – web guru.

While all of these events occurred, some details have
been changed to protect people involved.
For Mum, who can't sing, and Dad, who is tone deaf:

Thanks for listening.

Contents

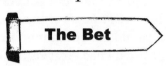

The Bet

door-to-door busker *n.* one who goes door to door, singing, hoping not to be told to bugger off. See: *beggar, bum, hobo, peddlar, homeless Kiwi idiot.*

Three hard things

Three of the hardest things I've ever had to do:
1. Do the opening act for Engelbert Humperdinck.
2. Sell my Mini even though I knew the lights weren't working.
3. Door-to-door busk my way around the UK in the middle of winter.

THE FIRST HAPPENED on a cold night in Wellington. I had been asked to do 15 minutes of comedy before the great Engelbert came out on stage. This is my break, I thought. This is the big time. Just me and Engelbert. I'm even staying in the same hotel; only he's on the eleventh floor and I'm on the first, looking at the back of a butcher's shop.

But that doesn't matter. I've got a mini bar and nice little chocolates on the bed, just like Engelbert. And I've got a room-service menu and Sky TV in my room, just like Engelbert. And I've got hair! Unlike Engelbert.

Then the panic set in. All the material I normally use on stage is targeted at young, drunk people on a Thursday night. As I looked around the Michael Fowler Centre there wouldn't have been a human under the age of 86; this was to be my downfall. I was devastated when I found out they were sober. Most were ladies with purple hair, their sons by their sides looking at me as if to say, 'You'd better be funny and you better not offend my mum. I paid $80 for this ticket.'

After singing my first song, entitled 'Kentucky Fried Kitten', I could see that I had indeed offended his mum and most of the audience. I'm sure if they weren't asleep the complaints desk would have been inundated.

Before the gig started I had great visions of Engelbert and me touring the country together, playing golf, drinking, and singing songs other than 'Please Release Me'. Instead, I never met him. The next morning I was just glad to be alive. It was as if I had been thrown into the comedy equivalent of going over the top of the trenches. I lay in the bath, eating chocolates and watching *The Karate Kid*.

Of course, selling the Mini was not as exhausting but was still mentally tough. I hate cars and the problem with selling one is that only the owner knows exactly what is wrong with it. Windscreen wipers scrape the glass, brakes don't work in the wet, clutch only works on Tuesdays. The problem with mine was a small one regarding the lights – they didn't work. At all. I always drove in the daytime. The only solution was to sell the car during the day.

'I'm calling about the Mini. Can I have a look at it tonight?' This was to be the only call I received all week. What's a man to do?

'Um, tonight?' I asked. 'When you say *tonight*, do you mean, when it's dark?'

'It's generally dark at night, yeah.'

I didn't like his attitude. It was a fair enough question. Night can mean a lot of things. It's dark 24 hours a day in Finland. Maybe I should sell my Mini up there?

'I only say tonight because I've got a lot of work to do when it gets dark. [Couldn't you be any more obvious! Why don't you just tell him about the bloody lights?] Can you drop by this afternoon?'

'I'll try,' he said.

'Great. Bring a torch.'

I sold him the car and walked home in the dark. The deal was made just as the sun was finishing work. It didn't feel good but I comforted myself by thinking that he looked like the kind of guy who could fix lights on a Mini. I don't know what that look is, but I definitely don't have it.

Door-to-door busking is something I tried in New Zealand when I was saving for an overseas trip. It is officially the hardest, most humiliating, most degrading thing I've ever had to do to make a buck. Instead of busking on the street and hoping people throw money, I decided a more personal way would be to corner them on their doorstep. This was five years earlier and, to be honest, I hadn't thought about it since. That was until a couple of months ago when a ludicrous, yet somehow alluring, bet with an Aussie mate grabbed my attention.

The bet is made

Auckland, Saturday, 11 August 2001
The game: All Blacks v Australia, Carisbrook, Dunedin

AS USUAL, ON the day of an All Black rugby test, the nation of New Zealand stops. Car salesmen lock their doors, real estate agents pack up their gear and supermarkets let their staff go home. The rest of the nation stocks the fridge with recently acquired additives.

Mates call each other to say, 'Have a good game', even though none of us are really playing. It just helps. It unites us. Makes us feel like we're in the dressing room and doing our bit to help the guys. Chances are we're as nervous as them anyway. Of course, the old rule applies: if the All Blacks win, we say *we* won. If the All Blacks lose, we say *they* lost. That's the luxury of being a fan and an armchair critic: you get the best of both worlds.

As I look outside I realise it's perfect rugby weather: cold, raining and miserable. The Australian team, hoping for blue skies and warm temperatures, will be in for a hell of a shock. Hopefully, the first of many today. To add insult to injury, they have to play in Dunedin, easily the coldest place in the country.

Unfortunately, or fortunately if we win, we have an Aussie who'll be sitting with us in the lounge. Mark's been a mate of mine for years, even if he does come from Melbourne. We met in a dodgy flat in Clapham, moved to a dodgy flat in Brixton and have kept in touch via dodgy emails. Mark's an actor and a very funny guy, but he can be extremely annoying, especially if Australia are winning. I don't mean ha-ha annoying, come-on-have-a-laugh-it's-only-a-game annoying. I mean it-normally-ends-in-tears-someone-will-have-an-eye-out annoying.

Things are going well. Everyone's getting along as I introduce Mark to my other mates. Once the sheep-shagging and rugby jokes are over the beer goes down well.

'So, Brownie, we gonna have a little wager on the game?' he asks me.

'Oh, yeah, suppose we could get a little sweepstake going. What do you reckon, guys?'

Nods of approval. Most are transfixed by re-runs of what the All Blacks did wrong last year. Why they show these before the real game I'll never know. Great for the confidence to see the Aussies win in the final minute, *again*. I just hope the All Blacks aren't watching it in their dressing room.

'Oh, remember that, guys, John Eales' penalty in the last minute? That must have ripped your nightie!' Mark says, opening another Fosters.

'Sheep-shagger!'

'So, come on, are we gonna get a wager going or not?'

'All right, all right, keep your hair on,' I say. 'Tenner each, closest to the final score?'

'Na, bugger that,' Mark says. 'That's chicken feed. Listen, let's get a real bet going here. Put your balls on the line, ya buncha Kiwi slackers.'

'Twenty?'

'Na,' Mark slurps.

'More than thirty? Mark, I don't want to take your money off you, mate. I know you're a struggling actor.'

That much was true. He had the great ambition of being the next Heath Ledger, but in the last two years had only scored one acting role: a priest in a Fuji ad.

'OK, what do you want to bet?' I ask.

'I was thinking about it on the plane yesterday. How we should have a bet that means more than just a free round.'

'Yeah … for example?'

'For example, what's the most embarrassing thing you've ever done?'

'Why?'

'Just tell me.'

'How do you define embarrassing?'

'You made a fool of yourself, something you'd never do again even if you were paid.'

'Why?'

'Well, instead of betting for money we should bet that, should the All Blacks lose, you have to re-enact the most embarrassing thing and vice versa. We'll have proper rules and everything. We've got witnesses. So, what's the most embarrassing thing you've ever done?'

'Door-to-door busking. What about you?'

'That's easy. I was with my mates at a rugby match in Oz last year. We were on the piss big time and someone dared me to streak across the field.'

'Did you?'

'Bloody oath I did. I was smashed.'

'You never told me that. You had no problem taking your clothes off?'

'Mate, I'm an actor. I probably take my clothes off once a week for ad auditions. I was out there before he'd finished the dare.'

'And what happened?'

The boys had become bored watching re-runs and were now listening to Mark's fable. 'The crowd went nuts, mate. I ran out to the middle, completely starkers, flashing it about and was taken out by a security guard just before I got to the players. Only problem was it was freezing and –'

'Don't tell me.'

'Yep …'

'You bloody idiot, don't say what I think you're going to say. You'll let us down as a species.'

'You better believe it. I had major shrinkage going on downstairs! In front of twenty thousand punters.'

'You streaked in the middle of winter, of course you're gonna get shrinkage!'

The telly was now muted. Everyone was hoping for a disastrous ending.

'By this time I had a sweatshirt draped across my face. Thank God, I thought, no one can recognise me. I was dragged off the field and the crowd got louder and louder as I got nearer to the stands. I was paranoid by this stage. I wanted to cover myself, started feeling like a right idiot.'

'Bit late for that, mate.'

'It got worse,' he continued. 'Just as I was thinking how lucky I was that no one but my mates were in the audience, I heard a cackly voice and a bunch of chicks laughing –'

'No! Get outta town. This is brilliant. Who was it?'

'Tanya, my ex, and her friends.'

'Brilliant. Oh, you've made my day!' I refilled my glass.

'All I heard was, "Hi, Mark. You a bit cold there, darling?" Then the security guard, smart arse, says, "Know those ladies, do you, mate? Bit of a shame she has to see you like this, or *not* like this as the case may be."'

'Couldn't have happened to a nicer guy.'

I sensed from the laughter in the room that everyone agreed.

'So, you reckon door-to-door busking is the most embarrassing thing you've done?' Mark asked, opening his sixth Fosters.

'Definitely,' I said.

'But that was in New Zealand, right?'

I nodded. The look on Mark's face made me shiver.

'OK, here's the go,' he continued to an attentive audience. 'If the All Blacks lose, you have to go to England in the middle of winter and door-to-door busk and make enough money for a flight home.'

'You're joking! How much would that be?'

'I dunno. 'Bout five hundred quid, I suppose.'

'That's impossible,' I said. 'That'll take me months. And what do you have to do?'

'You name it, mate, I'll do it. I just know the Aussies are gonna thrash the All Blacks.'

Thinking of a similar punishment wasn't difficult. All the pain and embarrassment of door-to-door busking came flooding back to me.

'OK, if the Aussies lose, which they will, you … have to go to Wimbledon and streak in the men's semi-final.'

'Get a life, Brown. You can't even get tickets to Wimbledon.'

'Not my problem, mate.'

'In front of millions? Yours is so much easier. At least you've done it before.'

'So have you. Look, for sheer endurance mine is harder. Five hundred pounds, Mark! Walking round in the cold for two months getting doors slammed in my face. You take your clothes off for ten seconds in the middle of summer. As you say, you do it every day anyway. Why not do it in front of ten thousand Poms?'

This is crazy, I thought. I can't go to the UK in the middle of winter and knock on people's doors. I've been to the UK, but that was summer, we were sitting outside a beautiful pub in the Cotswolds. We were drinking and laughing and socialising, *not* terrorising someone on their doorstep.

Then again, I do have confidence in the All Blacks and we do have witnesses. Mark was thinking; for the first time today he was pensive. A ray of light shone from the bottom of my beer glass – imagine if the All Blacks won and he did have to streak at Wimbledon. It would be fantastic!

'At least it'd be summer, mate,' I said. 'No shrinkage.'

'You're on. Hope you lose.'

'Likewise.'

As we opened a new tray of beer I decided this was ridiculous. Right up there with the most stupid thing I've ever done. I'm not a betting man, yet, now, everything was riding on 80 minutes of rugby.

Everyone was watching for a reason.

The whistle went.

The bet was on.

– 2 –

The Game

THE LOUNGE HAD taken on a different persona since the bet was made. True, this was an important match; New Zealand playing Australia always was, but now the room was brimming with anticipation, as if at any minute the walls might burst.

The more beer I drank, the better I felt about my decision. Every now and again Mark and I would try to ease the pain by slipping in a few jokes, but there was no point. It was only a matter of time, 80 minutes in fact, before one of our lives would change for the worse. Three things were heavily in my favour:

1. The Australian Wallabies had never won in Dunedin.

2. The Wallabies had lost to South Africa two weeks previously.

3. Um, there is no third, it's just that you always need three points to make an argument sound complete, don't you think? That last one should be the clincher, the argument winner; just like 'C' if you're using the more orthodox A, B, C method.

Anyway, I digress.

'– Tony Brown gets the match under way, New Zealand versus the Wallabies! Can the Wallabies beat the All Blacks for the first time ever in Dunedin?'

The game had started and we all moved to within six feet of the telly. The crowd, the commentary, the buzz of it all hit us like a drug at the same time. The All Blacks performed the legendary haka. If you've never seen the haka before, it's a Maori war dance used to scare the absolute hell out of a team before they even start the game. It's pretty scary all right. I just wish the New Zealand cricketers would use the same tactics; to see a haka at Lord's would be hilarious.

'Hell hath no fury like an Australian team who lost the week before,' Mark assured us. 'We're gonna waste the All Blacks. I can feel it.'

If he was faking, he was very good. Then again, he was an actor. Something didn't feel right. I was worried. Turns out I didn't need to be. Jonah Lomu chased a kick within the first five minutes and scored. The stadium erupted, the All Blacks embraced and Australian captain John Eales looked uneasy.

'You beauty, you little beauty. Goodnight Australia, thanks for coming!' the Kiwis in the room screamed.

'Shit,' Mark mumbled.

'What's that, Mark? Better buy that ticket now, big boy. You know how hard it is to get a ticket to Wimbledon.'

'Early days yet, mate.' He opened another Fosters. We moved closer to the TV.

'Early days? Jonah just scored in the first five minutes in his fiftieth test. You've got no chance. The All Blacks are back to their best.'

And you know what? I believed it.

That was until half-time. The Wallabies led 10–5, with

the only brilliance from the All Blacks coming from Jonah's try in the first couple of minutes. Now I really was worried. Heaven bless the people who don't even follow sport; they would never have gotten themselves into this mess. Look on the bright side, I try to tell myself. There's still 40 minutes to go, the beers are still cold, got your mates with you, still a prospect of a win, anything could happen. Most importantly, that's 40 minutes you still have a friend from Australia. Forty minutes when he and I can tell jokes and still be mates and *like* each other. But, in 40 minutes, it will all change. I will laugh. Or he will laugh. Either way we will no longer be mates. We will try to act impartial and say well done but it will end in tears. All over a game of rugby. All over a stupid bet. And the All Blacks are trailing 5–10.

The first points in the second half went to the All Blacks and all of a sudden things weren't looking so bad. I even saw the sun breaking through the clouds outside. Mark was wriggling around in his chair, the Kiwis were full of beans and the sound of a fresh beer being opened signalled, 'Wow, it's gonna be a great night, who cares about tomorrow?' That was until the Aussies scored next. Now when I looked at my beer it made me feel sick. It wasn't a happy beer. It was saying, 'You've had six already. Not only are the All Blacks going to lose, you're also going to feel like you've eaten the carpet tomorrow morning. Think about it. Have a juice.'

Australia was 13–8 ahead and I could feel our friendship starting to wane. Mark's bright yellow Australian cricket shirt was blinding me and making me feel like I'd *already* eaten the carpet. To be fair, he was outnumbered; everyone else was wearing an All Black shirt but for some reason his was glowing, like a light bulb at the end of a very dim corridor.

The TV was turned up again, as if somehow this solitary act of urgency would make the All Blacks perform better.

A two-year-old asks if someone will play with him; he's ignored. A restless girlfriend decides to head outside for a ciggie via the TV: 'Oh, get out the way will you, love? There's a game on. Can you be a sweetie and get me another beer?'

'Yeah, yeah, all right,' she concedes.

Despite the increase in volume, things are still going seriously wrong. Once upon a time, a few years ago, the All Blacks could have dug themselves out of a hole like this, but one has the feeling it's not going to happen today.

And you know the All Blacks have had a bad game if the ladies in the room, who, 80 minutes beforehand showed no interest whatsoever, can pick exactly what went wrong: 'Well, every time we have a lineout and have the throw in, we lose the ball. We have no go-forward and they looked completely disorganised.'

'Yeah, we all know that, darling. We just didn't want to say it out loud.'

'Come on, you guys, play like you used to. Stop pussyfooting around,' I yelled at the TV.

'Face it, Brown, you're gonna lose. Pack your bags.'

'To be honest, Mark, I don't even care about this team any more. I gave up on them last year.'

'So you don't care about them?' he repeated.

'Couldn't care less. I've watched every game for the last five years. I get up at three in the morning. I'm a dedicated and loyal fan. Now look what they do. They go and lose and play like the Argentinian Second XV. I give up. I can't do it any more. These guys are useless.'

All of a sudden Jonah had the ball and was running down the wing like a black truck on speed.

'Go, Jonah! Go boy! Run like crap!' I screamed. 'Pass it, pass it, oh pass it, you idiot! Oh, you bloody idiot!'

Mark raised his eyebrows. 'Not that you care, eh?'

'Yeah, well.' I hung my head in my lap.

I'd like to say the All Blacks made a miraculous comeback. I'd love to tell you Jonah scored two more tries and we flushed Mark's Australian cricket shirt down the toilet but I'd be lying. Jonah did assist in a try late in the game but by that stage Australia had won.

'And there we have it,' the commentator droned. 'The world champion Australians have done it again, beating the All Blacks by twenty-three to fifteen. John Eales has steered the Wallabies to their first Carisbrook win in eleven attempts dating back to 1905.'

'Cheer up, mate, it's only a game,' Mark said.

'Oh, don't start with that crap. It's *only* a game. It's not *only* a game.'

'No, let me finish. I want to say what you always said to me when the All Blacks beat the Aussies. It's only a game – but *we* won.'

The Australian captain came on screen for an interview. The elation in his eyes matched Mark's. I'm sure what I was hearing John Eales saying was different to the rest of the room: Everyone else – 'Yeah, well, it was a good game. We just tried to get good ball and keep pressure on the All Blacks. I'm really proud of the boys.'

Me – 'Yeah, well, it was a good game. We won. We're the best. Get packing, busker boy.'

'What a captain.' Mark opened another beer. 'You know what his nickname is?'

The room looked completely disinterested. I wondered where my long johns were.

'John Eales's nickname is "Nobody". You wanna know why?'

The lack of interest had now turned into a groan. As I

looked around I saw a serious case of the 'I don't want to go to work on Monday' blues.

''Cos Nobody's perfect,' he laughed. No one else did.

'Jeez, cheer up, you lot. At least you haven't just lost a stupid bet,' I said.

They smiled. So did Mark. John Eales was still on the telly. That long, angular, distorted face belonging to Australia's most successful captain would haunt me for the next six months. When I'm in the UK freezing my butt off, he would be on my right shoulder laughing, singing and telling me what it's like to be Nobody.

I looked outside. The rain had started again.

'Who wants to go to the pub?' Mark asked. 'Come on, I'm only in Auckland for one night.'

'Yeah, all right, might as well,' the guys mumbled. 'Drown our sorrows.'

'That's the way. What about you, Brown? Come on, plenty of time to pack tomorrow.'

The fresh air was great. Even the Kiwis started to feel better. That was until we walked past the service station and picked up the *New Zealand Herald*.

After nearly one hundred years of trying, the Wallabies finally beat the All Blacks at Carisbrook to retain the Bledisloe Cup. Not only that, a Kiwi idiot also lost a bet and now has to go door-to-door busking around the UK.

Stupid boy.

What have I done?

3

Flight or Fright

Auckland: cloudy, muggy, 22 °C

AFTER SAYING GOODBYE to my loved ones I headed to the airport. Now, normally when you go to the airport you at least have *some* idea of what will happen in the near future. For example, within three hours I will be sitting in the sun in Fiji. Within eight hours I will be checking into my hotel in Hong Kong.

Whereas in my case it was, 'In twenty-eight hours I will arrive in a country where I will freeze my buns off knocking on doors. Where I will eat and sleep I have absolutely no idea.'

As I wheeled my creaky trolley towards the lady at the flight desk I wondered (like you always do), have I brought too much stuff? But I had no one to consult. I mean, how much *should* a door-to-door busker take when travelling? I don't even know any door-to-door buskers! Maybe I should start a club: ('Hi, I'm Warren and I'm a door-to-door busker.'

'Lose a bet did you, Warren?'

'Shut your mouth.')

My pack seemed very heavy, mainly due to the duffel coat I'd purchased in a dodgy second-hand shop in K Road, Auckland.

'What the hell do you need this for?' the young shop assistant had asked me.

'I'm going to England.'

'It's *summer*,' he said, emphasising the very word that emitted the smell of beach, barbecue and beer.

'I lost a bet and have to go to England.'

I explained the bet, something I realised I would have to do many times over in the next few months.

'Why don't you just not do it?' he asked.

'I have to.'

'Why? *I* wouldn't.'

'Because he'll track me down and castrate me.'

'So, will you think twice before you make another bet like this?'

'Course not. Gotta live a little.'

As I walked out of the shop, wondering whether I should hire a small boy to carry this wretched second-hand rug with arms, I thought to myself, why *don't* I just stay at home? How the hell is Mark ever going to know if I don't do it? He's in Australia for God's sake. But then I looked at the duffel coat and my empty wallet. Oh, screw him, I've come this far. I'm psyched up now. It's like I'm waiting to bat and I've been in the nets for months. Priming up, getting fired up for anything that the Poms can throw at me. If I called it off it'd be like cancelling the game. Sure you can go home and get pissed afterwards but something would be missing. I'd feel like I'd cheated. Wait a minute – who am I kidding here? I'm a door-to-door busker for God's sake, you'd think I was talking about an Olympic event.

A few things had been happening at home that suggested I wasn't completely relaxed about this time in my life. For a start, I had been dreaming like a madman. Some of my more interesting dreams included:

1.   Imaginary dinner plates falling off the wall above my bed.
2.   Water coming through the wall.
3.   Dead guys waking up and spraying water all over my feet. (What the hell is it about water?)
4.   Walking around the back of an old woman's house, coming in the back door, scaring the hell out of her and suddenly her house starts to sink and there's water coming through the walls. Again, water.

And if I was to be completely honest, the prospect of door-to-door busking in the middle of winter in the UK presented me with more than a few anxious moments:

> Will I get beaten up?
> Will I ever get to the doorstep and forget how to play my guitar?
> Will I get to the doorstep and there'll be no door?
> Will I get beaten up?

Other things I worried about:

> The cold
> Mean people
> Cold fingers
> Finding somewhere to sleep

Things I was looking forward to:

> Warm pubs
> Warm beer
> Villages
> Finding somewhere to sleep.

IT'S WEIRD, BUT one major fear – even worse than getting beaten up – was that every doorstep would contain a scraggly old woman with a sharp broom; the kind of woman who'd had an extremely hard life; the kind of woman who in one instant could dismiss you with a witty one liner and make you feel as small as a toothbrush. She'd look at me as if I'd just committed a heinous crime, boot me out onto the street and shove snowballs down the back of my shirt.

Basically, I feared that what could go wrong would go wrong. Sometimes it made me sick just thinking about it. My last week in New Zealand was spent in the sun, playing golf, lapping up every moment where I wouldn't have to make an arse of myself. I'd wander around my neighbourhood where I saw old men watering (bloody water, I tell you!) their gardens. There they were with a cold beer in their hand, content, knowing that along with the best weather of the year would also come cricket matches on TV, barbecues, beer and flip-flops. I was intensely jealous and on more than one occasion wanted to stay home. Bugger the stupid bet.

Maybe the water theme in my dreams had something to do with New Zealand's physical place in the world, i.e. the arse end of it. Our isolation is extreme, which can be a curse and a blessing. There really is no other option than to jump on a jumbo. You live in France: you can get the train to England. You live in Spain: you can drive to Portugal. You live in New Zealand: you have to reserve three days of your life, sit next to a coughing, snoring, dribbling, wriggling, armrest-thieving stranger for 28 sodding hours before you can even think about walking down Oxford Street.

That chunk of water between New Zealand and the UK looks quite the romantic distance on the map, that is until you get on the plane and see that demoralising red line which tells you how far the plane has flown in the last hour. Sometimes you've got to wonder whether the plane has really moved at all. I mean, the scenery's not moving, we're not passing petrol stations and there are no traffic lights. Speaking of which, I wonder how long it *would* take to drive to London? How boring would the scenery be? How many toilet stops would you need? How many games of 'I spy' and 'My mother went shopping'?

'Darling, can you pick up some milk on the way home?'

'I would but I think I'm gonna be a while. Stuck in Tonga.'

'Oh, hell, that new road again, is it?'

''Fraid so. Why they do it on a Friday I'll never know.'

'Is the car going OK?'

'Not bad but the petrol light's been on since Hong Kong.'

'I think it's broken. Will you be late?'

'Just gotta pick up some fags in Melbourne ...'

During these moments of fear, hysteria and near nausea I decided to ring my mate Phil the Pom. He'll comfort me, I thought. He'll let me know what it's really like in the motherland. He'll tell me that door-to-door busking is a great idea and I'll get the money in no time. However, his first words didn't exactly inspire me: 'The Poms are very insular. It will be the middle of winter, people hibernate. They live in their cocoon and don't move. They're not going to open the door to some stranger with a guitar.'

Did I say *inspire*?

'And it's very cold up north. The country is designed for indoor living. They're not going to hold the door open and listen to you sing. Why don't you go in summer?'

'I didn't get a bloody choice, mate, I lost a bet. The reason he wanted me to do it in the middle of winter was so I'd freeze my balls off and embarrass myself.'

'Not much of a mate, is he?'

I was beginning to think exactly the same thing.

He continued: 'Just do it in Leicester Square. I've seen some great buskers there. You could make loads of money provided you were any good. Lot easier doing it on the street, you know. I've never heard of doing it door to door.'

'Exactly.'

'Well, mate, all I can say is you've got your work cut out for you.'

'Tell me, then, you're an outgoing guy *and* you're a Pom. What would you do? Please say, "I'd invite you in for a cuppa. I'd commend you on your bravery. I'd offer you a hot roast meal and get you to warm the bed for my half-Swedish teenage daughter."'

'I'd tell you to bugger off, I've got other things to do.'

'Like what?'

'Read the paper, watch TV.'

'Oh, how boring.'

'I'm serious. Be careful, you might get beaten up.'

AS I CHECKED in at the flight desk the girl spotted my guitar and asked, 'So, you're the in-flight entertainment, are you?'

'Something like that. Reckon I could rark it up at four in the morning?'

'Can always give it a try.'

Nice. Sense of humour. Something I may not see for a while. Maybe busking on the plane wasn't such a bad idea? I could be the world's first seat-to-seat busker. I can imagine the trolley dollies might get a little upset but at least I'd have a captive audience and drinks would be free.

Fortunately the coughing, snoring, dribbling, wriggling, armrest-thieving stranger wasn't on this flight, but the headrest-yanking grandma was definitely in full swing. I was busy watching the little red line following the plane's progress when my headrest was nearly ripped off by what can only be described as He Woman. He/she belted me on the shoulder like your mother used to do when she was at her wit's end. I'm sure there were bullet holes in my shoulders from where her nasty little digits had poked.

'Oi! Move your chair forward while I'm trying to eat!'

'All right, all right, keep your hair on,' I muttered.

'And don't put it so far back. I haven't got room for my legs!'

'All right, all right.'

Every time she got up (which was quite often, obviously the rest of her body disagreed with her as much as I did), she'd yank my headrest so far back I thought she was going to rip it off. Just as I was about to nod off, it was as if she knew – whoof! The headrest would spring backwards and my slumber would be interrupted.

I gave up trying to sleep and spoke to the nine year old sitting next to me. She looked excited. She didn't yank headrests. She never needed to go to the toilet. I liked her already. I explained to her and her mother about the bet. Confusion reigned on the mother's face while Alexandra, my new little friend, asked the bleeding obvious: 'Why are you going all the way over there knocking on people's doors just so you can earn enough money to get home again? Why don't you just stay here?'

I stared at the red line thinking, 'Now that *is* a bloody good question – '

Three hours into the flight, in a moment of panic and homesickness, I decided I should orchestrate some sort of plan. And since I was a busker, albeit not a very experienced one, maybe a song would come in useful as well. I only had one song I felt confident about – 'Kentucky Fried Kitten' –

the song I had sung at the Engelbert Humperdinck gig. But seeing as it went down like a lead balloon on that fateful night, I thought I should pen a new one.

I remember learning 'Yellow Brick Road' and 'Blowing in the Wind' in my bedroom till three in the morning, playing the same chords over and over again. I didn't pick up a guitar till I was 19. If you heard me play you'd believe me. I remember thinking I was the duck's nuts because I could run into a music shop and memorise the chords for 'Happy Birthday' without buying the book. I really thought that was quite a coup. I always imagined the music police (who would have a very tuneful siren I would think) would track me down at any minute.

'Oi, you get in there and buy *101 Campfire Songs*. Don't just steal the chords!'

But the music police never arrived and I continued to play 'Happy Birthday' illegally.

Even though I spent hours in my room butchering very average sing-a-long songs, never in a million years did I imagine I'd be flying to the UK having to knock on doors. I did, however, realise the importance of choosing a very good song to attack with.

In the meantime, a quiet beer and movie was on the cards. Amid the selection of crappy movies you wouldn't get out on video even if you had tonsillitis, I flicked on Dudley Moore in *Arthur*. I'd always heard about this movie but had never watched it. What a classic! It's true what they say, they don't make movies like this any more. Thankfully, political correctness wasn't around then. Let me set the scene: Dudley Moore is having dinner with a prostitute in a swanky restaurant. He is absolutely trolleyed.

Prostitute: 'My mother died when I was six.'

'Uh huh ...' says Dudley.

'And my father raped me when I was twelve.'

'Oh … so you had six years of relative happiness then.'

I howled. Even He Woman couldn't disturb me. I looked across at Alexandra who was reading *Harry Potter.*

Harry Potter! That's it, I thought. My song! It's topical, all the mums will give me money and kids will love it. Either that or throw tomatoes. But, hey, I'm a door-to-door busker. Can't be fussy.

I wrote a song called 'Grow up Harry Potter' on a used napkin. It's a touching number about how Harry will soon have to find a real job as magic won't pay the bills forever. Eventually he'll end up like Drew Barrymore, a child star and spoilt brat who in a moment of weakness turns to drugs, crime and debauchery. Don't get me wrong, I don't dislike Harry Potter (or drugs and debauchery). I've never even read the books. I also think it's brilliant that J. K. Rowling has encouraged millions of kids to read. I just felt it was time there was an evil song written about the over-achieving little blighter.

My mother, bless her, had given me a printout of *The Joy of Busking* by an American lecturer called Ray Dessey. She'd found it on the Internet and thought it would help me not get beaten up. Right about the time my nostrils were starting to seize up due to the air conditioning, I decided to concentrate on pudding and Ray Dessey.

Busking is a British term that means playing music for bystanders. Sometimes a licence is needed.

Not door to door it's not, Ray, although maybe I should check that once I get to London.

Certainly respect the sound radius of other buskers, particularly if you don't speak the local language well.

I'm hoping most home dwellers in England speak English; I don't even want to imagine the consequences if they don't. Trying to explain to some poor Polish immigrant that I lost a bet with a half-naked Aussie would be exhausting.

Don't try to compete at close distances with someone who is technically superior or who has a repertoire that is more attractive.

That's exactly why I do it door to door – I don't have a repertoire. I don't have more than three chords, let alone three songs. I'm also starting to fancy the idea of taking something other than the guitar. Bagpipes perhaps. Or a piano. What about juggling knives, that would get a reaction. Sorry, Ray, you were saying?

It's essential to match the wants and needs of the audience, not just play your own preferences.

Well, you see, Ray, this is a big problem for me. It's not a matter of choice, more one of desperation. I'm not going to learn 'Careless Whisper' and 'Unchained Melody' for the sake of one person. I have one song I will play the entire trip and that song is written on a napkin in front of me. It's rude, offensive and controversial. And a little tuneful.

Older audiences will enjoy well-known Baroque pieces, but younger audiences may require the Blues, Jazz, or something even harder. Old favourites go well, and songs from the turn of the century bring back memories to certain age groups.

What?

When the audience starts to fidget, that's the time to switch it.

That is, unless they're standing in their own house and their fidget turns into a quick grab for the nearest crowbar. I'm scared of getting beaten up, Ray. Are you busy over the next month?

Take the time to compare buskers. Shop around. Give money to the best one, then the others will try to perform as well as him.

You're having a laugh, Ray. What other idiot is going to wander around knocking on doors singing Kenny Rogers in the middle of winter? Honestly, how did you get that degree?

Maybe it was the lack of sleep and lack of real oxygen but Ray wasn't really making much sense to me. And I'd given up watching the little red line following the plane. It really was too depressing. We hadn't even gone a quarter of the way. I set about reading the so-called contract Mark had given me. It smelt of beer.

Busker Boy's Contract (Go the Wallabies! Ha, ha)
1.   Justin must door-to-door busk his way around the United Kingdom all in a vain attempt to make enough money for a flight home.
2.   He must not be there longer than two months.
3.   If this is completed successfully and Justin arrives back within two months, Mark will make a special trip to Auckland to congratulate him.
4.   If he doesn't bring ciggies and beer home, he's dead.

THEY SAY YOU should try and put positive images in your mind when you're facing a fresh challenge. Only problem was, every time I thought about my door-to-door busking experiences back home, I felt woozy.

I remember it as clear as day; that fateful afternoon back in '96. For some reason I thought door-to-door busking would be more *personal* than busking on the street. It meant I could just play the same tripe all day and the only head I'd do in would be my own. You might argue that buskers on the street play the same song all day as well, but we never really know; we can only walk past, look the other way and hope like hell we don't make eye contact. Something about cornering someone on their own doorstep intrigued me; plus if your performance stinks, at least a whole shopping mall isn't going to know about it.

I remember lying on the couch watching the cricket, drinking Coke and eating a well-crafted chicken and avocado sandwich.

'Get out there. You're supposed to be busking today,' my conscience said.

Another wicket fell. One more over, I thought. Then I'll get out there.

'Six runs! New Zealand only need thirty-five to win,' the TV screamed at me.

One more over. I'll even tune the guitar. That's a start.

'Four runs! New Zealand really have a chance now.'

Eventually I rolled off the couch and moped out the door. New Zealand were definitely going to lose, they always do in this situation. I strapped the guitar on and wandered into unknown territory.

I made a corporate decision with myself that the opening line is imperative. It must have a hook. It must have sincerity. The following few entered my head:

'Hi, I play guitar. Got any sausages in the fridge?'

'I see you've got a thirty-four-inch telly. Don't suppose you know the score in the cricket?'

'Hi, I found this guitar on your lawn.'

I finally settled on this: 'Hi, don't worry, I'm not from the Mormons or Amway. I'm here to sing you a comedy song. If you like the song, you can give me some money towards university. If you don't, you can tell me to bugger off.'

'Bugger off!' came the reply.

I got this response from the first six houses. I felt a very strong desire to retreat to the couch to find out how much New Zealand had lost by.

Then, finally, a woman gave me $2! I held the coin in my hand as if I'd discovered Rome.

'You're my first. This is a special moment. I won't forget this.'

I kept walking and had made about $8 when I came to a beautiful house with a new Jeep and Honda in the driveway, to be greeted by a big lady with a warm smile. A welcome change. I gave her my spiel and she said, 'Go on then, I've had a hard day.'

Her husband wandered out in his dressing gown, listened and told me he loved it.

'Can you play another one?' he asked.

'I can, but the next one's rude. Can you handle rude?'

'Listen, mate. I've got cancer, only a few months to live. I think I can handle rude!'

He ran inside to grab his video camera and taped me on his front lawn, chuckling away. He handed me $6.50 and as I walked down the street he yelled, 'You've made my day!'

The feeling was mutual.

One of the biggest worries about door-to-door busking is: what if you get to the stranger's door and you simply feel too nervous to do your spiel? For example, you can hear from the doorstep they've had to prematurely finish a phone call, slammed the phone down and now they're storming towards the door.

I normally start walking away but Murphy's Law never lets me down.

'Can I help you there?' they yell.

Now what do I say? I don't have the confidence to do my Amway spiel and I know they're wondering, 'What the hell is this jerk wandering around my house with a guitar for?'

My normal response is, 'I don't suppose ... John still lives here,' followed by flight.

I SAT THERE nursing my warm beer, seriously doubting what I had just embarked upon. I admired Alexandra next to me. I even admired He Woman. They're not scared out of their brains, I thought. They don't have to knock on doors and sing for their supper tonight. They can relax. They think I'm an idiot.

My guitar lay there like a new schoolmate. I wanted to ask him questions. Will this be an absolute disaster? Where do I start? Will you let me down? Will you sound good if I play with gloves on?

The harsh reality (and one that I'm sure Mark was aware of when he made the bet) was that I *would* have to wear gloves while I played guitar. It was, after all, the middle of winter and I'd be walking the streets for hours. Ask any guitar player, playing with cold hands is nearly impossible. You can't feel the frets. You don't know where your fingers should be landing. You're a lost lamb. And that's the good players, not to mention hackers like me.

Just like having to leave the couch when I was watching the cricket in New Zealand, I would have to make another executive decision and get ready to sing as soon as I hit London. Unfortunately, for the first time ever I slept like a baby on the plane and before I knew it we had arrived at Heathrow.

I checked my contract one more time. It's now or never, Brown. I strapped my guitar on and headed for the door.

'Good luck on your trip,' Alexandra said as we walked off the plane.

'Thanks. Thanks a lot.'

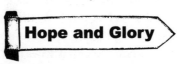

4

Hope and Glory

Stratford, East London

OK, SO I'VE never fought in a war. I've never milked a poisonous snake in the Congo. I've never been held at gunpoint crossing the Ethiopian border. All right, I admit, I'm a complete Nancy-boy. I've never even cooked for more than two people at once.

But I *have* had to open for Engelbert Humperdinck and let me tell you, it was no laughing matter.

The very feelings I experienced on that evening in Wellington were not dissimilar to the feelings I felt as soon as I arrived in London.

> What the hell am I doing?
> Why do I need to go for another shit?
> Why do I put myself in these situations?
> How will I sleep tonight?
> Where will I sleep tonight?
> Will people laugh at me?
> Well, of course, they'll *laugh* but will they, you know, *point* and laugh?
> Will I get beaten up?

IN SOME WAYS I was over the moon to get the Engelbert gig. I mean, opening for someone that big is something to be proud of, right? It's something to tell your grandkids. Hell, Engelbert could tell his *now*. But something didn't feel right on the night. Don't get me wrong; getting flown down to Wellington was lovely and reading the paper was very nice, but you knew you weren't going to Wellington for a boozy weekend. You were going to Wellington to commit comedy suicide. Reading the paper and enjoying the flight were my last rites as a fundamentally normal human being. You could even chat to people: 'Really, your son's twenty-first? That'll be quite a party.'

'Yes, he's grown up so fast. What about you, what will you be doing in Wellington?'

'Excuse me, I need to go to the toilet ...'

I talked twenty-first birthdays' food for as long as I could with the middle-aged mum, but as my last piece of quiche wriggled down my throat I realised we would soon be arriving in Wellington. I would have to introduce myself to Engelbert. I would have to make him laugh. He would ask me to play golf with him. Then he would invite me into his private limo and we would ride together as rock gods all the way to the Michael Fowler Centre, where we would breeze through sound check, order room service and practise our putting in his penthouse suite.

It wasn't entirely unlike that. Who the hell am I trying to kid? It was the complete opposite. Engelbert jumped into his white limo; I wandered down the street in the rain and paid for a shuttle bus.

However, there was one moment I will treasure forever, one moment I will definitely tell my grandkids. I walked into the Park Royal in Wellington, complete with pretentious sunglasses, second-hand guitar on back and wannabe rock star walk.

'Good afternoon, sir. Can we help you?'

'I'm with the band.'

I've always wanted to say that! It's like opening the batting at Lord's or kicking a ball around Stadium Australia. Stupid boyhood dream stuff that, no matter what swanky job we now possess, never, ever leaves us. I guarantee, if you gave your husband a choice of playing 40 minutes for the All Blacks at Ellis Park or a job for life with a salary of $200,000 a year, I know exactly what he'd do. I also know you wouldn't own a credit card. In fact, you'd be living in a cardboard box by the motorway. You, freezing your arse off trying to keep warm by inhaling exhaust fumes of cars passing by. Your sad, pathetic husband holding his team photo like some demented chimp, pointing to him with the ball, screaming, 'That's me, Raewyn. That's me!'

I was shown to my room, knowing that I would be on stage in less than three hours. A piece of A4 paper found its way under the door. What is that, I thought? Some kind of conspiracy, perhaps? Maybe Engelbert is inviting me out for pre-dinner drinks? Doubt it, it was just the room list.

Brown Justin Room	113
Humperdinck Engelbert Room	820
Dorsey Patricia Room	819
Dorsey Louise Room	715
Dorsey Bradley Room	717

As I said earlier, my room looked onto the back of a butcher's shop, but Engelbert stayed in the Penthouse on the eighth floor. Which was fair enough, I just thought he may have asked me up for a few G and Ts and some chips 'n' dip. We could even practise our seven irons by blasting them across Wellington Harbour.

And who the hell are all these Dorseys? Are they all family?

Are the Humperdincks not telling us something? I had read that when Engelbert was in his heyday he used the line 'Married but available'. He's been married 37 years but had two kids to different women in between. Maybe *he's* going out with all the Dorseys? Maybe he has some strange fetish whereby he has to date someone with the last name Dorsey.

You can imagine Engelbert, lying in bed after a mammoth love-making session: 'God, you're gorgeous! You're intelligent, bubbly, vivacious but there is one thing wrong with us.'

'What's that, Humpy Dinky?' she says stroking his chest.

'Your name's not Dorsey.'

'How do you know?'

'Well, is it?'

'No.'

'See, told you! It won't last. Humpy Dinky only dates Dorseys.'

'What a shame. I thought we had a love that could last forever.'

'What *is* your name?'

Backstage I felt like the kid at school who never got picked for the sports team. Roadies, technicians, make-up crew, backing singers. All these people knew each other. It wasn't fair. They were laughing and joking in stupid accents. They knew exactly what they were doing. This was just another day for them. Another show, another city. Whereas for the boy from Room 113, it was a time of nerves, anxiety and incontinence. I felt very, very unfunny. Not a good look if you had to get on stage and have people in stitches. At that very moment I wished *I* was in stitches; hospital looked a better option than singing before Engelbert.

Three middle-aged guys with ponytails asked me on stage as a sound-check was required. I was shaking. My guitar lead didn't work. I sang my song to two thousand empty seats.

Another man introduced himself as the stadium announcer. He's the guy that says, 'Laaaadieeeeess and gentlemen!' He needed to know what my last words would be. I explained to him, in the nicest possible way, I had no idea what my first bloody words would be.

I considered ducking up to my room to catch a bit of TV as a technique to stop thinking about my performance. Instead, I decided to socialise, and lucky I did because I met a Dorsey!

'So, what do you do here?' I asked the guy about my age wondering where he might fit into the Dorsey love triangle.

'Merch,' he replied.

'Merch, what's merch?' I asked.

'Merchandise. Hats, T-shirts, CDs, tapes.'

'Cool, so you travel around the world and sell stuff for Engelbert Humperdinck?'

'Dad? Yeah.'

'Dad? Wait a minute, back the truck up.'

'He's my dad.'

'But [this was getting stranger by the minute], but, your name's Dorsey, right?'

'Yeah, so is his.'

'No, it's not, it's Humperdinck!' I said proudly.

'His real name is Dorsey – Arnold Dorsey.'

Bugger me, I don't know what's worse. Changing your name from Arnold Dorsey to Engelbert Humperdinck is the equivalent of living in Chernobyl half your life, then moving to Rwanda in your twilight years. Then again, he's sold a ton of records. And I bet *he* wasn't shitting himself at this very minute.

'What's it like travelling the world?' I asked.

'Bit tiring. We were in Singapore two days ago and playing golf in Japan last week.'

'Sounds terrible.'

So, the gig came and went. I didn't die. No one was hurt. It probably wasn't as bad as I thought but when you're opening for someone so well known, obviously everyone wants to see the guy they paid money for. A tactic often used by promoters is to put someone shite on first, then the main band will look the business. It makes sense. I mean, how would Oasis feel if Dorsey and the Dorselfins rocked more than them?

Afterwards, I met Louise (daughter Dorsey), who was much better looking than her brother. She told me, 'We've had all sorts of problems with comedians opening for Dad. In England we had some guys who had bottles thrown at them, so you didn't do too badly.'

'Thanks,' I said, slurping my wine.

'Plus,' she continued, 'you now have something in common with Jimi Hendrix and Karen Carpenter.'

'What's that?'

'You've all opened for my dad.'

Wow, bloody hell. How cool is that? Then again, maybe not.

Jimi Hendrix: drug overdose, dead.

Karen Carpenter: anorexia, dead.

I poured my wine down the sink.

IT WAS WITH these flashbacks running through my head that I woke in East London to a feeling of absolute dread. What the hell am I doing here? This is not possible. This is a bad dream. This is a bad life. Mum! Why can't I just buy a small piece of land in New Zealand and milk cows and shear sheep. Why have I put myself in this situation? Bloody John

Eales. Bloody Jonah Lomu. Bloody beer.

I had chosen Stratford as a starting point purely because a good mate of mine, AJ, was living in a flat there. Thankfully, he provided me with a couch and a free ride from Heathrow.

Meanwhile, rain pelted down. The man on the radio told me it was 5 °C with a chance of showers. Obviously he wasn't looking out the same piece of glass as me. It was also about this stage that I started to wonder how difficult it really would be to streak at Wimbledon. It would all be over in a matter of minutes. Sure, you would get arrested but you'd be chauffeured away in a nice white van and, hell, you might even make the papers. I realised all too late that Mark had definitely pulled the wool over my eyes, which although not uncommon for someone coming from a nation of sheep, still didn't feel good.

I looked at the guitar in the corner of the room. Bastard. Just sitting there, aren't you? Just coming along for the ride? Well you're going to freeze your balls off as well, you know, so I wouldn't get too comfortable. You might even get used as a weapon if things get out of hand, like the guitar guns in *Desperado*. No, that would be door-to-door hustling.

Or maybe I should grab a broom and shovel and become the world's only door-to-door duster?

'Excuse me, ma'am, your veranda looks a little grubby, mind if I give it a quick once over?'

Brainwave – there was nothing in the bet to suggest I had to be in the UK for two months, that was just a random number plucked out of mid air. In Auckland when I door-to-door busked, I made $40 a day (on a good day), so if that was to be the case in England and I made half that, say £8 a day, that would be at least 62 days – 62 days in the rain! AHHH! I needed coffee.

Double brainwave – if I picked a rich area in London, say Chelsea, this could be all over in a couple of days. I could even make a couple of hundred quid extra and head to Spain for a week. Eat olives, drink Sangria and lie on the beach. Then fly home to watch cricket, wear shorts and fire the BBQ up. Of course I'd have to go via Melbourne to tell Mark to go screw himself.

That's the answer, I thought: Chelsea. Home of Bob Geldof and Liam Gallagher. In fact, bugger the busking, they might hear the Harry Potter song and offer me a record contract. I'd walk into the house to see naked chicks, a live band and cocaine being handed out on serviettes.

'Justin, we've just had a call from Radio One. They love the song, we're gonna make you a star.'

I felt tired and just wanted to go to a pub and get pissed. Even if it was ten in the morning. I put on a new CD.

I decided to call a travel agent. I admit by now I was using a technique familiar to all of us: doing anything other than your homework used to feel great. You knew the calculus test was tomorrow but all of a sudden washing the car and doing the dishes became moments of absolute joy: 'Wash the dog? Sure!'

'Take the rubbish out? Not only delighted, but honoured!'

'Oh, Mum, I wanted to scrub the bowl!'

Your mother saw a whole new side to you. She wasn't stupid. Was this a complete change in character? Is my son finally growing up? No, he's just avoiding hard work.

And that's exactly what I was doing. I should have been out there busking. I should have been fulfilling my side of the bargain. But it was still raining. And it was cold. And I hadn't listened to the whole CD. Plus I had research to do, so I thought I may as well find out how much a ticket would cost: 'How much for a one-way fare to New Zealand, please?'

'Let me just check. First class, business or economy?'

'First class, please.'

'First class, let me see. Heathrow to Auckland via Singapore ...'

'Easy, love. I'm having a laugh. Budget, economy, down the back with the goats and chickens.'

'The cheapest flight I have, sir, is four hundred and ninety-seven pounds.'

Coffee left my mouth. Hope left my heart.

'Do I get a busker's discount?' I pleaded.

'No,' she said blankly.

Amazing, she didn't even entertain the thought or ask what the hell I was on about. Just a blank 'No'.

'I bet you don't treat pensioners that way when they ask for a sodding discount!'

Although she had now gone and I was talking to myself.

Right, fuck it. Where's that guitar? Where's my jacket? Where's my scarf? I'm leaving. I'm doing it. What's the worse that can happen? A slammed door in my face? Big deal, our grandfathers ran over the trenches, all I have to do is make a fool of myself. I'm pumped, I'm ready, give me your best shot East London because I'm a loaded cannon full of dodgy R18 songs. I am officially ready!

'The Poms are very insular.'

'You'll get beaten up.'

'No one is going to open the door to a guy with a guitar.'

Just as soon as this CD is finished.

Putting my second-hand duffel coat on actually filled me with hope. I was moving, I was now picking up the guitar. I was now putting my scarf on. Things were looking up, I was on a roll. I'm really going to do this! A huge weight lifted off my shoulders as soon as I ventured outside. There was no turning back.

Four hundred and ninety-seven pounds, here we come.

For the first time, I really felt I'd arrived in London. Greasy spoons offered bangers and baked beans for three quid, Travis played on Capital Radio. Boys were selling *The Sun* on the street, old men selling fruit and veggies, setting up their stalls. 'All right, guv?' they'd say. Litter, homeless people lying under cardboard boxes. I felt like I was in a Jeffrey Archer book. I was hitting London on a Tuesday morning with a clean pair of eyes.

A sudden rush of happiness punched me in the stomach: this was going to be a great time.

I saw a guy handing out a parking ticket so I went and bugged him for directions. Where to I didn't know exactly as I had no itinerary. I think I was just looking for a doorstep where I wouldn't get beaten up. He was white but had African features and a thick Jamaican accent. Must be albino, I thought, then I remembered reading somewhere that albinos don't actually live that long, which begs the question: if you knew you weren't going to live that long why would you spend your time being a parking warden?

He had no idea where I should door-to-door busk. It was probably a stupid question anyway.

How many times have you been asked, 'What areas are good for door-to-door busking around here?'

Might as well have asked the meaning of life while I was at it.

The traffic warden did, however, point me in the general direction of residential housing. Townhouses, lined up one by one; two up, two down. I was scared. Some schoolgirls walked past singing, 'I will survive, I will survive.' I was thinking, *I won't, I won't.*

Don't get me wrong, I'm sure there were lovely people in some of those houses but to me they looked old, cold and inhospitable. There's no other word for it; I was crapping myself. I walked past some teenagers dressed like Ali G doing dodgy deals, me ol' china.

I heard them say, 'Then I got him in a headlock and fucking kicked his head in.'

Right, OK then, nice place to start.

Vernon Road, East London
Time busking: one hour
Earnings to date: nothing

FOR SOME REASON I couldn't stop thinking about the number 497. It was a depressing thought; if out of one hundred homes one in ten people answered the door, and if out of those ten, one listened to my song and gave me a pound, I would be here for approximately ... seven months!

I felt like being sick as I walked down Vernon Road. Will they have Rottweilers? A gun? Will I lose my life in East London? I was shaking. The cold dark doors were staring at me. Who lives in there? I knocked on the first door. No one answered. It's the silence of the 'no answers' that scares me.

Then, finally – a bite! The very first door opened in the UK is a lady from ... Peru!

'Hi, I'm from New Zealand and I'm a door-to-door busker. Would you mind if I sung you a song?'

'What is busker?' she asked.

'I sing door to door, you give me money.'

'Sorry, I have to go out, otherwise I would.'

I can't tell you how much better I felt getting that first door out of the way. Classic case of 'the fear of attack is worse than the attack itself'. I likened it to sitting a maths exam: I knew I was always going to fail but if I was in the classroom answering questions, there was nothing to worry about. The pain would be over, the results would be in the mail and I'd soon be losing bets instead of making spaceships.

At the next door I was greeted by an old lady with yellow teeth. She half opened the door; I gave her a half smile. She looked worried, nervous, apprehensive and suspicious. I explained my predicament, still shaking.

'I don't actually live here,' she said.

'Can I sing you a song?'

'No, I don't live here. But I'll check with my husband.'

He was hidden. I couldn't see him but knew straight away he'd say no.

'Would you like a song, there's a busker ...'

'NO!' he yelled.

She looked startled, taken aback.

I yelled out, 'I'm from New Zealand!'

'NO!' he yelled.

I saw more of her yellow teeth than I needed to. She closed the door.

Mentioning the bet may also be a good idea at some stage. Maybe I can win some sympathy that way. In the meantime, things were not going well in East London. My feelings of ecstasy and exuberance had been squashed in a matter of minutes. All I needed was one person. A smiling Londoner, keen to listen, would make my day. Unfortunately, it wasn't about to happen on this street.

Three little black kids walked past me.

'You can't even play guitar,' the tallest one offered.

'Can I have a go?' the other one asked.

I walked on.

Cheltenham Terrace, Chelsea

Chelsea was looking more and more like a better option. I would find Bob Geldof and we would sing and drink in his backyard. One small problem: I had no idea where he lived. Surely someone around Chelsea would know, I reassured myself.

It was cloudy, windy and cold but Chelsea was on its best behaviour. Kings Road looked a picture with its subtle yet festive decor. Not over the top, just enough to make you realise it was Christmas and you were a sad loner. There may have been no sun to speak of, but that didn't stop the million-pound homes gleaming in the afternoon grey. Every house sported a big black door and majestic gardens. What a change from East London. This was the land of Mercedes and Audis. This was the place where privileged kids with clean uniforms compared their Harry Potter school bags.

Those big black doors gave me confidence. Unlike East London, with houses all squashed together, these homes offered space and grand entrances, and made you smile when you looked inside. Then again, they probably did cost a little more than those on Vernon Road. On the doors lay knockers the size of horseshoes (so to speak). This didn't mean sociable, welcoming beings lay on the other side but at least these trees on hinges made me feel good.

The small problem beyond my control was that no one appeared to be home. Finally, I heard someone activating an alarm. Here we go, someone's home! I put the bait on the rod and scurried over. The big black door dwarfed me. I knocked with authority, three times.

An attractive woman answered. I offered her a song. She had a four- or five-year-old boy standing behind her. I had a good feeling. Could this be my first pound in the UK? Would this be my debut performance on the doorsteps of the motherland? She was now looking in her purse. Bloody hell!

'So, you'd like a song, is that right?' I asked.

My confidence soared, all of a sudden East London was a thing of the past.

'No, please don't sing,' she said. 'I'll see what I've got.'

I mentioned the Harry Potter song; the kid looked very interested.

'No, no, I'm serious. Please don't sing,' she insisted.

The kid still looked very interested. I could tell he really wanted to hear 'Harry Potter'. Sorry, kid, but I don't get paid if I sing. Talk to your mum.

'This is all I've got,' she said, handing me £1.73.

£1.73! Wow, I'm on my way! I put it straight in my pocket where it couldn't be stolen. It was closely followed by my hand. I felt the coins jingle around; they felt amazing. This was *my* money. All mine and I hadn't even sung a song yet!

I thanked the lady and headed to the neighbours. There was no answer. I looked across at the little boy who was now watching from the window. Poor little bugger. All he wanted was the Harry Potter song. He'll probably remember this strange man for a number of years. Just don't go losing bets, kid.

The next ten rejections didn't faze me at all. Checking my coins every two minutes became my new routine. A Cockney geezer with no teeth drove past in his beat-up Renault station wagon.

'Give us a song, mate!' he yelled.

Just as I was about to sing the light went green.

Timing is everything when you're a door-to-door busker …

I was astonished to find Chelsea was full of Spanish maids who couldn't understand me. Trying to explain a stupid bet in English was bad enough, but translating to a recent arrival from Madrid made me feel like I was at a party with spinach in my teeth.

I approached some builders working on a Chelsea mansion, thinking they'd be up for a laugh.

'No thanks, but we've got a Kiwi here. I'll see if I can find him,' one said.

They never came back so I walked on, checking the coins in my pocket one more time.

As I was about to approach a new black door, I heard a voice: 'Oi, you gonna sing a song or what?' It was a Maori guy wearing earmuffs. Describing the bet and singing 'Kentucky Fried Kitten' was my next obligation. He concentrated on the lyrics, not smiling. To be honest, I didn't even think he was enjoying it at all until the British builder said, 'Very good mate,' and my new Kiwi friend offered, 'You got balls doing that shit.'

The Maori guy passed me £2. Rock 'n' roll, that's £3.73! Less than £494 to go.

Prince of Wales Drive, Battersea

I quickly discovered that the cold made my guitar waft out of tune on a regular basis. The strings would bend and I'd find myself constantly tuning on the footpath with cars screaming past. Everyone was looking at me as I tuned and re-tuned my badly needed prop on Albert Bridge. I also continually asked where Bob Geldof lived.

'Bob Geldof?' they'd say. 'Oh, he's loaded. Good bloke. He lives around here somewhere.'

I know that but *where*?

The first house in Battersea presented an Indian man who peered through a half-open door. Funny thing was, he didn't even look surprised to see a door-to-door busker at his doorstep. He approached it as if it were part of his daily routine.

Get out of bed.

Have cup of tea.

Say no to door-to-door busker.

'Hi, I'm from New Zealand, do you mind if I sing you a song?' I asked.

'Sorry, I'm having a bath,' he said with the door half closed. Let me get this straight, this man was so obviously *not* having a bath. He was dressed for God's sake! Good excuse, though, I'll give him that. I let him close the door in peace. I laughed to myself. He looked just like Mr Bean.

I met Sam the lovely mother a few doors down. Her black lab loped down the stairs, soon joined by a young girl wearing a fairy outfit. She was shy at first, hiding behind her mum, although when I started singing she relaxed a little and even did a dance. They clapped at the end but offered words I didn't need: 'Sorry, I've got no money,' Sam said.

I find that hard to believe. This is Chelsea – write a cheque! I accept Visa or if you like we can set up an automatic payment. I can also give you the option of taking my account number and next time you're passing by the bank, just make a deposit.

Continuing down the road I saw an Australian flag on a window. Flowers, Triumphs and BMWs filled the street. Lots of houses were for sale, wheelie bins were left out. A *Stop the War* sign attracted my attention. I threw a rock through the window.

A lone builder on a roof glanced at me. He had a headphone in one ear. Judging by the good response the builders down the road gave me, I felt he'd also be a good prospect for a song.

'What are you listening to?' I smiled.

'Football,' he mumbled.

'Chelsea?'

'No, Arsenal.'

'Wanna hear a song?'

'Not really.'

'Sure?'

'Sure.'

I wasn't going to push it; he was holding a nail gun.

It was now starting to get cold. I had no gloves and the guitar continued to go out of tune every two minutes. In some ways I didn't blame people for not giving me money; this thing had a mind of its own, especially where shrinkage of strings was concerned. I was starting to realise that walking around London for an hour or two did test your endurance factor. And if you're not feeling that confident you just kept walking. You'd start thinking of different excuses for why you shouldn't go into houses: driveway is too long, curtains are drawn, looks like a haunted house, killer budgie, that sort of thing.

I approached a woman delivering leaflets. I started to walk alongside her and sing; a new tactic she didn't seem to object to. Only problem was, like the rest of the people in Chelsea, she had no money. Bloody hell, a cashless society is no good to a door-to-door busker. After singing a freebie I discovered she was just like me: a busker, though of the 'leaflet' variety. I told her she should count herself lucky she didn't have to sing, just pop a nasty piece of junk mail under the door. Janine had lived in this street for 14 years. I was astounded to hear she'd never met anyone on her own road.

'People are just too busy, no one has time to talk,' she said.

'Have you got any advice for busking around here?'

'You have to find houses with toys out the front. That means they'll have kids. Kids means mums means, hopefully, money.'

'Good thinking, 99.'

I could tell she was quite embarrassed having no money. She informed me she was actually moving to New Zealand in three months.

'I'm sick of London, sick of sitting in the car for half an hour just to go a mile down the road. Do you know how much a dodgy, one-bedroom flat costs in this road? £250,000.'

My mind went ballistic. Imagine living in the middle of London next to Bob Geldof.

Let's just get to £497 first, shall we?

NOT SURPRISINGLY, THE young gardener I accosted at the next house had never heard of a door-to-door busker. Some people you just have a good feeling about, he was a smiley chap and I knew he wouldn't say no to a song. I'm normally in such a rush to mumble what I'm doing in the UK that he said, 'Sorry, I'm just trying to take this all in. You're a what?'

'Door-to-door busker,' I proudly repeated.

'Right, door-to-door busker. I see.'

He said he could relate to my situation. He busked in Spain years ago and had to raise enough for a flight back to the UK. Mostly Bob Dylan songs, he said.

I told him about my limited repertoire, which he related to fondly. He said, 'Looks like you're coping pretty well.'

'Yeah, well, you didn't see me yesterday. Do you want to hear a song?'

'Why don't you play something different than the Harry Potter song? I'm sure you're sick of it yourself? I'm sure everyone asks for the Harry Potter song?'

'Um, yeah, I suppose so.'

'Have you got a traditional Kiwi song?'

'What's wrong with "Harry Potter"?'

'Nothing, if you want to play something else that's cool. I'm just saying you must be bored with "Harry Potter".'

'What about "Kentucky Fried Kitten"?' I offered.

'Why not?'

He whacked his hands together to clear the dirt, rummaged in his pocket and handed me a shiny £1 coin.

After an hour and a half of walking I came to the conclusion that while normal buskers may turn into fat slobs, I'd be fit and toned. And tired and hungry at this rate. Regardless, I felt great. After a day of rejection I now had £4.73 in my skyrocket. It was burning a hole so bad I only had one thing to do: buy a beer.

It was approaching evening anyway and my legs were starting to ache. I chose a bar called the Cross Keys in Lawrence Street, Chelsea. My pint tasted bloody brilliant. I asked the barman about a sign I had seen as I came out of the toilets. It said *Rupert and Lucy*.

'There's a private function upstairs. Up there,' he pointed.

I looked up to the second floor and could see people milling around, dressed in checked sports jackets and seventies slacks.

'Is it free booze?' I asked.

'Well, I suppose so, if you know Rupert and Lucy?'

'Oh, is *that* Rupert? Hardly recognised him, haven't seen him for years.'

He continued to dry champagne glasses, then said, 'Even if you did know Rupert I'll bet you a million pounds you don't know the guy leaning against the bar?'

'No, who is he?' I squinted.

'You're not from round here, are you?'

'No, New Zealand. Come on then, who is it?'

'James Hewitt!' He was obviously supposed to whisper but it came out as a loud hiss.

'Who the hell's he?' I asked.

'You're *definitely* not from round here. James Hewitt, army guy, famous for shagging Di?'

What the hell, I thought. I decided to go and meet Rupert and Lucy. No one knows me around here anyway. I've been making an idiot out of myself all day, why stop now? The barman described in detail which one was James Hewitt. I must say I was tempted to straddle up beside him, maybe buy him a jar and ask, 'What was she like then?', but when I arrived in the posh setting drowned out by posh-speak I chickened out.

This wasn't my party; I had no business being here. I just wanted free beer. I had now officially turned into a bludger as well as a busker. I left via the door and heard, 'So, do you play croquet?'

'No, sorry I don't.'

'Oh you should, *wonderful* game.'

I never met Rupert and Lucy to wish them well.

Suppose it would have helped if I knew what they looked like.

5

Tottenham Court Road, London

Earnings to date: £2.13 (change from beer in Chelsea)

MOST PEOPLE PROVIDE one of two responses when I explain the bet to them: 'You're very honourable for doing it – I wouldn't.'

'Do you have to live on this money as well?'

The answer is yes, I do have to pay for food and, as was the case last night, beer. I have to be very frugal indeed. Let me just say to avoid confusion that I will have to subsidise whatever I make. I have to reach the dreaded amount of £497 and that money will be kept in a closely guarded bank bag at the bottom of my backpack.

It was cold outside and even though my coffee was also cold, I came to the conclusion that sitting in a warm café was more inviting than getting rejected on the streets. I did, however, need a plan for the day. Half an hour earlier I was going to try to busk around Tottenham Court Road, the only reason being that I had scored a ride there that morning. But upon inspection I quickly became aware that not many people live in buildings named James Smith & Sons and The Housing Corporation Library.

On the other hand, I have done stand-up comedy in a library. It was a bizarre event. During the Auckland comedy festival they put me in the library as all other venues were taken. Maybe they were trying to tell me something? The library may have been clean and it may have been short of hecklers but let me tell you: when you're used to singing songs and telling jokes to a bunch of pissed workers in a pub, it's quite a challenge entertaining irritable students, confused pensioners and an oversized, drab librarian who is quite at home telling you to 'Ssshh down!' every two minutes.

A sign at McDonald's across the road caught my attention: *Employees needed – £4 an hour.*

Hell, that's more money than I've made from two London suburbs, I thought. Could I flip burgers and sing at the same time? No, door-to-door busking might be a lousy gig but at least I have my dignity. They reckon you should work at KFC or McDonald's at least once in your life. It gives you good grounding and a good work ethic, they say. It also opens your eyes and gives you a good appreciation of how to deal with the public.

I say bollocks to them. I'd rather get beaten up.

Just as I was scouring my pocket for more change, hence more coffee and yet another excuse to keep warm, I met Josh who was delivering papers. He sat at the table next to me. He couldn't stop staring at the guitar.

'From Down Under, eh?'

'Yeah, New Zealand.'

I had strategically placed a New Zealand sticker just below the strings. I was hoping it might put Brits at ease knowing I was from a relatively safe country. That I wasn't going to blow up the house or shoot the dog or torch the garden shed. Maybe just raid the fridge.

I had no idea whether this tactic would make a blind bat's difference but it was worth a try. This was unknown territory. I needed all the tactics I could muster.

After I explained to Josh what I was doing in the UK he nearly fell off his chair. He wasn't a small man and the table jiggled about the place while his steaming hot tea found its way onto his *Daily Mirror*.

'You're a bloody madman,' he said. 'A door-to-door busker? How much have you made so far?'

'Um, let me see. Two, four, carry the five … times six … minus expenses …' I took a deep breath. 'Six pounds,' I said proudly.

Which was actually a lie. As we all know it was £4.73, but I took the liberty of rounding it up. Which was pointless anyway, as I'd bought a beer in Chelsea last night.

Mental note: if I spend money on beer there will be less money for a flight.

'Have you ever heard of Don Partridge?' Josh asked.

'No.'

'Oh, you must have. Don Partridge, he's the King of Street Singers. Everyone in England knows about Don Partridge. Back in the sixties or seventies he had a number one hit, with, oh, what the hell was the name of that song? "Rosie"! That's it, "Rosie".'

Then he started singing it. It really was quite sweet.

'You should track him down,' he continued when he realised 'Rosie' was the only lyric he knew. 'See if you can get in touch. The door-to-door busker meets Britain's most famous street singer!'

'Could give it a go, I suppose.'

'I bet he's still around. He'd be a great bloody laugh. He's mad. He plays all sorts of instruments, guitar, drum, tambourine, mouth organ. He's a one-man band. I bet he'd be right up for a meeting with a madman from Down Under.'

'Where do you think he lives?'

'Oh, shit, now you've got me. I think, don't quote me on this, but I think he used to live in Brighton. Definitely south. He used to sing in shopping malls, that's how he got his break. One day he's singing in the mall, the next, some high-flyer record-company geezer takes him away to record a single. Don Partridge, King of Street Singers; he was called that for years.'

What the hell, I had nothing else to do. No meetings, no appointments; just a lonely, unemployed guitar begging to be played properly. I took Josh's advice and turned myself into the nearest Internet café. I found two Partridges, both were in the south. I tried the first one: 'Is that the world's most famous busker?' I asked.

'I bloody wish, mate.'

'That's not the Partridge household then?'

'It is but there are no buskers here.'

'So, you're not related to Don Partridge, the street singer?'

'Never heard of him, mate.'

Damn, I only had one more number. What to do if I couldn't get hold of him? Josh had raised my hopes. It now felt like a pilgrimage I had to undertake. I needed advice. I was going to see the Messiah, the King of Buskers. I was Luke Skywalker and he was Obi-Wan Kenobi, er, Obi-Don. He would teach me and guide me. Don't let me down, Don Kenobi, you're my only hope. Help me, Don. I can't budget. I bought beer last night. I'm fucking desperate here! Please help the door-to-door busker.

The phone rang three times: 'Hail to the chief?' came the reply.

'Is that Don Partridge?'

'Certainly is.'

YES! YES! YES! Thanks, Lord, I promise I'll never ask for anything again.

Although now that I finally had Don on the line, I didn't know what to say. I froze. My memory went blank. Please, Lord, let me know what to say. Last favour, promise.

'Wow, fantastic, wow … this is … Don … gee … I … I … this …'

Thanks, Lord, but a few more adjectives would be swell.

'My name's Justin and I'm the world's only door-to-door busker and I heard that you were Britain's King of Street Singers. What say we meet up for a beer or something?'

Five more minutes of mumbling and adjective searching provided me with an answer that was music to my ears.

'I'll just check with Pam and we'll get the bed made up,' he said.

My pain was over. Pack your bags, Luke Skywalker. Don has officially felt your presence.

I found out Obi-Don lived in Seaford, about 30 miles east of Brighton. So there I was, running late on the 1.46 p.m. from Victoria. The man opposite me had chosen a bad place to sit. Not only did he have to open the door for all passengers, he also had to answer the same question every two minutes: 'Is this the train to Gatwick?'

'I hope so,' he would say, folding the sports pages of his paper together so they could squeeze past.

I felt sorry for him. Surely he realised his choice of seating had been a bung decision, but, then again, it was a window seat and maybe he enjoyed the social interaction this exercise provided. I then realised *I* had done exactly the same thing when I boarded. I had asked him if this was the train for Lewes, which is where I would change for the train to Seaford. Honestly, all these bizarre places I was discovering in Britain! Another person jumped on: 'Is this the train to Gatwick?'

'I hope so,' he replied. I must say I admired his patience.

He'd obviously done this for a number of years and had it down to a fine art. Maybe he'd been employed by the Railways as 'Confirmation Inspector'?

'Mr Morgan, your job is to read the paper and put people's minds at ease by telling them they're on the right train.'

'Right, and um, what … what train *are* we on?'

Luke Skywalker was running late and had to make a phone call. I didn't want to let Obi-Don Kenobi down. After all, I was the apprentice and surely Obi-Don had other songs to sing and other buskers to train. I just hoped Darth Vader wasn't going to be in the same class. I bet he knows some wicked chords. I could just imagine myself strumming 'Kumbaya' to Obi-Don just as Darth Vader, joint hanging from his lips, plugged in his amp and played an AC/DC riff while groupies hung from his cape.

Obi-Don Kenobi's answer machine kicked in: 'Hi, Don and Pam can't come to the phone right now. Please leave a message after the beep. Justin, if that's you, I've just popped into town to do a few songs, then I shall pop down to the Wellington pub till four o'clock. It's easy to find, just ask at the train station. Hope to see you soon, old chap. Bye.'

Wow, that was Obi-Don Kenobi. I arrived in Seaford with a smile on my face and headed straight to the Wellington. I'd heard that he often played at Seaford shopping mall but obviously Don decided sitting perched at a bar was a far more attractive option. I'd tend to agree. Just as Obi-Don had suggested, I asked for directions at a newsagent's by the train station. Seaford was obviously a small town with small town stories judging by the local rag's front page: SEAFORD WOMAN IN CAT MYSTERY.

I didn't even read the story. I didn't need to. Surely it would be a let down. It was just such a pleasant surprise not to see

SIX KIDS SLAUGHTERED IN TOWNHOUSE.

I was pretty pleased with my listening skills as far as how to get to the Wellington pub was concerned. Normally, I'm useless with directions. I don't listen. I just nod like an idiot and wonder whether the kind person offering me their valuable time realises they've got a wandering eye and corn in their teeth.

The pub must have had twenty people in it but I knew Don was the one at the bar with his back to me. There he was enjoying a pint of Spotted Chicken. Cowboy hat, boots and glasses – Don Kenobi, the master, my Jedi, my only hope as far as busking was concerned. He insisted on buying the first beer. I opted for a Spotted Chicken as well, even though it sounded like something a vet would deal with. Mind you, I was more than sure I could adequately deal with whatever was put in front of me. Six or seven times even.

So here we were, in the Welly, Don's world, where he meets all his friends. I felt honoured to have been welcomed into it.

'So, how did it all start, Don?'

He lit up a cigarette. Everyone in the pub was watching. Not gawking, just quietly observing. Who was this stranger asking Don all these questions in our local?

'Well, Justin, I started busking in 1964.'

I liked him already. He wasn't in a rush. This was his local and he was comfortable. Just Don, his Spotted Chicken and a few stories. It was a shame I would only be in Seaford for a few hours. It may have been pissing down outside but it was nice to get away from the go, go, go of London.

'There was no new blood coming onto the busking scene since the Second World War so a mate and I started singing together. We'd pop down to Devon and sing our songs. It was just the two of us plus an artist who collected for us. By the end of that summer we came back fully fledged buskers.'

'What sort of songs did you sing?'

'Everything, mate – folk music, gospel, blues. You know, good, strong folk songs.'

'And had you always played music as a kid, Don Kenobi?'

'Don who?'

'Don Kenobi. *Obi*-Don Kenobi. I'm Luke Skywalker and you're the master. I'm here to learn off you. I've heard all about you. I need some help with door-to-door busking.'

'Well, don't expect too much, old boy. What you're doing is crazy. I don't know if I can offer any words of advice when it comes to what you're doing.'

'So, you've never been door to door?'

'I've played to a lot of people, Justin. I've played a lot of different situations but never door to door. I couldn't imagine doing that. Not now.'

'Any advice will be great, Don. You've got to remember I have no idea.'

'You'll have to be careful, son. You'll get copycats wanting to do the same thing. Guys who are hard up will try busking door to door.'

'They're bloody welcome to it, mate!'

Bless him, he thinks this is a good idea.

'Was music in your blood, Obi-Don?' I asked.

'Definitely. I started off on a ukulele banjo when I was seven. All my family on my father's side sang and played, and on my mother's side my grandfather was a poet and a songwriter.'

'Did you know you wanted to be a busker?'

'Busking was just a very natural thing for me to want to do. I used to play folk clubs but after a while I wanted to bypass all that crap. You needed an agent and a manager to book you. And if they didn't like your face they wouldn't book you. So, we went straight to the people in the pub and said, "Here we are, this is what we do." We had to take a reduction in pay, but in the end it paid off. We discovered you could make more that way. Plus, you could play when you like and what you like. And that was important.'

'Freedom,' I said.

'Yeah, freedom.'

'Plus, we realised very early on that we actually had a lot of power. Sometimes we'd walk into a small bar and ask to play. The owner never seemed to mind, so we played and they fed and watered us. Then all of a sudden punters wouldn't let us leave. People started fighting. Drinks were thrown. It was only then that it clicked, *we* had caused all this to happen. We had power. This was magic, not your high, flown out of the wind, Harry Potter stuff, but earthly magic. The more powerful you are the more you can excite people.'

Luke Skywalker was all ears. This was the speech I had been waiting for. The hairs on my back were standing on end.

'On a Tuesday night, which was the hardest night to perform, we had caused people to be as joyful as if they were celebrating some kind of party. And you, Justin, you can make all those people happy as well.'

'Do you still get nervous?' I asked, hoping like hell the answer would be yes. I was hoping we could discuss worst pre-stage bowel movements and how to overcome them.

'Not busking, no. Busking's home. Promoting records I get nervous.'

I had read on the web that for the first time in 34 years Don Partridge was releasing an album. He presented me with one as we enjoyed our second Spotted Chicken. I laughed at the name of track 11: 'The night I met Elton John'.

'That was terrible, that night. I had been off the booze for a month but I decided to have a few drinks. I ended up shitting my pants in front of Elton John. Woke up in hospital wearing nappies.'

My new teacher definitely wasn't boring. And I loved that. I had to ask about 'Rosie', the song Josh the newspaper deliverer in Tottenham had forgotten the lyrics to.

'It came at a time in my life when I had busking down to a fine art. I was earning good money in Hastings and I remember they used to sell apricot and peach wine by the barrel at the local grocer's. We'd get the fire going and have a drink and a sing. We were talking about what's involved writing a pop song. I said, well it can't be that hard. So I went off into another room, came back twenty minutes later and "Rosie" was born.'

'You wrote "Rosie" in twenty minutes?'

'Pretty much, yeah. A producer who worked for Essex Music heard it and wanted to record it. It went to number three and stayed in the top twenty for fifteen weeks. Eight pounds was what it cost to make the album.'

'Bloody hell, Don Kenobi, they turned you into a superstar!'

'For eighteen months I had a glorious, hedonistic time but I never felt I earned the money. I spent it very quickly. It's a very fraudulent job, this. I was getting paid a thousand quid a week for half an hour's work. I felt like a fraud.'

'Yeah, but you wrote "Rosie", no one else. So you deserve whatever accolades you got.'

He fell silent.

'But, Justin, look at all these actors awarding themselves prizes. They have money and they still want more. What about all the ex-plumbers and ex-builders, where are their accolades?'

A Jedi with a conscience; I haven't got a chance.

I don't know why, but in New Zealand we don't seem to have many buskers. Although, I do remember one old guy in Auckland who used to play the recorder worse than your three-year-old brother and still expect money. I'm not being unfair, I just think it's essential to play more than one note in a four-minute song. Poor bugger never seemed to have any money in his hat either, which prompted me to ask the master about busking tricks.

'Don, what do you reckon about the money in the hat? Do you think you should show people all of the money you've earned that day? Surely, you don't want to appear too well off, otherwise you won't get any more?'

'People should know you're making money. Sometimes, if you keep some of the big stuff in there, other big notes appear. One fiver is followed by another. I have a friend who insists on taking all the large stuff out, but that's a bit like begging, don't you reckon?'

'I guess so,' I said.

He lit up another cigarette and we sank the last of our Spotted Chickens at the same time.

'You've got to remember, back in the sixties busking was looked on as begging. Although we did a reasonable show and by rights the money was ours, there were still laws enforced to get buskers off the streets. It was a movement Charles Dickens started in the nineteenth century. He and his friends got together and signed a petition that would rid the streets of organ grinders. The organ grinders counteracted this by putting their organs so intensely out of tune they'd be paid to be sent away.'

'I can relate to that,' I said.

Don laughed. 'Even now we get associated with people that stick their hands out.'

After securing fresh ales I took the opportunity to have a good look through his new album. Obviously I wasn't the only one interested; a middle-aged man with a beer belly and a pint wandered over.

'Have you got any of those new albums there, Don?'

'Sure, here we go.' He reached into his jean jacket and produced a cellophane-wrapped CD. As Don's first customer today enjoyed his beer and CD sleeve at the bar, I asked him how much he sold the albums for.

'I'm supposed to sell them for £14.99 but I think that's a bit steep,' he whispered.

'How much, Don?' the guy asked from the bar, waving the CD in the air.

'For you, a tenner.'

'Oh, cheers, Don!'

You're a top bloke, Don Kenobi, but remind me not to let you take over the budget side of my trip.

I had wondered on my train trip to Seaford what the most I'd get from one doorstep might be. Judging by yesterday, not more than £1.73. Surely someone will give more than that. Like back in Auckland when I sang to a guy in a swanky house who didn't have anything smaller than a $20 note.

'Do you have any change?' he asked.

Once my laughter had stopped he handed me the crisp, clean note saying, 'Good luck. You'll go far.'

Yes, yes, yes, that's all well and good but that's in the past and it *was* in the middle of summer. When people are relaxed and happy. Middle of winter is a little different. Who the hell is going to open the door to some dodgy idiot wearing a duffel coat and strumming a guitar when the rest of the country is interested only in how cold they will be that day?

I was doing this all wrong. Sure, Don's stories had inspired me, but now I wanted to be a *normal* busker. I wanted to get discovered by Essex Music at Seaford Shopping Mall and write songs about shitting my pants in front of Elton John. I wanted to feel like a fraud! That's rock 'n' roll! Door-to-door busking is just, well, it's pants really, isn't it?

'What's the most you've made in one day?' I asked Don.

'One time I was busking in Paris and this guy came along who was the head of some flash company. He had about twenty associates with him. Twenty Americans in posh suits. He says to me, "Do you know 'Dixie'?"

'I say, "Yeah, I know it."

"I'll give you fifty bucks if you play 'Dixie'."

'So I played the song and sure enough, he threw fifty bucks in. Then all his mates felt they should put money in as well. First a ten, then a twenty, then a five, then another fifty. I earned seven hundred dollars for one song! *And* lifelong friends because they took me out for drinks and a meal afterwards.'

Now was the moment I had been building towards. Before the beer took an effect on me, I had to extract whatever I could from the King of Street Singers. After all, a train ticket to Seaford wasn't exactly cheap and Luke Skywalker can't claim expenses. So, before my pockets became lighter, hence saving myself the embarrassment of saying I was skint, I asked Obi-Don Kenobi for three 'Gems of Busking'.

Here they are:

1. 'Stay sane when you're travelling. When I was busking I was a one-man band and I carried around all this musical equipment. It weighed eighty pounds, it was the equivalent of doing SAS route marches every day. Course, I was also on the old whisky and beer like you wouldn't

believe, but I compensated for that by doing exercise. Because I was carrying all my gear around, I was staying fit. The doctor reckons that's why there's nothing wrong with me now.'

2. 'Always have a song on the boil. There's nothing worse than stalling with a crowd in front of you. The worst thing is stagnation as a busker. If you're bored the crowd will be. A lot of buskers have a set programme. Unlike Shirley Bassey, who can't even see her crowd for the lights, a busker has to assess the situation and adapt accordingly. You have to read the crowd. Half the time in Seaford I'm just talking to people. Some come past that have already heard me and throw some money in. Pam thinks I get paid more when I don't sing!'

3. 'Don't drink before a gig. Don't let the drink take ya. A lot of nights the only time you'll see companionship is in the bar. It's a good place to find out the buzz of the town. But don't forget, your body has to be revitalised every day. Eat good food. You can get as pissed as you like afterwards, just not before a gig.'

'Or a doorstep in my case?'

'That's right,' he smiled, shaking his head.

I could have stayed in the Wellington pub all night, but I had to make the decision to leave. Three or four beers soon turns into five, turns into six, turns into rum and Coke, turns into whisky, turns into kebab, turns into no money, sleeping in a bus stop and shitting your pants in front of Elton John.

And although I'd expressed delight at that very feat not so long ago, I can't imagine anything worse.

For him *or* me.

So Don and I swapped phone numbers and wondered if we'd see each other again. He said Pam would be disappointed I wouldn't be joining them for chicken casserole. I apologised but said I really had to get back to London. It was sad that last couple of minutes. I liked Don and I think he liked me. I shook his hand and he hugged me.

In true Jedi style he said, 'May the chords be with you.'

6

Victoria Station, London

Earnings to date: £2.13

BEFORE I LEFT New Zealand, Andrew and Jacque (who do the breakfast show for Classic Hits, Auckland) had listeners call in who had sons and daughters doing their Overseas Experience.

I then received a phone call from Andrew and Jacque, and it soon became apparent I wasn't just a door-to-door busker, but also a postie and, effectively, Santa. The day after I bargained for my duffel coat, I also screamed around the circumference of Auckland and met mums and dads who, despite loving their kids very much, couldn't be arsed paying for postage and stamps. The plan was that I'd arrive in the UK clad with chocolates, chips and lollies with love from their mums and dads back home.

I didn't mind. After all, presents could become very good bribes.

And that they did.

Crumpled at the bottom of my backpack was a list of names that would take me all over London:

Paul Goldfinch, builder, brother of Vanessa.

Carl Woodman, son of Raewyn. Studying media communications in Arsenal.

Paul Cameron, son of Nan. An interesting one. When I

picked up the parcel that was bound for Paul, Nan told me a photo of her brand-new apartment was in the envelope. She said it was effectively Paul's inheritance. Bloody hell, she trusts me with it!

Narissa Prasad, daughter of Chris. Willesden Green.

Justin Brazier, son of Mary.

Graeme Kilgour, runs The Glasshouse nightclub in Blackfriars. Son of Trish.

Just before 8 a.m. I arrived at the address Paul Goldfinch's sister had given me. I had five more addresses in my bag that would see me start my day at 7 a.m. and end at three the next morning.

Now, if you're a Londoner, you hardly need to be told Chapel Road, SW1 is an exclusive area. Every house looks like 10 Downing Street. Buckingham Palace and Westminster are just down the road. A *Daily Telegraph* lies on every doorstep. This is the London you see in the movies. This is also the London where Paul would hopefully be expecting a door-to-door busker and a present from his sister. Telling his mates to clear the mothballs out of their wallets wouldn't go astray either.

The smell of sawdust led me to six big-handed builders. Luckily, one of them was Paul. Titty calendars lined the walls, empty Fanta bottles scattered the floor and a copy of *The Sun* lay on a workbench. It was a Saturday morning and not surprisingly these six Kiwi builders were hung over. None of them wanted to be at work. They told me about the £6million, six-storeyed house they were working on.

'Bloody expensive around here, mate,' they told me. 'Prime real estate. This place is six stories, servants' quarters on the floor above us.'

'Servants' quarters?' I asked.

'Yep. These guys are loaded.'

Paul was very excited to see me. The others were just confused. Or intrigued, one of the two.

'So, how do you know Paul?' one asked.

'I don't. I've just got a present for him.'

'Who from?'

'His sister in Auckland.'

'How do you know his sister?'

'I don't, I'm just a door-to-door busker delivering presents.'

Hangovers obviously weren't helping their situation. These six big-handed builders looked like they were trying to work out some sort of algebra equation. Door-to-door busker? Delivering presents? Who the hell is this freak? I was just hoping no one in the room suffered from homophobia because, in the next couple of minutes, I'd find myself serenading six strapping young men.

When I finally started singing they all reacted differently. One couldn't look. One read *The Sun*. One continued to work out algebra.

And although nerves still accompanied my song and singing to these fellow countrymen didn't make me feel entirely at ease, what followed cheered me up no end.

Paul handed me £10 – £10 for God's sake! I was about to burst. I felt like I was six. I wanted to skip around the room and dance with the builders. £10! This was easy. All of a sudden the happy memories of Auckland busking came flooding back. It all felt so primitive and raw; like being a lion chasing a sobbing antelope. I mean, we all go to work and we all get paid, but correct me if I'm wrong, when you open your payslip you don't specifically know what that money was for. Was it for replacing the toner in the printer? Was it for photocopying those memos? It could be for any number of things. With door-to-door busking it's very simple; I sing and either get told to bugger off or get money. Next minute you're holding ten pounds sterling in your sweaty little mitt and you know exactly how you earned it.

You have evidence. It's very animalistic, very basic, which is just as well for me, I suppose.

The best thing about Paul giving me £10 was the rest of the builders felt obliged to give just as much. Paul had set the precedent and a very fine one at that, I must say. The big-handed builders searched their pockets. I always feel uncomfortable when this is going on. Sometimes all I really want to say is, 'Oh, don't worry about it guys. You have a good day,' and walk off.

But you can't be proud when you're a door-to-door busker. This may be the only money I get today. There's a lot at stake here; not least, beating an Australian.

Builder number two handed me £10, the next three, £5 between them. One said exactly the same as the builder in Chelsea, 'You've got balls, I'll give you that.'

I still wanted to skip. I wanted to hug them. The last builder was obviously struggling with the budget side of things. Finally, when at least a few of his mates weren't watching, he placed some coins in my hand: 'Sorry, mate, it's all I've got.'

I gave Paul his present, probably the most well-travelled chocolates and Lotto ticket I had ever met. Who cares if it wasn't a gold watch? It didn't matter, it was from his sister and it had her handwriting on it. That's all he needed to know. Those chocolates and Lotto ticket had flown halfway around the world, accompanied by a song. Meeting Paul's sister, Vanessa, then meeting him now felt very strange. Only a few days ago, 12,000 miles away, he was just a name on an envelope; now I was singing songs to him and his workmates on prime real estate in the middle of London.

At that moment it occurred to me that I had absolutely no idea where this busking trip would take me. Who would I meet? Where would I end up? What town or city in the UK would give the most?

I was excited for the first time.

I discovered quickly that the thing about London is everyone's lost! You can't exactly ask the person next to you where Green Park is because they themselves are looking at their map as if it is written in Russian.

I was about to ask a woman in front of me for directions, but she was obviously in her own world. Maybe that's stretching it a little, this woman wasn't even in the same universe. Her hair needed a wash, she wore stovepipe trousers and was carrying Safeway bags. As she walked past a dozen black cabs at Victoria Station she yelled, 'Why don't you all fucking fuck off? Look at you all there lining up in a row. Looks like you're all fucking going to a fucking funeral. It's all right for you, isn't it?'

Maybe I should take her door to door? Shock tactics.

Mind you, then I think I really *would* get beaten up.

A BUSKER SHOULD never count his money in front of people so I waited till I got inside Victoria Station to see how much the big-handed builders had given me. It came to £26.83! I was ecstatic.

I even threw a couple of quid at the first busker I saw. He was a saxophonist and a bloody good one at that. His big black cheeks puffed out like Louis Armstrong's while acoustics bounced off the walls of the old tube station. It made people smile. You couldn't help but give money.

That's the thing about Britain: busking is an age-old art. I mean, look at Don Partridge, touring the country in the sixties and even then it was nothing new. There are singers, jugglers, comedians, pianists. Britain's got them all. They put a hacker like me to shame. The sad thing is, half of them would be good enough to play on any stage in the world.

It was a stunning morning in London. Sure, it was cold but the sky was blue and crisp. Having pounds rattling around in my pocket made me feel like a king. I could buy British things with British money. However, I steered clear of the first pub I saw; I learnt that lesson in Chelsea. Being Santa for a day was rewarding, not to mention satisfying. My bag would weigh less after each house visited and at least I felt I was achieving something.

Carl Woodman, son of Raewyn, would be my next victim. All I knew about Arsenal (where he lived) was what I had seen on Nick Hornby's movie, *Fever Pitch*. And that's exactly what I found when I got there. This place *says* Saturday. North London, football mad, chips, beer and escapism. No matter how bad your week's been, once Arsenal run onto that field on Saturday afternoon you can forget your job, forget your bills, abuse the ref and, hopefully, depending entirely on whether Arsenal win, go home a happy punter.

If not, go home, quit your job and burn your bills.

The advantage I had on this particular day playing Santa Busker was at least I knew I'd be greeted with more than a lukewarm reception. Unlike Chelsea, where people either weren't home or just told me to bugger off, these Kiwis had no choice; if they wanted Mummy's present they'd better be nice.

Corrupt? Yes. Necessary? Most definitely.

An attractive girl answered the door. She looked Eastern European and was wearing only a nightie. Singing to her seemed a far better option than serenading another man. But that's exactly what I ended up doing. She invited me into the lounge where I waited for Carl, alone. Eventually he pounded down the stairs wearing a T-shirt and jeans, bare feet and wet hair.

'So, what's this all about?' he asked. 'Mum mentioned something about it.'

'I lost a bet with a mate and have to door-to-door busk my way around the UK, all in a vain attempt to make enough to fly home.'

'Some mate,' he laughed.

'Exactly.'

He opened his present while I sang to him from the other sofa. I got the feeling he was glad he had something to do while I sang; otherwise the very same place that held memories of wooing Eastern European women was now a place where he'd look into the eyes of some weirdo in a duffel coat singing songs about deep-fried cats. We were both relieved when it was over. It's a contractual obligation. I would feel I was cheating if I didn't at least sing something. OK, I admit, I sang a shorter version but to be honest, we were both better men for it.

During the song I had been eyeing up a £10 note on the coffee table and was hoping it wasn't going to be used for the next phone bill.

'Here you go, mate,' he said, passing it to me.

'Wow, thanks, that's great,' I gleamed.

'You're mad, but you're gonna have a lot of fun.'

I left knowing he was about to shag that Eastern European girl.

MAKING £34.33 FROM two residences was really too much for me. After rejections and blank stares the day before, this was overwhelming. My calculations in Stratford had now gone completely out the window. Initially I thought

I'd be here for 497 days, now I was thinking a couple of weeks. At this rate, I could even take a trip to Spain! What's the saying – if you want to make God laugh, make a plan. I had to be footloose and fancy free if I was to make this money. Wherever you go, there you are. I had to let the guitar lead me.

Providing the fucker stayed in tune.

The other thing that became bleeding obvious was that if people actually let me into their homes, half the battle was won. I could chat, make them feel at ease, maybe have a cuppa on the couch. The longer I stayed, the more they'd pay me, surely.

Suddenly, a dark cloud descended on my silver lining. Who the hell was I trying to kid here? The only reason these people were letting me in at all was because I had gifts from Mummy, not because of my charm and not because of my (God forbid) music. These poor Kiwis felt obligated to let a desperate, guitar-wielding maniac into their house; the only reason and rather tenuous link being that they were born in the same country as the mad bastard.

Well, let me tell you, if that *was* the case, I would have to milk this day for all it was worth. In the grand scheme of things this may end up being one of the easiest days to accumulate funds. So be it. Water off a duck's back. Shooting fish, whatever. If these tenuous New Zealand links held us together then bring it on because I'm ready to raid your wallet like there's no tomorrow. I've got nearly forty quid in my back sky rocket and I'm not afraid to use it.

Shut the gate, hold the phone, lock up your daughters, I'm ready!

PAUL CAMERON LIVED in Cricklewood. He would be my third stop in an already full-on day. I knew I had to be at his flat by midday as he was leaving for a pub crawl. He was most disappointed I couldn't join him.

I said, 'Paul, Santa Busker is a busy boy and sprinting between North and South London is bloody tiresome for a flightless Kiwi.'

A stocky South African greeted me and threw a beer into my hand. Paul ran down the stairs and welcomed me into the lounge. Two girls were having greasy hangover breakfasts consisting of baked beans, sausages and cardboard-looking hash browns. *Smash Hits* was hissing away on the telly.

'Nice TV, for a flat,' I said.

'Yeah well, it's going tomorrow,' one said with half a sausage in her mouth.

I had to compete with *Smash Hits* when I finally sang my song. But I was counting my blessings that there were at least females in the room. Four people in fact, a record crowd for the door-to-door busker.

I had just enough time to embarrass Paul with his mother's present. It contained a photo of him as a baby, the whole flat laughed and passed it round.

'Isn't there something else in there from your mum? About her new apartment?' I asked, remembering that his mother Nan had mentioned back in New Zealand to be very careful with the envelope. He rummaged through it, reading various bits of paper.

'No, nothing. What about her new apartment?'

'No … inheritance?' I stammered.

'Inheritance? What do you mean?' he asked.

'Oh, nothing.'

Maybe I should just shut up, sing and deliver.

Another £10 found its way into my pocket. That made today's total £44.33.

With three more Kiwis to visit I decided to splash out and

get a cab to Willesden Green. I know what you're thinking – you bloody idiot! Save your money. You're a bludging busker, for God's sake, not a rock star. But my legs were tired and I had to save my energy for meeting people and singing. Quite stressful meeting strangers, you know. It's all right for Santa, he gets reindeer and a schedule.

So, forgive my extravagance but have pity on me.

Thankfully, I wouldn't have to dig too deeply, as Narissa's house was not too far from Cricklewood.

Not having to entertain for the next couple of minutes was a real luxury, although my Nigerian taxi driver wasn't about to go unnoticed: 'New Zealand, huh? Always picking up New Zealanders in this area.'

'Really?' My eyes were closed and my legs were resting. I'm sure my guitar was taking a nap as well.

'Kiwis, right?'

'That's right, Kiwis.'

'Yeah, thought so. Kiwis, always drinking beer. Always drunk.'

I opened my eyes. He had caught my attention. Always drinking? Always drunk? I was about to tell him his country folk weren't exactly angels when I realised he probably had a point. Of course, being a Kiwi I never noticed it but it's a fact, Kiwis and Aussies live in London, drink in London and fall down in London. His comment hit a nerve; I suppose drinking is better than starting a civil war but it makes you wonder why we tank up every weekend and fall into taxis.

My new Nigerian friend didn't waste any time weaving between subjects either. No sooner was I adding up the taxis I'd thrown up in than he was on about how Europeans take life too seriously.

'I used to be in the forces,' he said. 'Had a great time. I

went all over Africa, we used to love it when there was a war on because everything was free.'

'Really? How lovely.'

'Plus there were loads of women,' he laughed a deep, hearty laugh. 'I live in the UK for six months and Nigeria for six months.'

Someone obviously forgot to tell me this was an episode of *This is Your Life, Mr Nigerian Taxi Driver.*

'I don't like seeing old people grow old alone,' he continued.

This guy was really getting his money's worth. I hope he did debating at school.

'Too many old people have to look after themselves in this country. My question is this – when you're seventy or eighty why should you go through that by yourself? Your excuse not to look after them, they're old and you have a busy life to lead. Well, when you were weak and vulnerable you were looked after, so why shouldn't you do the same?'

That actually made sense. Quite touching as well. I handed him £5 and read my piece of paper which would lead me to Narissa's house, the fourth Kiwi today.

True to form, the first thing the Kiwi at the door passed me was a beer. I walked through the six-bedroom flat that housed God knows how many Kiwis, thinking: did Mr Nigeria have a point? *Are* we all pissheads? It would be rude not to accept a cold brew so I sat on the couch, met Narissa and explained my busking predicament to the unisex (thank God) crowd. Sympathy and admiration followed. The first thing they did was look up a travel brochure lying on the coffee table to see if they could find a better deal.

'Four hundred and ninety-seven pounds? You can get a better deal than that!' one said.

A blonde Australian girl glided into the room on her latest

acquisition, shoes that transformed into roller skates. Little wheels popped out from the bottom when you pushed a button. Great for door-to-door buskers, also great for doing runners from restaurants.

'Where'd you guys get your Christmas tree?' I asked after singing 'Harry Potter' to them.

'It's not really a Christmas tree at all. We found it on the way home from the pub the other night. Some guy had chopped it down, and we thought it would look good in the lounge.'

'Smashing,' I said.

These were nice people. They looked after me. I felt welcome and my blessed day of easy money wasn't over; Narissa passed me a £5 note and some coins.

I left with a warm glow in my heart.

I nestled into a quiet corner on the tube and felt the warm coins in my pocket slide through my fingers. Mine, I thought, *all* mine. Another quick calculation was in order. Narissa's house had handed over two beers and £7. That made the grand total for today of £51.33!

Four down, two to go. Santa Busker was knackered. His itinerary said that Justin Brazier would be the next lucky punter to receive a pressie from Mum back home.

In the meantime a guy had sat next to me with his own guitar. He asked me what songs I played.

'Just the one, mate,' I conceded.

'I fucking love music, man. It's my life! Here, listen,' he said, taking his guitar out of the rather elegant case. 'This is a Gibson Hummingbird, especially fitted with a Fishman pickup, just like Thom Yorke uses.'

'From Radiohead?' I asked.

'Course, Radiohead. Best band in the world. This is the plectrum he uses as well. Listen to this.'

And with that he proceeded to strum, sing and scream a full range of Radiohead songs even Thom Yorke would be proud of. He sweated like a woodchopper. I thought the veins in his temple were going to burst. Sometimes he looked in complete ecstasy, other times he looked like someone had just dropped a sledgehammer on his big toe. One thing was for sure, this man had passion. His enthusiasm was like a drug. He was totally oblivious to Mr Jenkins in the grey suit reading *The Guardian*. He couldn't give a toss that someone was trying to resume their grumpy 'tube face'.

This man was on fire. His stage was the Jubilee Line to Green Park. I looked at my pathetic guitar and just tried to enjoy the free concert. He finished too soon.

'That was brilliant, mate. Do you play in a band?' I asked.

'Na, just at parties and stuff. I'm playing tonight at my friend's twenty-first.'

'How long have you been in London?' I asked, figuring he was from somewhere in the States.

'Only five weeks. But I'm trying to make a real go of it here, see if I can do this for a living.'

Sweat poured from his forehead into his eyes.

'Oh, shit, my stop!' he said, placing his Gibson Hummingbird fitted with a Fishman pickup back into his case.

'Don't forget your pick,' I said, passing him the plectrum he had dropped on the seat. 'And good luck!' I added.

'You too, brother!'

What an all-you-can-eat smorgasbord of people I was meeting today.

Justin Brazier was next on my list. I guess I should have purchased a map somewhere along the way. Instead, I ended up walking two miles from Vauxhall tube station. Another sensible thing to do would have been to jump on any number of buses that whizzed past me every five minutes, but for some reason I didn't trust them. I mean, what if they were going to Manchester? I don't trust buses; they're … well, dodgy.

Needless to say, by the time I arrived at Justin's flat I felt like I'd walked two miles with a guitar on my back. The chocolates, cards and Lotto tickets had taken their toll on Santa Busker. I was so hungry I could have eaten a reindeer. I asked myself time after time: why the hell didn't they just send these presents? Then I remembered the warm coins in my pocket. And the people I'd met.

Justin walked me up the stairs to where flatmates were either watching TV or ordering pizza. It seemed cold and dark, cars whizzed by and the odd untrustworthy bus. All the inhabitants of the house seemed a bit too cool, or maybe it was just the way I was feeling. Repeatedly I asked myself what the hell I was doing. Sitting with strangers in the middle of London waiting for them to turn the TV off so I could sing to them? Suddenly this whole bloody thing seemed too ridiculous to be true. What in God's name *was* I doing?

Two more songs, I thought, then I can relax.

'Show us your stuff, mate,' one flatmate said in between abusing a pizza delivery guy on the phone. Initially I thought, who the hell do you think you are, asking me to strut my stuff? Although, he did have a point; I was a stranger in *his* house invading *his* pizza-eating time, about to take *his* money.

I would have done the same.

The others had a look that said, 'You'd better be good.'

I sat at the kitchen table and sang to a crowd of five. Luckily, they laughed and loosened up. As the pizza arrived and cars continued to whizz by, the pizza orderer told the rest of us a story that Gav (who was also in the room) was obviously not keen on hearing again.

'You know what Gav did last night, eh?' said Pizza Boy.

'Shut up!' said Gav.

I knew whatever it was had to be true because Gav was defending it so staunchly. Pizza Boy told the story with a certain amount of glee, knowing the punch line wouldn't let anyone down. He took his time and demanded the floor's attention.

It turned out Gav had been snogging a girl at the pub the previous evening. Nothing wrong so far, good on Gav. Although what Gav didn't realise was that the girl he was snogging had been standing on a stool the whole time he'd been courting her. It's fair to say Gav was pretty tanked but that still didn't cover his surprise when his snoggee excused herself, climbed down from the stool and went to the Ladies.

She was less than four feet tall. Pizza Boy proudly named her Pygmy Woman.

In a quieter moment I asked Gav whether he'd be seeing her again. He passed me £10, saying nothing. His smile told me he'd seen the funny side of it. Unfortunately, so had the rest of the flat, who were now fighting over the phone for people to ring.

Justin also gave me £5, taking my grand total to £66.33.

Five down, one to go.

Knowing I'd have a few hours to kill before I could meet my final Kiwi (Graeme who ran The Glasshouse nightclub in Blackfriars), I decided to call my good mate, Tim, who was living in London. I was pretty knackered after a huge day so a quiet meal sitting with someone I didn't have to act the fool in front of appealed.

Graeme had told me to meet him at the nightclub after 10 p.m. I looked at my watch; it was now midnight after starting the day at 8 a.m. I'd been on the go for 16 hours.

The Glasshouse seemed to have more security than a U2 concert. The staff were looking at my second-hand duffel coat, scuffed shoes and guitar. Not exactly nightclub attire.

'I'm here to see Graeme,' I said at the front door.

'Come this way,' said a big bouncer with a fancy walkie-talkie thingie hanging from his ear.

I was led down a labyrinth of corridors to where the boy from Takapuna in Auckland would be embarrassed by a present from his mum 12,000 miles away. Tim was still with me at this stage; he was my pimp, my manager, making sure no one asked for autographs at the wrong time and making sure I had Evian water and rum 'n' raisin ice cream in my dressing room.

Graeme seemed a top bloke. We were now in the office at the back of the club. He gathered everyone around, about 20 staff altogether. They treated me like a celeb. Everyone knew why I was there. All of a sudden I felt very nervous. So nervous in fact that as soon as I sang the first line of 'Harry Potter', my mind went blank. What was probably only two or three seconds seemed a lifetime. Shit! What was I going to do? I had 20 people waiting for the next line. There was nervous laughter, the staff looked at each other: 'I thought this guy was a good busker?'

'Maybe this is part of the song?'

'Why has he stopped?'

'Shall we beat him up?'

Then for some reason, for some lovely, lovely reason, the office door opened and a guy popped his head in.

'All right?' the guy said.

'All right, Dave,' everyone said.

'Sorry, didn't mean to interrupt.' Then he closed the door.

Thank you, Dave! Thank you, thank you, I owe you one. I don't know what Dave did or why he was sent down from heaven at that particular moment but as soon as he left I remembered the whole song no problem. I completed it and everyone clapped.

I needed fresh undies and deodorant. Graeme handed me £20 and invited Tim and me into the top bar to have a drink. A quick calculation proved a very successful day – £86.33.

Just like meeting the other Kiwis so far from home, it was humbling meeting Graeme, whose mum I had only met last week. She had been working in a tuck shop at an Auckland secondary school for boys. Here I was talking to her son who ran a flash nightclub and wore a flash walkie-talkie thingie in his ear.

Free beers arrived, we met Danny the DJ who'd be cranking the tunes up in the small hours and Graeme told us stories about girls who hid drugs under their bras.

'We don't like dealers,' he said.

'So, do you get famous people in here?' I asked.

'Yeah, Paul McCartney had a big party here just last week. Prince has been here, a few other guys. You guys want some shooters?'

'Um, yeah, why not?' we both said, eyeing up the tequila on the top shelf.

I couldn't help but think of humble beginnings. Here was Graeme, once upon a time going to school in little old New Zealand, now organising parties for Prince and checking girls' bras for drugs.

Before I started delving into my busker funds, Tim and I decided it was probably best to leave. We thanked Graeme and the staff and although they were all top people, I didn't admire the fact they had to be there till 8 a.m. Then again, judging by their faces when I explained my bet to them, I'm sure they were glad they weren't sodding door-to-door buskers.

I suppose at that stage I should have hit the sack as well, but I had a feeling something was just around the corner. Like the old story, the best parties are impromptu ones, and when you don't want to go out, *that's* when things happen. Unfortunately, I also suffered a disgraceful example of busker discrimination.

It happened as Tim and I ventured into the back door of Savoy Hotel. It all seemed very posh and for a while there I thought we may have been a little under-dressed, but our confidence was riding high after our successful endeavours with Graeme at The Glasshouse.

Tim still looked like my pimp as our search for whisky on the rocks scaled new heights. Things were going well. Then, out of nowhere a well-dressed penguin disguised as a doorman started questioning us.

'Can I help you, gentlemen?'

'Yes, that would be lovely.'

'What are you looking for?' he asked.

'The bar, good sir,' we said. 'Can you tell us where it is?'

'Upstairs.'

'Excellent, these stairs?' Tim asked, pointing to a grand staircase that probably wound its way up to some sort of 1920s ballroom. The well-dressed penguin disguised as a doorman then looked at the guitar hanging off my back. Then at my duffel coat.

'I'm afraid the bar is actually closed,' he said.

'Oh, that's a shame. What time does it close?' I asked.

'Um.' He looked at his watch. 'One … forty … six. Yeah, quarter to two, normally. Can I suggest another bar that may interest you?'

'Would you?' I asked.

'Be my pleasure, sir.'

He then led us through the rest of the hotel, giving us a

free tour as our lips became more parched than ever.

'This hotel actually dates back to 1889, you know?' he told us.

'Is that a fact?' ('Now, where's the brandy?' we should have said.)

Through the flash revolving doors we went. He showed us the Strand Hotel across the road where he suggested we could drink as much whisky as we desired.

'That is the politest way I've ever been kicked out of a hotel,' said Tim as the penguin closed the door behind us.

Blatant busker discrimination; I know exactly how the slaves felt.

AFTER SCRUBBING UP in the little boys' room I came out to find Tim in the reception of the Strand Hotel with fifty or so very, very drunk patrons. I knew we were in trouble when I discovered a middle-aged man with bloodshot eyes attempting to play 'That's Entertainment'. He was thrashing the guitar so hard it looked more like he was trying to start up a second-hand chainsaw rather than attempt anything tuneful. Obviously he thought he was the man; the fact that everyone was holding their ears didn't deter him in the slightest. Then he fell asleep. Which was lucky for the guitar; I may be a very average player but I've never publicly thrashed my baby like that before.

'Brown, I'm going to get us a drink. You play these guys a song,' Tim said to me.

'No bloody way. I'm finished for the day.'

'Come on, this is your job. Fifty drunk people are waiting.'

I scoured the room. These people were almost in a coma. It's like they'd all been told this was the last night alcohol would be available on earth. Some were asleep, others swayed. Others said things they'd only say at an end-of-year piss-up.

Tim soon arrived with whisky and was pleased to see I had started playing to a sell-out, if not altogether sober, audience. I struggled through some numbers I remembered from my songbook when I picked up the guitar eight years ago. Namely 'La Bamba', 'Help', 'Hide your Love Away' and a few party favourites from the Rolling Stones.

'Do you know any Elvis?' someone yelled.

'Only if it's got the same chords as "La Bamba",' I replied.

I urged Tim to work the room with a hat. After all, he was my pimp and a pimp's job was to make money for the performer. Between instrumental breaks we met a few of the more sober patrons. There was a Don McKinnon (politician from New Zealand) lookalike and his wife. We told Mrs McKinnon lookalike that we were both door-to-door buskers living on the streets of London in cardboard boxes.

'I don't believe you,' she said. 'You're too well dressed.'

The hotel staff were now attempting to call Security. I'll be honest. We were making one hell of a noise. No one was holding back. We had nothing to lose; these people were drunk and I didn't live in the country.

Just as my voice was starting to disappear, a man with a bleeding face walked up to me and said, 'Your music made my lip bleed.'

I would like to think this was true, that my natural musical prowess was so intense that it had inflicted physical damage on a fan. But the sad truth was he'd smashed the top of his beer bottle when he opened it and every time he took a swig he just made the cut deeper. Blood was pouring down his face. Rock 'n' roll.

He continued drinking out of a smashed bottle. That's commitment. That's dedication. That's alcohol.

My pimp arrived back with a measly £4.50. I decided to

pass the guitar to anyone game enough to argue with Security while we attempted to get food from reception (which was probably a bloody stupid idea considering we had, as a group, scared off any customers that may have arrived in the last half hour).

A Chinese waiter must have felt sorry for us.

'You want sandwich?' he asked.

'Yes, please.' Just getting served, not getting kicked out, felt wonderful.

'What do you have?' I asked.

'Chicken? Ham? Cheese?'

'Ham and cheese, please.'

'One ham, one cheese?'

'No, I'm not finished. One ham and cheese –'

'One ham, one cheese? Yes, got that. And to drink?'

'No, listen up. We want one ham and cheese, twice.'

'OK, OK, double ham and cheese. No problem. What about you? What you want?' he said to Tim.

Tim looked at me, saying nothing. I continued: 'No, we want one ham and cheese, times two. One for him, one for me. Got it?'

'Ahh! OK, OK. One ham and cheese,' he said, pointing proudly to me. 'And one ham and cheese,' he said, pointing to Tim.

'That's right. Good,' I said.

Thank God that's over. My head was about to explode.

'And to drink?'

Oh, no, not again. Something simple. No cheese, no ham.

'Two gin and tonics, please?'

'Two … gin … and … tonics.' He wrote slower than my four-year-old niece.

'So, one gin for you … and one gin for you?' he smiled. Was he taking the piss now?

'Yes, Maestro, that's right. One each,' I confirmed.

'What room number?' he asked.

'We're not staying here. We'll pay cash.'

'Ah, no cash! Only food if room number.'

'Well, we're not staying here.'

'Sorry, no stay, no food.'

Well fuck off then and don't ask if we want any!

Bloody hell, £4.50 and I can't even spend it.

'Hey, you know Don McKinnon's wife over there?' Tim asked.

'Yeah?' I said.

'Don't you reckon she's got nice tits for a sixty-year-old?'

'I think it's time we left, Tim.'

7

Harlington

Earnings to date: £90.83

ARRIVING BY TRAIN in the small village of Harlington in Bedfordshire, I realised I'd seen the last of the golden weather. Sure, the last week in London may have been colder than the South Pacific but at least the sun was shining and it was dry, crisp and clear. Here, it was a different story. It was like pea soup: cold, damp and heavy. Choosing the next town to busk in took meticulous planning; i.e. throwing a dart at a map of the UK.

Harlington: where the fog hung low and old brick houses, hundreds of years old, looked good enough to eat, like they were made of candy and featured in *Hansel and Gretel*. Immaculate gardens and narrow, winding roads circled their way around the village.

Unfortunately, none of this physical beauty washed over the fact that I had to knock on doors and ask for rejections. Nerves were always present at the start of the day and today was no different. The only way to get around it was to jump in the pool and not worry about how cold it was. In a way it was exciting; I wonder what people I will meet on the doorstep today? In other ways, terrifying; will today be the day I run into trouble?

My mammoth day in London had definitely given me

confidence, but as I said before, they were all Kiwis, they knew I bore gifts and knew I wasn't a freak. To the people of Harlington, however, I was a weirdo in a duffel coat who may use that guitar as a weapon. Now, considering just two days ago I complained about lack of funds, today I had a new problem, albeit a rather luxurious one: being weighed down by 3000 coins but not having the freedom to spend them is a curse. Of course, I could actually do what I bloody well liked with them, but then there'd be no flight.

Today was also my birthday. I considered carrying my passport door to door and singing myself 'Happy Birthday'. Maybe people would feel sorry for me? It's easily one of the more bizarre birthdays I've ever experienced. I couldn't help but wonder, whatever happened to simply sitting around a table with friends, eating lollies till you were sick, playing pass the parcel and sleeping for a week?

Here I was in an unknown village with a wet instrument, lost and cold, wondering how many exotic ways there were to be told to fuck off.

I can't do this today.

I can't walk up to these houses.

I can't be a door-to-door busker.

Where are my presents?

I need Don Partridge. His advice would have to get me through:

Don't drink before a gig.
Always keep a song on the boil.
Keep your body in good nick.

I'D BEEN TOLD where the vicar of the village lived. This made me feel more at ease, a man of the cloth wouldn't tell me to bugger off, surely. Chickens and ducks waddled around on dead leaves outside the church. The old boy offered no response, just like the next six houses in the village. The next three at least opened the door but wanted nothing to do with me.

The next abode sported a brand new yellow convertible in the driveway. Great, I thought, at least they've got a sense of humour! I comforted myself by thinking they'd be bright, perky and good-natured, just like their car. I bet they also have loads of money, especially for buskers.

I knocked on the clear leadlight door and heard someone thump down the stairs. To be honest, this is when I shit myself. What sort of person is it going to be? *Should* I use my guitar as a weapon?

I saw a woman through the glass. I knew she was watching me. Does she not think I can see her? She sprinted to the next room. I waited a couple of minutes. How long should I wait? She's obviously gone. She's shit scared. She won't be coming back. What could a man in a long black coat possibly offer her that she can't find in a public park late on a Friday night?

I wouldn't have answered either.

Dejected and hurt, I moped off like a lion that failed to catch the antelope. She'd be watching through the lounge curtains. She'd see me try next-door and the next door and the next door. Who is that strange man, she'd think. I'd just try to keep my chin up and hope my guitar strings didn't burst due to the cold.

A man with teeth bigger than his dog's answered the next door. Even though he seemed to have a friendly disposition, it was all just a cover; as was the owner's.

'Hi, how are you, sir?' I asked.

'If you're anything to do with entertainment the answer's no! I'm in the thick of something and can't stop,' he said.

'You'd even say no to a door-to-door busker?'

'Yep.'

I had a feeling I could twist his arm. Surely he couldn't say no. After all, it was my birthday and I hadn't made any money today. I tried patting the dog as a tactic.

'Have you ever seen a door-to-door busker?' I asked.

'No, but I'm really in the thick of something and it's not a good time. Anything entertainment, the answer's no.'

I'm sure his dog was sniggering as he walked into the warm house with his master. In a world full of war and despair it made me wonder, what's this man got against entertainment?

Maybe the woman hiding behind the curtains was still watching me. It wouldn't surprise me. She'd be having a right old laugh at the fool with the guitar who couldn't get anyone to listen. Better than a soap even, this is real life, right in front of your eyes. The next door would have pleased her as well if that was the case: 'No, no, no, I don't want a song.'

Slam!

And the next one where a burly security guard peered through a gap in the door.

'What?' he grunted.

'Hi, I'm from New Zealand and I'm a door-to-door busker. Would you like to hear a song?'

'Na.'

Slam! Lock. Rattle.

My fingers were now goddamn blue. I had been walking around Harlington, a quaint little village where you'd expect to find relaxed out-of-London folk, for over half an hour. I was cold, hungry and my guitar had gone out of tune for the eighth time today. Happy birthday to me.

Even the coins in my pocket couldn't cheer me up. You're

only as good as your last performance and they were from yesterday's. I wondered how far I could get for £90. Maybe I could jump on one of those cargo ships that take three months to get anywhere? Or maybe I could fly to Spain? Busk, drink *cervezas*, hit the beach and nibble on tapas. One problem – no Español.

Oh, come on, surely all Poms weren't this inhospitable. This was getting ridiculous. Here I was on my birthday, wandering around a strange town starting to lose my marbles.

An old man revived my faith in the human race at the next house. Dick handed me 50p and listened at the door. His sick wife lay in the lounge with a smile on her face. This gave me a huge boost. Thanks, Dick, you're nearly 90 and you haven't become so set in your ways that you won't open the door to a desperate Kiwi. Respect, old boy. I hope I have half your courage when I'm that old. Who knows, I might still be here!

It may have only been 50p but often that's all it takes when you're desperate for human interaction. Dick had quite possibly saved me from a certain white coat and pink padded room. I was happy. Well, at least *happier*. In the grand scheme of things I was still up shit creek but I had earned my first coin in Harlington. Dick must have sent some good karma next-door as I hit it lucky once more.

An Essex girl with big teeth and curly hair asked me what I was up to. When I mumbled my way through my opening line, stopping only to shiver and teeth chatter her face lit up. She was speechless, then yelled, 'Well, I'll be. Kids, you'd better come and see this!'

I hoped they weren't expecting the Elephant Man or the Hunchback of Harlington. I also hoped my limited repertoire wouldn't disappoint them. I was just happy not to get a negative response. I didn't even care that people didn't give money; a smile and a gold watch would be fine. Just getting someone not slamming the door in your face does wonders for your confidence. Course, I wouldn't object to a ham and cheese sandwich and a cuppa by the fire, but I thought that might be pushing it.

The kids enjoyed the song and laughed in all the right places. Hanging onto one of Mum's legs and hiding behind the other was a sight I was getting used to.

'How come you're friendlier than the rest of the people around here? Everyone else slammed the door in my face.'

'I'm not from round here. I'm from Essex, that's why I'm so kind,' she laughed. 'You haven't exactly timed it that well either. Santa comes past every night, collecting for charity.'

'Bloody charities, eh? What about the poor door-to-door busker? What the hell does Santa do anyway? Does he dance? Does he sing? No, he just dresses up in a dodgy costume and harasses kids. Maybe I should say I'm collecting for charity?'

'No, I don't think so,' she said, handing me a shiny £1 coin.

Look at that, a 200 per cent increase in a matter of minutes. How many businesses can boast that? I must say, though, I was now starting to get extremely cold. Purple fingers, cold toes and a constant dripping nose signified I would have to call it quits before I made a spectacle of myself. Collapsing in a village 12,000 miles from home wearing nothing but a second-hand duffel coat and hand-me-down long johns would not be a good look.

I spotted an old man tidying his garage. This was always a good sign; somehow yelling out to someone who's already outside is a lot easier than standing at the door and interrupting their morning routine.

'Go on then, I'll meet you at the front door,' he said after I'd told him what I was doing.

He must have been mid-seventies, his piercing blue eyes burned straight through me. He found a gold coin in his pocket and passed it to me.

'Don't you want a song?' I asked.

'Oh, go on then, but hurry up,' he said, looking at his watch.

I wanted to say, 'You're old! Don't worry about the garage. No disrespect, but the garage can wait. What have you got planned tomorrow afternoon and the one after that? Will it matter what day you clean the sodding garage? Talk to Dick over the road, with the sick wife and the open mind. You have a door-to-door busker, a fucking freezing one at that, at your beck and call! Have you ever *seen* a door-to-door busker? Make the most of him. Ask him to sing, dance or clean. Just don't be in a hurry, old boy. The garage is going nowhere.'

'Well, you gonna sing or what?' he asked.

Was I just *thinking* that?

The guitar was now so far out of tune it resembled a pregnant seagull. The notes weren't just flat, they were below sea level. My nose was a grade two rapid and my toes no longer felt they were part of my body. Ol' Blue Eyes continued to look at his watch and fidget. He wasn't enjoying the song at all; I could tell by the fact that halfway through the second verse (right about when the seagull was finally giving birth), he slowly closed the door, saying, 'Lovely, all the best, boy.'

Poor bugger. That was quite possibly the worst rendition of any song I'd ever heard. I'm surprised farmers didn't shoot me from afar, mistaking me for some stray marsupial stuck in a fence.

I'm just glad I got the money upfront.

You're only as good as your last performance, and as my last performance was a bunch of arse I decided to duck into the local. The Carpenters Arms was warm, inviting and although not entirely pumping, i.e. just the barman and myself, it had a good feel to it. Eventually workers skived in to have a beer in their lunch break. It was Monday, 11 a.m. Half of them dragged mud through the floor on their work boots. Others proudly paraded holes in their socks your nana would get excited just looking at.

I ordered a Guinness and sat down, thanking my lucky stars I was still alive. The three workers at the bar said nothing, just sipped occasionally. There was no music to speak of, the only warblings coming from the live snooker being played on the TV next to a pre-nineteenth-century photo of Harlington. Unfortunately, in order to pay for the Guinness and the next one, I had to delve into busking funds; I hadn't learnt my lesson.

The £93.33 had now become £88.33, but damn it was a good drop.

An old guy had found his way to the bar and while waiting for the snooker to start up again, enquired about my guitar. After the normal, edited version of this stupid escapade I was on, I also told him I would be anticipating some trouble from carol singers in the near future. After all, Christmas was only weeks away.

'Carolers? Oh well, you'll just have to beat them up. Most of them are only kids anyway.'

I liked this man. What a life, watching snooker in the pub at lunchtime.

I asked, 'How come people don't get pissed at the snooker like they do at the darts?'

'*I'm* always pissed at the snooker,' he said.

Just as the busy workers at the bar ordered another beer, a big float came past the window. This must have been what the lady from Essex was talking about. I could hear a Cliff Richard song screeching from the speakers on the roof. A grubby old man dressed as Santa waved from the top. He was throwing a bucket around, doing his best to attract attention to himself. Bugger off, Santa, this is my patch, you try doing it *without* the truck. And don't think people will give money just because you've got a pillow shoved down your gut. We can all see past you, Santa. It's all mirrors and smokescreens from here, fatso.

God, I hate buskers.

'Never mind carol singers, boy. There's your competition,' my new snooker buddy said.

'Tell me about it.'

I changed the subject back to the snooker. It wasn't as stressful as watching a fraud collect money off innocent people. My mate didn't seem to mind; he was hooked on the game.

'You know, my mother watched snooker on a black and white TV for years,' he said. 'She finally got a colour TV but had no idea what the hell was going on.'

'I reckon that's why dogs don't play snooker,' the older man at the bar offered.

'Why?'

'Well, they're colour-blind aren't they?'

I could have sat with these guys all day.

A NEW PLAN was in order. Sure, London was a success, but my effort in Harlington had been nothing short of pathetic. Was it my singing? Was it the cold affecting my guitar? Who knows, all I knew was I needed a new plan of attack if I was to make my flight back before Bush was re-elected. I decided to ring Chiltern FM in Dunstable, which I'd heard on while in the pub, my plan being that if I could get on some sort of local radio show, maybe people could prepare for my arrival and hastily remove money from their Swiss bank account in time. Thankfully, I got through to Andy who ran the morning show. He very kindly said I could join them the next morning on air for a chat and a coffee; see if the people of Luton were kind folk.

Chiltern FM was tucked away in an elaborate shed of sorts with rabbit warrens and cubbyholes populating the building. I was led into the studio where I met Andy, Sarah and Steve. As a team they did the morning show but, best of all, provided me with coffee. I sat in the corner of the studio guzzling away, stressing about what the hell I was going to say to possibly hundreds of people. I'm sure Chiltern FM had more listeners than that; just not so sure they'd want to listen to what *I* had to say.

One thing was for sure: there was no way my bastard guitar was ever going to go out of tune in this tropical studio.

And it didn't. I sang 'Harry Potter' and 'Kentucky Fried Kitten' to a microphone, three real people and God knows how many others either cooking breakfast or shovelling ice off their windscreens. It was a bloody marvellous success. I felt great. No one slammed a door in my face. No one abused me. My guitar stayed in tune!

And things only got better. After coming down from cloud nine I suggested I should hit the streets of Dunstable. They went one better.

'Well, where are you heading next?' Andy asked.

'Um, good question. Wherever this leads me,' I said, pointing to my guitar.

'How 'bout Reading? Our boss is heading there for a meeting in ten minutes. Thought it might save you a bus fare. Plus, we have another radio station there, you might like to sing your song to those guys as well?'

Reading? I knew nothing about it. Where would I sleep? Where would I eat?

'That'll be great. Cheers, Andy,' I said.

'Not a problem. More coffee?'

Bloody hell, these guys drink a lot of coffee. So that's the trick to the early mornings.

8

Reading

Earnings to date: £88

NOW, EVEN THOUGH I had made no money in Dunstable and even though I spent my hard-earned cash on Guinness yesterday, things were definitely looking up upon arrival in Reading. What a strange name for a city, I thought. I decided during my stay that Reading would be renamed Singing. Far more appropriate, don't you think? Singing is far more lucrative than reading. I mean, how many door-to-door readers do you know of?

'Hi, I'm a door-to-door reader. Keep the light on, will you, I'm trying to finish this chapter. Won't be long.'

So there I was visiting my second radio station in a matter of hours. I felt like a right old anorak. Now, I'll be the first to admit, my timing is usually lousy, proof being that I was freezing my tits off in the motherland at the wrong end of the year. But stumbling across the friendly crew at 2-Ten FM in Reading saw me arrive on the best day of the year, the annual radio station Christmas party.

I was so excited I even considered having a shower for the big night. Maybe even a clean T-shirt?

'Come along,' they said. 'Sing a few songs.'

Don't mind if I do, I thought. Bring your wallets.

DUE TO THE fact that people in the radio station had to actually *work* and couldn't take me out for a long, boozy lunch, I thought it best that I hit the streets of Reading before the sun retired. About time I added to my £88, and no place to start like West Berkshire. The first thing I noticed down a road called Thompson Walk was the cars: BMWs, Mercedes and Volkswagen Golfs were parked outside immaculate gardens. Sometimes a boat. More London commuters; I was hoping they'd have more heart than Harlington.

Wrong! Now, I'm really sorry I have to say this but, Reading, you sucked. You comprised of heartless, horrible, rich, stingy people who collectively had less heart than a roast lamb. All a bit too good for the rest of the world, are we? We work in London. We live in Reading. Na, na, na, na, na! It's only an hour away, you know. Bob's a chief executive, I'm a first impressions manager. Have you seen our new Volkswagen?

Oh, fuck off!

Proof: the first two houses.

1. A stale, middle-aged couple who looked at me like I was some kind of leper, fresh off the boat. Initially, seeing a launch and numerous European cars gave me confidence to knock on the door. Receiving a crowd of two also gave me confidence. Normally, if one doesn't go for the song you can always work on the other. But, unfortunately, I had found the unhappiest marriage on the planet. OK, OK, we all have bad days but these were the people responsible for giving *others* bad days. You wake up grumpy for no apparent reason? Look no further than this road in Reading. These are the people responsible. The bad karma in this household was overbearing. The

atmosphere could have nuked cockroaches. Birds avoided trees, dogs shat on other lawns, leaflet deliverers preferred to take their own lives.

'Hi, I'm a door-to-door busker from New Zealand. Would you like to hear a song?'
  'No, we would *not!*'
  You'd think I'd just asked for a threesome in their Mercedes.

2. A mother who looked at me like I *was* having sex in her Mercedes. I smiled and asked if she'd like a musical number from a bet-losing Kiwi.

'Look, you've got me at a really bad time. We're about to go to a nativity play.'
  'Well, maybe I can sing a song for you before you leave?'
  'Why should we listen to your music, we've got our own music, haven't we, love?' she said to her daughter, hiding between her legs.
  'Yes, Mum.'
  Suit yourself.

SO, NOT A good start to West Berkshire. Didn't exactly put me in a festive mood for the Christmas party. A sudden wave of exhaustion and lethargy hit me as I queried which road to next try rejections from. Nothing like a couple of slammed doors to know you're alive. You knew you weren't doing well if you couldn't even get past your opening line. Just when I was about to take Reading off my Christmas card list forever, someone finally gave in. It came after a whole road of solid rejections when an attractive mother (also with a BMW outside) said, 'I've only got twenty minutes to pick the kids up. It's a very sweet idea. I'll get some money.'

She passed me a pound. It warmed up quickly as I clenched it tightly in my fist.

I wandered aimlessly around suburbs I knew nothing about. Closed doors and negative responses followed me like a shadow. No one wanted a bar of it. Again, I was cold and hungry and just looking for someone to offer me a transfer from their Swiss bank account. Curtains remained closed, TVs flickered. I wanted to be inside those houses, having a cuppa by the fire, warm, at home.

I wanted to be the one to tell the door-to-door busker to fuck off.

And they kept coming thick and fast: 'No thanks, not interested.'

'Try down the road.'

'I'm not home.'

'Do you have identification?'

'Do you have a busker's licence?'

'Certainly not.'

Close. Lock. Walk away. Start again.

A man standing on a ladder saw me approaching. Who's this weirdo with a guitar, he was probably thinking. He was doing his best to hang Christmas lights via the garage roof. I locked him in my sight and smiled. I had him, he couldn't turn me down. If he did, consider the ladder a goner.

'Would you like a song?' I asked.

'I'd be very embarrassed if you sang a song. If my daughters were here I'd let you.'

Definitely one of the more bizarre responses I had received; I can only listen to music if my daughters are around. Better than piss off I suppose; to be honest I'd prefer it if his daughters *were* here. Singing to three British beauties was a far more endearing prospect than looking up a man's crotch while he attempted amateur Christmas decorating. Listen to me, I sound like an old man. Give the man a break, he doesn't want a song, I thought to myself. *He* doesn't have to knock on doors. *He* has a life. He's also been told if he doesn't get those bloody decorations done there'll be no supper.

So, just leave him alone.

Just like Dick coming to the rescue in Harlington, so a bubbly lady kept my spirits alive in the next street. The song 'Hallelujah!' rattled around my skull.

'Oh my lord, what have we here!' she said, throwing open the door.

Relief would not be the right word. I wanted to cover her in roses. I wanted to fill her chubby cheeks with expensive European chocolates. This kind-natured woman had single-handedly saved Reading's reputation.

'George Harrison used to live around here,' she said. 'Maybe you should try his house. New Zealand, oh, lovely place. My husband went there a couple of years ago to do the BT Global Challenge. Is that song an original?' She stopped to take a breath.

'Yeah, "Harry Potter" is an original.'

'Hmm, I was just wondering about some of the lines. Maybe you shouldn't sing it in front of kids?'

Like most people, she didn't know where to look when I sang. She focused on the strings, then on my jacket, then the New Zealand sticker. I knew she was uncomfortable, but at least she had an open mind. She was my new best friend. As you can probably tell, it doesn't take much to be my new best friend; if you want to be covered in roses, just listen to my song and shower me in money.

'I'm not surprised you haven't had a good response

around here, love,' she said. 'We've lived here fourteen years. They're not that friendly to be honest. They would never have heard of this before,' she said, pointing to my guitar.

'That's the problem, no one has,' I conceded. 'I tell you what else, though, you've got crap neighbours! Over the back with the boat and the Mercedes – unfriendliest people I've ever met. Don't you dare say hello to them tomorrow.'

'I won't,' she laughed.

THE SECOND GOLD coin of the day sent my total rocketing to £90. An hour and a half in Reading had proved fruitless. One more street, then that would have to be it for today. But what the hell would I say back at the radio station? They'll all ask how their hometown stacked up compared to the rest. Would I say Reading was great? Would I tell them they lived in the best part of the UK?

The last street presented just as many negative responses. A man who looked a painter of sorts peered at me from a front room. There was a white decorator's van in the driveway and numerous second-hand cars. I get scared when I see lots of cars, I don't know why, I should be thinking big crowd, more money. Instead, I think of how many people I'll have to interrupt.

'Yeah all right, go for it,' was the response when I finally got the nerve to knock on the door. Two guys, one about twenty, the other younger and obviously his brother, about fifteen. The older brother sported a cowlick like I used to have when I was a kid. It stuck up like a blade of grass on a windy day despite vain attempts to gel it down. I know what you're going through, I thought.

I sang 'Kentucky Fried Kitten'. Even the painter in the front room gave me the thumbs up. Amazing how quickly people's suspicion changes when they know you're not gonna shoot them.

Cowlick Boy fished around in the drawer by the front door and came up with three marvellous, lovely, heavenly pounds.

I SPOKE TO a woman called Barbara in the warm reception of 2-Ten FM upon return.

'How did you go?' she asked.

'Not so good, five pounds in two hours.'

'Look, if it makes you feel any better, if someone came to my door I'd be highly suspicious so I'm not surprised people don't open their doors. It would be different twenty years ago. We used to leave money on the bench for the butcher and the milkman, we would trust them completely. But people feel under attack these days. We're actually all very nice, you just have to prove that nothing nasty is going to happen.'

She was dead right of course, but it just made me sad that as human beings our first instinct is to wonder what harm the person at the door is going to do instead of, 'Hello! Welcome to my home. What have you got to offer?'

A person's first move is to clam up and act suspicious. It was never meant to be that way. Your first reaction should be one of surprise and warmth. Welcome stranger …

A very kind offer came my way in the form of a shower and bed for the night. The man offering this was Andrew who also worked at 2-Ten FM.

At their place, as he and his wife dressed for the Christmas party, it occurred to me that I could wash my clothes in the shower. Mmm, maybe not a good look on the first night.

They were dressed to the nines; I sat in the back seat wearing a smelly T-shirt and grubby jeans. I felt privileged to be going to their party – lucky timing.

'Just gotta pick up our mate on the way,' Andrew said, pulling into a driveway that looked familiar.

Too familiar.

'Don't suppose you did this street this afternoon?' Andrew said.

'Wait a minute,' I said, sitting upright. I spied a white decorator's van and second-hand cars. I knew exactly where we were. And with that, Cowlick Boy who gave me £3 not two hours ago was looking at me through the window!

He nearly fainted. *I* nearly fainted.

'Not you again! Holy shit!' he yelled.

Here was a man deep in shock. He had never seen a door-to-door busker before and now within an afternoon he had seen one twice! He didn't talk all the way to the party.

The Donnington Valley Hotel, a beautiful old castle, was the venue for the Reading Christmas party. About a hundred people had been looking forward to this all year; I'd just turned up on the right day. The DJ sported a mullet haircut that a 1980s Jon Bon Jovi would have been proud of. Guy and Robert from the Morning Crew grabbed the microphone and introduced me to an audience well on the way.

'Ladies and gentlemen, here we have a desperate New Zealander. He has lost a bet, which means he has to door-to-door busk his way around the UK all in a vain attempt to make enough money to fly home. So, come on Reading, empty your pockets for the poor bastard!'

I grabbed my guitar. The barman passed me a Midlands Bank bag.

A shocking day on the streets meant I was now desperate. Guy and I worked the crowd, table after table.

I knew if I didn't take money home tonight, I would have to hit the cold streets again tomorrow.

Now, you might think this is actually breaking the rules of door-to-door busking, but remember, this particular Christmas party was in a hotel and the hotel had doors and I knocked on them before I entered.

Luckily, the song I was attempting to sing only had two chords; it was a shocking version of 'Thirteen sleeps to go, thirteen sleeps till Santa'. When this tactic started to wane we sang (to the same tune) 'Give us your bloody money, give us your bloody money!' and when they did, when the bag became heavy with coins, we sang, 'We are off to Spain, we are off to Spain!'

Now, you better sit down for this because the amount we managed to scam in ten minutes may cause cardiac arrest. David Beckham, you'd better be seated as well. Sure, you may earn £10 million a year, but the door-to-door busker, against the odds, performing to pissed radio people, earned £76 in the time it takes for the average person to have a cup of tea. Unfortunately, the first thing that crossed my mind was, I wonder how much a night's accommodation at Donnington Castle would cost?

NO!

A very friendly Reading local even bought me a brandy to celebrate. We ended up throwing mince pies and bread rolls. I hadn't had this much fun since I was six. Robert from the Morning Crew reminded me that I was due in the studio at 6.30 a.m. for an interview about my busking adventures. I looked at my watch; it was now 10.30 p.m. Now, this would have been all well and good if Andrew (my new housemate) hadn't stopped off at a petrol station and said, 'I'll just get some Coke for the whisky.'

Needless to say, we finished the bottle, got drunk, told lies and sang rude songs.

Before we knew it, it was 3 a.m.

All I remember was the sound of 'Kiwi … Kiwi' in my ear. It was Cowlick Boy letting me know it was 6.30 a.m. I'd had three hours' sleep and we were due on the radio. I threw on some deodorant, brushed my teeth and Andrew drove me to the studio. As I ran into 2-Ten FM I saw the *On Air* light on and Rob waving at me to come in. I felt like I'd eaten the carpet.

'So, tell us why you're door-to-door busking around the UK, Justin?' Robert asked, looking decidedly more healthy than yours truly. Somehow I got the answers out. Somehow I sounded half-human. I needed water, badly. I felt like I had 17 builders renovating a kitchen in my temple. Bloody Andrew, bloody whisky; typically, it had all seemed such a good idea at the time.

I was quite happy just to ride my luck and count my money from last night. Unfortunately, the Morning Crew had other ideas. They sent me out in –2 °C to do some 'live' door-to-door busking. Not only was it freezing, it was also pitch-black. Let me tell you, if you thought busking in the light of day produced unsociable people, you should have been a fly on the wall at six-thirty in the morning.

A woman who'd obviously had a bad life had opinions she desperately wanted to express at this ungodly hour. She jumped out of her car and started abusing me. If I hadn't been hung over and actually had energy to laugh, her Wiltshire accent would have had me in fits. If you don't know how to emulate the Wiltshire accent, this wonderful bastardisation of the English word, just roll your *r*'s like a pirate.

Repeat after me: 'Oim a farrmerr and Oi droyve my truckterrr!'

Very good.

The woman spitting these words at me was now only a few yards away. My head hurt. I was cold. It was dark.

'Why don't you play rugby?' she spat.

'Pardon me?' I asked.

'There's a lot of old people around here that don't appreciate what you're doing.'

'I'm from New Zealand. I'm just trying to busk –'

'If you're from New Zealand, why don't you play rugby!'

'I'm a door-to-door –'

'I don't care.'

'I'm hung over. Would you like to hear a song?'

'No! Why don't you play rugby or something?'

She jumped in her car and slammed the door.

Fortunately, Andrew saved me from this embarrassment on the street and we drove to the nearest bus stop where we could sing without offending New Zealand rugby fans. Thankfully, I made £12.

And even better than the bottle of whisky that Andrew had provided was the greasy spoon breakfast which sent me straight to sleep.

9

Canterbury

Earnings to date: £181

I DECIDED TO head to Canterbury for no other reason than there's a Canterbury in New Zealand. What a meticulously well-planned trip this was turning out to be; nothing left to chance!

It was a Saturday and, as I walked the streets, I wondered: would the folk of Canterbury be more relaxed on their day off?

The Tally Ho pub was only metres from where I was going to start. It was tempting to head in, not for beer, far from it; if I could just sit in there, read the paper and sit by the fire that would mean I wouldn't have to hit the streets. The rain continued to fall as I dodged Friday night's chicken tikka masala on the footpath.

First door, a twenty-something girl answered in her pyjamas.

'Yes?' she queried.

It's moments like this I really wondered what I was doing. OK, so it was a bet, big deal. People have bets every night, it doesn't mean you have to carry them out. Remember playing the game Truth or Dare?

'I dare you to run in front of that car.'

'OK!'

But you never actually *ran* in front of the car, did you? Maybe you did. Maybe you're reading this from a hospital bed with both legs in plaster. My point is: most people don't go through with their bet. Sometimes I wish I hadn't. And if I tried to think rationally about what it was I was doing my head would explode. I wasn't just running on stupidity, I was running on blind faith. I was knocking on strangers' doors in the middle of the pissing rain, trying to convince girls in pyjamas to listen to warped melodies.

Oh, well. Who cares?

'Hi, I'm a door-to-door busker. Can I sing you a song?' I asked.

'Um,' she fidgeted with the door, obviously wanting to close the thing as quickly as possible. 'If I had my clothes on I'd listen.'

'Come on, just one song.'

'You can, but I'm gonna close the door.'

'You'd really close the door on me?'

'Yep, I'm having my lunch.'

'Anyone else in there?' I looked inside and saw a man in his dressing gown sprawled on the couch watching cartoons.

'My boyfriend,' she said.

'Will he listen to my song?'

'Look, you can sing all you like but I'm going to close the door.'

'You'd really close the door on me?' I smiled.

'If I had clothes on I'd listen.'

'But …'

Close.

A man with a fox terrier greeted me next. The dog was desperately trying to nuzzle his way between his owner's stubborn grasp.

'No, I don't want a song,' he mumbled.

He looked hard. I didn't want to push it. Some people have that 'I'm only gonna say this once' kinda look. He definitely had the 'I'm only gonna say this once' kinda look.

After half an hour I had made no money. This town felt extremely inhospitable. It had also started to snow. Again, due to the cold, my guitar had decided to emulate the pregnant seagull noise it had become so famous for in Harlington. I needed a motto and after frequent rejections already this morning, I thought of one: door-to-door busking – when one door closes, another one follows soon after.

Yes, the light at the end of this tunnel was definitely out of service until further notice. And the embarrassing thing about this particular street in Canterbury was the fact that the houses were so close together. This meant that after being rejected from one house, you'd literally take two steps to the left to try again. I hated to think those very people were sitting in their lounge listening to me getting a bollocking from their neighbour. Thankfully, the next neighbour didn't believe in such a thing.

Here was a man definitely in Saturday mode: messy hair, bare feet, unshaven. I spotted him cleaning out his garage, although to be honest he should have been cleaning the cat hair off his hand-me-down jersey. After listening pensively, then handing me a pound, he told me how his classical piano skills had earned him a spot on Radio Three just two days previous. A musician: I wanted to hug him. No, that's a lie. I wanted him to pack his bags and join me. He'd have to carry his own instrument, though.

'So, how has Canterbury shaped up, busking wise?' he asked me.

'Honestly?'

'Yeah?'

'Terrible,' I said. 'You are the first person in town that has listened to my song. I've been trying for just under an hour.'

'Typical,' he said. 'Bloody typical. Everyone is so far up their own arse in this country. That's why I want to move. You go to places like France and Spain, they're so much more hospitable.'

'You really think so?'

'Oh yeah, everyone's too busy trying to climb the ladder here. It's materialism, everyone's in a hurry. It's claustro-phobic.'

I think this man wanted to move.

'This is great what you're doing, though!' he said as the snow started to drift down onto my guitar strings. 'Good luck. I'm sure you'll make it.'

Not letting the snow deter me, I spotted a middle-aged woman in a shawl walking towards me. She didn't look that friendly but I was getting desperate. Sure, my classical pianist mate had proved a hit, but that didn't detract from the fact that I'd made a solitary pound in one hour. I decided to try my spiel walking beside her; sometimes it's harder for them to say no that way. You just start singing and hope for the best.

'Did you just see Dave down the road?' she asked.

'Is he the pianist?'

'Yes, very good musician is our Dave.'

Yes, and he wants to move.

'Would you like to hear a song?' I asked.

'No, not really.' She was fumbling around in her handbag looking for her keys. I gathered we must have been near her house. I didn't have a lot of time before she'd disappear so I explained the bet, making the obvious mistake of talking like a foreigner.

'Oh a *bet*! I thought you said *bit*!' she hollered.

This had been a major problem in the last week. Every time I said *bet*, people thought I was saying *bit*. Hence, when I said I lost a *bet* with an Aussie, they asked, 'You lost a *bit* of what?'

I was considering changing it to, 'I've lost a wager.' It may cause less confusion and God knows I needed that.

I managed to get her to listen to 'Harry Potter' and was looking forward to my second coin in Canterbury when she said, 'Sorry, but I've broken my collarbone and I'm saving for a holiday.'

Oh, bloody hell! I've heard them all now.

If my daughters were here I'd listen.

I'd listen if I had my clothes on.

I've broken my collarbone and I'm saving for a holiday.

Where do they find these excuses!

'How did you break your collarbone?' I asked.

This was a cover up for, 'Get your hand in your purse, lady.'

'How did I break my collarbone? Falling off a horse, of course!' she said. 'How else would you break your collarbone?'

I don't know, not giving money to a door-to-door busker?

I was starting to lose my patience in Canterbury. I heard some yappy dogs bolt down the stairs at the next house. No one answered, although I knew someone was home. I didn't really care if they were feeling uncomfortable on the other side of that door, I wasn't about to give up. I waited. And waited.

Finally, a woman opened the window on the second floor and leant out, holding a small dog. Is it just me or does everyone own a dog around here?

'Did you knock?' she asked.

'Yeah, how about a song on this lovely Saturday morning?' I didn't feel like being cheerful but it was my only option.

'No thanks,' she mumbled.

'I want to sing for you! Don't you want to hear my song?'

'No, not really.'

'Oh, you're joking! Come on, this could be the perfect *Romeo and Juliet* moment.'

'No, no … no I don't think so.'

'You're going to leave me out in the snow? In the cold? Come on, please, one song!'

I nearly thought I had her, but just as I was about to strike the first chord the dog's bark had become less audible; a dull thud signalled that the window had closed.

'What else are you gonna do? Oh, be boring then!'

It was all in vain; she had gone. And I was not happy in Canterbury.

I walked past a barber. He'll be friendly, I thought. He deals with the public all day. Plus I'm freezing. Maybe I can sit in the chair and do a free serenade for the guy getting a mop chop? I could be part of a barber shop quartet. I was a tad nervous walking in.

'Can't you see the sign outside?' the barber asked.

'Pardon?' I smiled, thinking he was joking.

'We're closed.' He didn't smile.

'I thought I'd just come and sing a song for you and warm my hands up.'

'The sign says closed, right?'

'Right,' I said. 'But I thought –'

'So?' he motioned to the door, holding a comb in his teeth. 'Sorry, bye.'

Did this whole town wake up on the wrong side of the bed this morning? I felt like an idiot; kicked out of a barber's shop, for God's sake! Sure, getting kicked out of a nightclub for being intoxicated? Fair enough. Booted out of a supermarket for guzzling grapes? Acceptable. But a barber's shop? What the hell was going on?

I moped along another curry and kebab-laden footpath, admiring some of the beautiful old cathedrals and buildings. What could be better than looking at a piece of history and smelling fish and chips and vinegar at the same time? I walked past a pub that bore a sign saying *Charles Dickens drank here*. For a Kiwi, this is staggering, absolutely staggering, to think that a hundred and fifty odd years ago one of the greatest writers ever used to pop in here for a quiet tipple. I never knew Canterbury would be so stunning, and like Chelsea the town was awash with Christmas decorations. The China Reject shop quickly became my favourite, purely for the name.

Imagine, you're at a party with Oxford and Cambridge snobs who for the last hour have been sipping Pimms and toffing on about inheritance, polo and houseboats in France.

'And what do *you* do for a living?' they ask, looking down at you.

'I'm a China Reject manager,' you proudly say.

'Oh, really? How … how, lovely.'

Sightseeing aside, I still only had a pound after an hour of busking. This called for desperate measures and a slight spin on the rules. I spotted a pub and all I needed to know was the pub had a door.

I swaggered up to the bar, not saying much, and ordered an orange juice. I'd been drinking too much lately and some vitamin C wouldn't go amiss. Don Partridge was right, the only time you'll see companionship is in the bar. You always ended up in them because that's where people were. That was my excuse anyway.

To get to this particular bar I had to brush past five locals who were having their midday Saturday pint.

'Oh, I wouldn't bring that in here,' one said, eyeing the guitar.

'Yeah, no busking in here, mate!' said his drinking buddy.

'You won't get any money in here, boy!'

Oh, we'll soon see about that. I'm not here for the atmosphere. A fat, red-faced man leaned against the bar next to me. The air smelt of smoke and old beer.

'What's your local drop like?' Fat, red-faced man asked.

Let me tell you, the last thing fat, red-faced man needed was a local drop. What he really needed was a local anaesthetic. This man had discovered too *many* local drops. His nose resembled a mashed plum and he smelt like a brewery; my kinda guy. Then again, if he'd survived this long drinking copious amounts of dodgy fermented ales, why the hell was I on OJ?

Meanwhile, my mates who had told me not to bring the guitar were in full flight at their lager-sodden table.

'What weighs thirteen pounds and won't be plucked this Christmas?' one said.

'What?' the others asked.

'George Harrison's guitar!'

'Oh that's fucking sick, mate.'

They all laughed. George Harrison had lost his fight with cancer in the last couple of days. Ironic that only a few days ago, my favourite lady in Reading had suggested I knock on the great Beatle's door, as he lived in the area.

Eventually, the barman's curiosity got the better of him and he asked about my guitar. I had purposely not walked into the pub with a hiss and a roar. Subtlety was the answer, especially when dealing with friends of the drink. You'd look a right tosser if you rudely burst into a pub and announced your presence in the following way: 'Good morning, Ladies and Germs! My name's Justin and I'll be your door-to-door busker this morning. Anyone celebrating a birthday? Excellent, don't tell me, you're eighteen with forty years' experience. Ha, ha! Hey, mate, ugly shirt, looks like you've thrown up. Don't clap by yourself, maam, someone will throw a fish at you. OK, here's one for the ladies!'

The barman pissed himself when I finally told him about my misfortune.

'My God, I've never heard of that before. What the fuck are you doing!'

I shrugged. I couldn't answer that question. I often wondered the same thing. My toes were still thawing, I was hungry, I had recently been kicked out of a barber's shop and had made one measly pound in an hour.

The barman continued: 'Streaking wouldn't be that hard anyway. He could get in *The Sun* for that. You've definitely got the short end of the stick. Listen, why don't I turn the stereo off and see if anyone wants to listen to you?'

Exactly what I was hoping for, me old china. He turned the music off. Nerves spread through me. Everyone kept talking. I turned to an old lady and her husband. 'Do you wanna hear a song?' I asked.

'No,' she said, slurping her G and T.

'Really?' I persisted.

'Is it any good?' her husband, nursing a half-pint, asked.

'It's bloody brilliant,' I lied.

The fat, red-faced guy at the bar kept talking to his mates. I stood at the front of the pub and sang, hoping like hell I wouldn't forget the lyrics. An audience of seven clapped at the end and I scoured the tables for spare change; my least favourite part of the busking routine, but an essential one. Proudly jingling the money in my pocket, I went back to the bar where the barman was also applauding.

'Great work, you'll make it for sure,' he said.

'Thanks,' I said, a weight having been lifted from my shoulders.

'Why don't you go down the road, there's another pub there. They'll help you out.'

There was indeed another pub down the road and I found it with relative ease, although my barman friend had confused me a little when he said to go past the 'sleeping policemen'. What a far less boring way of saying speed humps.

I had now made £6 in just over an hour. Canterbury was coming to the party. I was feeling better.

The pub was run by a lovely girl who, like her counterpart, offered to turn the music down while I sang. I found this overwhelming. They had no obligation to turn the music down for some idiot who lost a bet and only knew three chords. But they did, and for that I'm grateful.

Plus, I was out of the cold.

An American chef with those funny black-and-white checked longs wandered in with a steaming hot coffee and a music mag. Robbie Williams came on the stereo. He sighed, got up and changed the song.

'Don't you like that song?' I asked.

'Sick of Robbie, sick of shit music,' he said. He sat down and continued reading. Unfortunately for him, the next tune was also Robbie.

There were only three people in the pub, and two were staff. I was hoping two others that came in complaining that the football wasn't on Sky were going to stay and add to my busking kitty, but they left via the door. So it was up to me to impress the small but appreciative crowd. The chef didn't seem too impressed; to be honest, if Robbie couldn't please him, I didn't have a shit show in hell.

'Go on then, sing your damn song,' he laughed.

And I did.

The only customer in the pub asked me if I had penned the song myself, adding that it was 'bloody good'. I'll keep you on, I thought.

'You can play here tonight if you want. Do you want a room?' the girl who ran the pub asked.

This was very tempting, I've got to say. Even if I played to 30 people that night, I could potentially make £100, easy. But I felt that singing in pubs was not the nature of the bet. Sure, they had doors but I wasn't *really* door-to-door busking; I was performing in pubs. With £15 from these kind people and £5 from the other pub, that meant Canterbury had treated me to 21 big ones all up.

Although only one from door to door.

Again, I had been recommended another pub to busk in down the road, but when I arrived I didn't feel comfortable taking centre stage and disrupting an otherwise nice atmosphere. It was a big pub, people were eating, loud music was blaring from the jukebox and the barmaid was snogging a guy and looking through photo albums. I chickened out and sat down to rest my weary feet.

NEWS TRAVELS FAST and for some reason, when you're away from home, alone, bad news is harder to cope with. I first heard about Sir Peter Blake, KBE, when I was heading back to London from Canterbury. Sir Peter, who might as well have been the King of New Zealand, was tragically shot and killed by pirates on 6 December in Macapa at the mouth of the Amazon River. He had just embarked on a three-month study of wildlife and eventually ended up in Brazil aboard his boat *Seamaster*, where the shooting occurred.

There are all the usual reasons why Sir Peter was so incredible: regarded as one of the most successful sailors in yachting history, in 1995 he helped Team New Zealand become only the second non-American team in the America's Cup's 144-year history to take the trophy.

The whole country went nuts. Here was a man who influenced a whole bloody nation to wear red socks after we all found out that when Peter Blake wore red socks on the boat, the team won.

Every Kiwi household owns a pair.

But the real reason, I believe, is this: Peter Blake epitomised New Zealand. We loved him because he wasn't afraid to get stuck in, get his hands dirty and do what he loves. He had a famous saying: 'If it wasn't difficult to achieve then why bother doing it.' It was a sad day. He was an explorer and in all of us. New Zealand had lost its favourite son.

It was for this reason that a few mates and I made the decision to go to Sir Peter's funeral in Emsworth. We had no idea where the place was or how to get there. We didn't even know Peter Blake. We were just fans and wanted to pay respect. The guitar could stay at home.

What I didn't know about Sir Peter, as a New Zealander, was that he spent so much time in England. I always thought, naïvely, he just stayed in New Zealand till the next America's Cup rolled around. But in 1970 he moved to Ol' Blighty and for the first time competed in the Whitbread Round the World race. He became the only person to compete in the first five Whitbreads, that run ending when he won the event in 1989. Here was a truly incredible man.

We arrived in the southern town of Havant (just outside Emsworth) and caught a taxi with a local guy to St Thomas à Becket Church. A few other locals told us they couldn't believe the amount of people infiltrating this otherwise quiet town to celebrate a truly great life. Cars backed up, parking miles from the church. People walked in silence.

I felt very out of place wearing jeans and a sweatshirt as I had brought no going-out clothes with me, but I think Sir Peter would have appreciated that. He wasn't a suit man. As I looked around I realised I wasn't alone. Some people wore long winter coats, others Team New Zealand jackets and a couple of Kiwis were wearing Swanndris (iconic bush shirts).

More than a thousand people gathered around the thousand-year-old church, including representatives of the British Royal Family and the United Nations Environment Programme. Red socks were at half-mast. No one said anything but I'm sure people were concerned about their toes falling off. It was –2 °C and a bloody cold southerly swept straight off the ocean. Just the elements for Sir Peter; he would have been proud.

He was described as a gentle giant, father, mentor and leader. His older brother told of the time Sir Peter asked, 'How high is the sky?'

The general feeling at the funeral was one of disbelief and anger. How could one bullet from one dickhead in South America take the life of someone who, as one yachtie described him at the funeral, 'was only beginning to hit his stride'?

Toes frozen and eyes watery, the service finished and our friendly local directed us to Emsworth Sailing Club to join the rest of the mourners for drinks and food. Old men walked around with bottles of red and white wine, continuously filling our glasses. I had barely taken a sip when old Cyril had replaced it with more. Fantastic, keep this guy on. In the corner of the marquee a video showed Peter Blake sailing in the America's Cup. New Zealand songs blasted through the stereo.

As we were just fans and didn't actually know the family, we pretty much kept to ourselves. Just being here felt privileged enough. We also knew there'd be a celebration of Sir Peter's life back in New Zealand, but it was a special feeling being here at his English home. We sipped quietly and toasted Sir Peter.

This wasn't to be the case for the two West Auckland builders wearing the Swanndris, though. Once the rum and Cokes (Sir Peter's favourite drink) started to flow in the boat club, they grabbed a guitar each and brought the house down with renditions of 'Stand by Me' and New Zealand singalongs 'Weather with You' and 'Whaling'.

Respect to you guys; I would never have had the balls to do that.

It was a special day in a special place.

Sir Peter Blake would have loved it and I can guarantee he wouldn't have worn a suit.

10

Paddington Station, London

Earnings to date: £202.54

I KNOW WHAT you're thinking; how did the 54p get in there? OK, I'll come clean. A yachtie at Sir Peter Blake's funeral was so fascinated by what I was doing he dug around in his pockets apologising for such a small amount. He insisted I take it. Plus, if I converted it to New Zealand dollars I could buy a small car.

Bad news as I arrived at Paddington: carol singers. It had to happen, I was just hoping not so soon. I never anticipated competition from carol singers. We never get them in New Zealand. How the hell was I supposed to compete with an out-of-tune five year old and his grandma singing 'The First Noël' for the millionth time? There they were, a sizeable group churning out the same hits as last year, collectively forgetting the words, playing the wrong chords, the older ones peering out from the top of their glasses and making a meal of songs people were glad they only had to endure once a year. Honestly, how can someone sing the same old crap every year and get paid for it?

Then I remembered what my repertoire consisted of.

Heading west was my next challenge, hence buying a ticket at Paddington. On platform number eight I met a lady from New York who must have been in her forties. Upon inspection of my guitar and backpack she admitted she was jealous of young people today. She said she wished she could do the same, just take off around the world. I tried to convince her it was no different for her and her healthy body, but she didn't believe me.

'So, how *is* the busking going?' she asked.

'Lots of grumpy people. A few open their doors.'

'Really? I can't believe more people don't open their doors and have a laugh.' She paused, then continued. 'But saying that, I had some guys come around the other night wanting to sing a song and I didn't open the door.'

'Exactly,' I said.

'They said they were carol singers. They were about 16, three of them.'

'Balaclavas?'

'No,' she laughed.

Would look a bit suss, wouldn't it? Three carol singers confronting you on your doorstep singing in unison: 'Oi, give us your money, lady! I mean … Jingle bells, jingle bells …'

Eventually I wanted to end up in Wales but for now my train ticket would take me to Swindon. I'd heard so much about Swindon – all bad. The football team (?), the magic roundabout and the very close families. Oh, come on, that's not very fair. To be honest, the poor people of Swindon had to listen to my dulcet tones every morning five years ago as I somehow fumbled my way through a breakfast show. Eventually the county of Wiltshire revolted and had me evicted quicker than you could say: 'Will someone teach that Kiwi to sing!'

I told them I would be back so here I was. But would Wiltshire give more than Reading?

Steve, my old boss, met me at the door of the radio station

and looked a little surprised to see a forlorn-looking Kiwi with a guitar draped around his back and a duffel coat some poor grizzly bear was living without.

Unfortunately the words, 'Welcome back, let me shout you lunch,' wasn't the first thing Steve said.

However, what he did say would supply me with employment the next day.

'I'd love to sit and chat, Justin, but I'm just going to drop some doughnuts off to a turkey farm.'

'Run that by me again,' I said, hearing an opportunity rattle around in my otherwise unoccupied mind that seemed too good to pass by.

'I said, I just have to drop off some doughnuts to a turkey farm. They won them last week and we forgot to deliver them.'

This man wasn't going anywhere without me.

'I'll get my guitar,' I said.

The turkey farm was in a small hamlet called Bushton. I tuned my guitar in the car and thought to myself, wow, I've never sung to turkey people. Selecting a song from my dwindling list was a piece of cake: 'Kentucky Fried Kitten' seemed perfect.

The first thing I noticed was bird shit, everywhere. A fox terrier yapped at my feet and true to form, as soon as I got out of the car into the cold, my guitar decided to de-tune itself. Dodging mud, more bird shit and feathers, I made my way to where the turkey pluckers were in full swing. In a shed about the size of a double bedroom were men and women, young and old, ripping feathers off recently deceased birds. Did I mention feathers?

I crouched under the tiny doorway, attempting to re-tune my guitar. This was not a happy bunch of workers. All were knee high in feathers, facing the wall just praying this hell would soon be over. No one seemed very interested in what they were about to hear either, my main competition being the constant sound of pluck, pluck, pluck and Terry Wogan telling a joke on Radio Two. They continued to face the wall and pluck as I sung 'Kentucky Fried Kitten'. Forget the Auckland City Library, forget serenading builders, even forget Engelbert, *this* was now the most bizarre gig I'd ever done: singing to ten live humans and ten dead birds.

Now, call me old-fashioned but one small prerequisite I ask from my audience is that they stay alive during the entire performance, otherwise, like the cheapskate turkeys here, they walk away with a freebie.

And that's hardly fair on the rest of the punters.

Terry Wogan was still talking by the time I'd finished my song. The sound of one-hand clapping was almost audible, although that was overshadowed by the rip, rip, rip of feathers being yanked from a Christmas dinner's back. As you can probably gather, this was not a nice place.

I felt a little uncomfortable at the conclusion as no one said a thing. They just looked at me, then at their turkeys. Either they were extremely dedicated to the job or just completely brainwashed.

'Your guitar's out of tune.'

Yes, they speak! Yippee! Give that man a prize.

'It's your G-string, way flat,' the man with turkey feathers through his hair, kindly offered.

A few muffled sniggers bounced around walls, obviously laughing at the sexual connotation he had provided. He was right, though, not only was my G-string flat, every bloody string that had the misfortune to be laden on my guitar was. The man with feathers in his hair turned out to be Dave, a self-proclaimed gypsy who played the mandolin, hence the musical advice.

Behind me a girl brought over a live bird. She was an attractive girl and seemed completely unfazed holding a huge, plump turkey by its feet. It would eventually end up with the big boss (who looked exactly like the boss in *Chicken Run*), who in turn would warm up some sort of machine where the turkey would perform its last gobble. This machine made me feel sick. OK, so I ate turkey but I never knew they electrocuted them as part of punishment for having two fine breasts and a couple of corker legs. The bird was placed head-first in a big funnel of sorts, legs hanging in the air and *Chicken Run* man would then push the red button.

Right about now, that turkey was shitting itself. I couldn't help but wonder what he was thinking: 'I never thought it would end like this! Who will I leave the farm to? Bugger … did I leave the oven on?'

The red button was pushed with relative ease, an electric current ran through the poor bastard's little bird brain, his legs went stiff with shock, then he hung limply waiting for the attractive girl to pull him out, hang him on the wall and give him the full body wax. We're bloody sick sometimes, don't you reckon?

This whole torture scene had interrupted my train of thought somewhat. Well, it's not every day you see an animal being killed. I just couldn't understand how *Chicken Run* man did it all so matter-of-factly. I know, it's only his job and he does it every day but does that make it OK?

Only if the gravy's done just right.

During this hideous scene I had forgotten to ask the pluckers to contribute to my depleted fund. Blank faces resulted. Some waited for someone else to make the first move.

'Come on, I don't mean to be rude but I'm door-to-door

busking around the whole country.'

All of a sudden they were emptying their pockets, and the guy who was a real smart arse just ten minutes previously turned out to be the first to give.

'You should come and work here tomorrow. I'll give you two pounds a turkey,' *Chicken Run* guy said, putting another bird in the electric chair.

'Yeah, come tomorrow, I'll bring my mandolin,' said Dave.

I looked at workers covered in shit and feathers, wondering why in God's name I'd want to spend even five minutes in the most disgusting, inhumane, barbaric, not to mention smelly, shed of horror I'd ever set my naïve eyes on and resoundingly said, 'YES!'

I was now, officially, the world's only door-to-door plucker.

I didn't sleep much that night, and kept dreaming about birds and aviaries and slicing poor canaries' heads off. Why canaries, I don't know; you try and figure out what goes on in your subconscious after visiting a turkey farm.

I was nervous the next morning. What would I wear? More to the point, what would I be happy never to wear again? It's not as if I had a portable washing machine with me as I busked around the UK, and the chances of me carrying feather and shit-covered jeans with me till I found a Laundromat were very slim indeed. I felt like it was my first day at school. Would they laugh at me? Would I even be able to touch a bloody turkey? Would it scar me for life? Would it scar the bird for life?

I don't know why, but I expected some sort of standing ovation for actually turning up to the farm today. 'Wow, he made it, he's really going to do it.'

Instead, the very sounds that repulsed me yesterday were still as loud as ever: Pluck, pluck, pluck. Rip, rip, rip.

Most were silent in their work apart from my long-haired friend who gave money yesterday. He was listening to Radio Two and singing Van Morrison's 'Brown Eyed Girl'.

'Good morning,' he said.

'Hi.'

He was no mug. He knew I was shitting bricks. He also knew he could be the school bully and harass the new boy who had never plucked a turkey before. You see, already, these people had an advantage, they had at least handled live and dead turkeys before. I'd only had it placed in front of me with roast potatoes and wine. Even though it was −1 °C, sweat was dripping from my brow.

It was around 9 a.m. and judging by the amount of feathers in the workers' hair, most had been here a while. I still couldn't for the life of me work out how they got feathers there. It made me laugh.

Procrastinate! Quick! Anything to avoid actually starting, I thought to myself.

'I'll see you guys soon,' I stumbled. 'I've … just got to … go over here,' I said, pointing to nothing in particular. I can hang my jacket up! That's what I can do, that'll take a good five minutes.

At least a hundred dead turkeys were hanging upside down in the storeroom next to the main plucking shed. *Chicken Run* man was also in there on the phone. He acknowledged my presence and, slowly, I hung my coat up, taking particular care with the jacket only yesterday I didn't give a toss about.

'They've got to look like this when you're finished with them,' *Chicken Run* guy said as soon as he was off the phone. He was pointing to the hundred dead turkeys that were stripped of anything that resembled a feather.

'No problem,' I said.

Shit. Shit, shit, shit.

'Well?'

'Well what?' I asked. *Chicken Run* man was drinking his tea in the storeroom.

'You gonna start or what?' he said, again motioning to the dead birds.

'Yeah, hell yeah. Just gonna hang my, um, jacket up. I think it's fallen down.'

I sidled over to check my jacket was still hung up. Yep, no problem there, firmly in place. That jacket is definitely well and truly hung up. But *do* I need to go to the toilet?

'What do most of your mates do?' *Chicken Run* man asked.

'Back in New Zealand you mean?'

'Yeah, New Zealand, or you must have some working in London?'

This was good, very good. Conversation, keep it coming.

'A few of them work in IT,' I said.

'What, computers?'

'Yeah.'

'That sounds a bit boring. So, not a real job like this?'

We turned around to see the recently deceased turkeys hanging upside down with blood running to their heads.

'Yeah, I guess so,' I said.

During the time it took to check and re-check my coat, I also met *Chicken Run* man's wife. She was carrying a newborn baby around her neck and walking around with a needle and thread. I had to ask Dave what the hell she was doing.

'She's fixing the turkeys that get ripped,' he told me, pulling fresh feathers from a bird.

'How do you mean, ripped?' I asked.

'Well, the cardinal sin when plucking is to pull a feather out too hard and rip a piece of the meat. The breast is the worst.'

'So she goes around repairing ripped breasts on turkeys?'

'Yep,' he smiled.

'All day?'

'Yep.'

'And looks after the baby at the same time?'

'Uh huh.'

What a way to see the world in your first month of life.

Unfortunately, I had exhausted all possible stalling tactics. The time had come to pluck one of these godforsaken birds. *Chicken Run* man told me to go and get one from the shed.

What, *I* have to? I imagined they just sort of arrived hung up. I walked up the ramp to the shed feeling very vegetarian. Thirty turkeys eyed me. What bothered me more than anything was they didn't look nervous at all, despite half their mates having been absent for days. Ironically, I was crapping my pants; they were oblivious to death row just around the corner.

'Just grab one by the leg and bring it over here!' *Chicken Run* man yelled.

Easy for you to say, I thought, but which one? They all looked at me. I can't just grab one. This is horrible. I want my bed. I want my guitar. Door-to-door busking might suck but it's not this bad.

I grabbed a turkey by the leg and then grabbed the other leg. I couldn't believe he wasn't stressed or flapping. I made him say goodbye to his mates, then I took him to the electric chair.

This is the part I couldn't watch.

But had to.

'Now, grab one of these,' *Chicken Run* man said, pointing to some string after he'd executed my new friend. 'And tie it round his legs like this and get plucking.' He handed me the bird, which, even though killed only two minutes previous, already felt heavier.

It pains me even to think about this next part of my life. Think of the worst thing you can and multiply it by a thousand. I really didn't want to be there.

My terminal feathered friend and I ventured into the plucking shed. Twelve other people were ripping, plucking and swearing. I plodded my way to a spare corner, knee high in feathers. No one really spoke, I think most were depressed knowing there were 3,000 turkeys to get through. I hung the turkey up on a spare hook. The guy next to me, knowing I was a new recruit, explained how to rip the wing feathers off first.

'Before they get too cold,' he said. 'Too hard to pull off if they're cold.'

The old guy to my right offered more advice: 'It's all right, we've all had our first one. Things get easier.'

How sweet, it felt like he was dropping me off for my first date. What really bothered me was, what the hell was this old guy doing here in the first place? Why wasn't he at home smoking a pipe and watching the cricket?

I was really hoping my long-haired friend two turkeys along would take me under his wing (so to speak) or, even better, do the whole job for me. Unfortunately, he was busy in his own hell. Meantime, a dead bird lay upside down in front of me, blood quickly rushing to its pimply neck, making it a deep purple.

'Do you like doing this?' I asked the younger guy to my left, who couldn't have been more than 16.

'Hate it, but it's money in't it?'

'Do you look at turkeys differently in the supermarket?'

'Food's food.'

'Do you get bored?' I asked.

'Shit, yeah.'

'How do you keep going?'

'Just try and make it to the next break.'

Stop stalling, Brown! Start plucking. A sudden burst of energy had me ripping, pulling, yanking, tearing and grunting. This resulted in leaving the turkey looking no different than five minutes before. I hadn't even touched the surface. It was as if the feathers had grown as quickly as I plucked them. Oh, yes, you may laugh but do you know how many bloody feathers are on a turkey? I discovered all too quickly what my neighbour meant about pulling off feathers when they were cold; almost impossible. Like trying to pull a tree stump out of the ground. I couldn't believe we weren't wearing gloves.

Is it possible to get salmonella in the arm?

I was also starting to seriously doubt the payment for this less than graceful job. Only £2 a turkey? Should have been £2 a feather; what these people were putting up with was unimaginable. Unfortunately, it also became bleeding obvious why the workers had feathers, not just over their legs and clothes but all *through* their hair. Only yesterday I had been quietly pissing myself looking at Dave who looked like he'd been rolling around the inside of a pillowcase for the last two weeks.

Now I knew why.

Every time someone brought a new, recently deceased turkey into the plucking shed, chances were that it would have one last fit. Now, you'd think if you were to flap around like a madman for two minutes, one of the worst possible places to do it would be in a shed full of workers up to their knees in feathers, right?

So there we were, plucking away, hating life, listening to 'Fairytale in New York' on the radio, when a new turkey arrived on the scene. Struggling to hook it up on the wall, the plucker had to accept that the dead bird was in need of one last send-off. Feathers went everywhere! In your eyes, in your mouth, in your ears, in your hair. This was a snowstorm. You couldn't see for feathers. Eventually, when it went beyond a joke and someone was in fear of physically inhaling feathers and choking, they'd yell, 'All right, Brian, just kill the bloody thing, will ya!'

I was exhausted after 20 minutes of yanking feathers. Meanwhile, the 16 year old next to me was onto his second and the old guy to my right offered more kind words: 'If you need these pliers to get the last wings off, let me know.'

Thanks, Pop, but right at this very moment I need more than pliers. I had a situation on my hands.

Now, I should warn you, if you're at all squeamish, skip this next paragraph.

For it is the turkey's anus that I left till last. The boss had made it quite clear that every single feather had to be stripped from the bird. Don't ask me why but I stupidly left the backside till last. I suppose I was living in false hope. I just figured it was akin to eating roast lamb and potatoes when you were a kid and leaving your vegetables till last. You always hoped the courgettes and leaks would do an amazing disappearing act. But they didn't and neither, I'm afraid, did the turkey's anus. Not only that, my one shat itself after it died. Hence, I had to pluck around his bum, taking extreme care not to rip the breasts. To make matters worse, sometimes when you pulled the stubborn, twig-like feathers out, bits of marrow squirted over your clothing.

Most of the time the body was still warm.

More stuffing, anyone?

Judging by the amount of songs I'd heard on the radio I must have been stripping this bird for over an hour. I was sick of fucking plucking. My sense of humour was nowhere in sight. I yanked the bird off the hook and took it to *Chicken Run* man. Again, I was hiding my leaks and courgettes under my knife and fork, hoping the boss wouldn't notice that this bird wasn't entirely bald, but pretty close.

'No no, no!' he said upon inspection. 'Got to be as bald as a badger, like these ones.' Again, he was pointing to the prized trophies hanging up next to my coat, which, come to think of it, I hadn't checked for a while. 'Keep going, that's not good enough, boy.'

Bloody hell. This was not fun any more. Joke's over. Bet's over. Screw you, Mark, you win.

Finally, it was time for a cuppa. Everyone washed their hands and tucked into the doughnuts that my old boss, Steve, had delivered yesterday. Mother and baby were still repairing torn breasts. She soon showed what a true pro she was when, upon discovering *Chicken Run* man was nowhere in sight and seeing a worker (obviously not keen on a tea break) holding a new victim ready for the electric chair, scoured the shed for appropriate assassins. Proof that not just anyone was allowed to murder turkeys, she motioned to the man behind me eating his third doughnut.

'You couldn't just kill a turkey for Dave, could you? I'm a bit busy.'

And she continued sewing while baby slept.

No sooner had I started on my third cuppa than it was time to hit the damn shed again. Again, I used delaying tactics. I spoke to the dog. I washed my hands. I remarked on the cold weather. I asked how many turkeys they'll do this year.

'Three thousand, really? Isn't that lovely? What's your dog's name? Wow, nice name!'

'Are you gonna do another one?' *Chicken Run* man asked. Damn.

I ended up doing two turkeys in just under two hours. The young guy next to me had done at least seven.

Eventually I said, 'Bugger this, I'm going busking.'

It would have looked bad just doing one, hence going through the pain of doing a second. I asked to use the phone and called Steve at the radio station. I wanted to leave and never come back. While waiting for my ride, Dave asked if I'd like to meet his mates who were living in caravans down the road celebrating winter solstice. I took his number and said I'd give him a call.

At least I think that's how the conversation went; I was a little preoccupied, thinking only of sleep and a shower. *Chicken Run* man eventually put his hand in his pocket, after ten minutes of small talk, and handed me a £5 note. Before he could ask for change it was in my back pocket.

Hardest money I'd ever earned.

Saying goodbye to my co-workers was not difficult. I was busting to get out of there. I walked past 20 turkeys in the holding pen where I had earlier selected my two victims. They all looked wonderfully naïve and curious, as if to say, 'Wonder what's going on next door? What are we missing out on? Please tell us, mister!'

Trust me fellas, you *really* don't want to know.

I must have looked like a homeless person as Steve drove into his car park. Actually, no, that's unfair to homeless people. I had bird shit, feathers and bits of dead bird on my apparel. The feathers in my hair obviously confused a few people at the radio station; I'm sure they didn't know whether I just had really bad dandruff or highlights.

'Turkey feathers,' I said to a bunch of corporates who had just come out of a meeting.

'*Right*,' they said, thinking, 'who let this one in?'

Good news followed; I had a bed for the night and things were looking a whole lot better for tomorrow. Unknown to me, there was actually a village called New Zealand in Wiltshire. Even better, someone from the radio station was going to drop me there first thing in the morning. Would my country's namesake give money to the door-to-door busker? At this very moment I didn't care. I had a shower and a bed and a view unobstructed by a dead turkey's arse. I was happy.

To think those poor bastards were still plucking.

11

London Road, Devizes
(via New Zealand)

Earnings to date: £210

I SPENT LAST night with Steve and Susanna, a lovely couple who had no problem with a door-to-door busker sharing their home. In fact, as the night wore on I wished that I had knocked on *their* door when I was busking. Reason being, about 7 p.m., a door-to-door pedlar turned up with various wares that you wouldn't touch with a barge pole. I mean, who the hell would buy five golden dusters, a smart clean mop, 20 disposable cloths, a de-mister pad, a shammy and a handbag torch made of halogen?

Forty-one pounds later, Steve and Susanna had enough junk for a garage sale before the weekend even started. I stood on the stairs marvelling at the pedlar's selling technique.

'Please, if I sell just one more thing I will get my bonus,' he would say.

Stiff shit, looks like you won't be getting your bonus, I would have said.

The clincher was the halogen torch, which I'm sure our pedlar friend had been trying to shift for months. A born salesman, he left it till the very last and, hoping Susanna would buy one more thing so he could make his bonus, pulled it from the bag adding, 'Here's one for the ladies!'

The link between ladies and torches was beyond me but Bonus Boy didn't care. He had emptied half his bag and was off to the pub. He thanked us and wished us goodnight. My mouth hung open at the amount of money that had exchanged hands in the last couple of minutes, all for a couple of dishcloths. I hadn't made that much in three days.

Susanna closed the door, locked it and said, 'What the hell are we going to do with all this shit?'

Thanks for the bed guys and sorry about the bath – damn feathers.

Waking up and not having to pluck turkeys had a profound effect on me. I felt like the luckiest man in the world. Every now and again I'd think about the shed and the electric chair and those poor bloody workers who'd be wishing Christmas was over. Although today, I did have a TRI (turkey related injury), in the form of cut hands. Never again, I thought to myself.

Upon arrival at the radio station, I was shocked to hear there was a phone call for me. Luckily it wasn't bad news, but instead was Dave the gypsy, my mandolin-playing friend. How he got the number in the first place was beyond me; later I'd found out he'd enquired which radio station the winning doughnuts had come from. Walking into an office after two weeks of hustling and bustling at doorsteps was a luxurious feeling.

'Hi, Dave,' I said, tempted to put my feet up on the desk like those wannabe bosses.

'Hi, listen, are you going to come down and join us for winter solstice? It'll be great, we'll get a bit stoned and play some music.'

'Sounds good, Dave,' although I knew someone from the

radio station was keen on dropping me off in the village of New Zealand. Maybe I could meet the gypsies after that? 'Why can't I just come down with you when you've finished plucking turkeys for the day?'

'Can't mate. I'm flat on my back. I'm still *at* the turkey farm lying in my caravan. Me back's gone. Do me a favour, when you get down to the fields, can you tell Pete to come up here so he can ride my horse back? I can't move.'

Looks like I'm going to see the gypsies.

But not before Craig, the journalist from the station, dropped me off in New Zealand. He also told me he'd be heading to a town called Devizes for a press conference and would be quite happy to take me there if I was ready in an hour. Wow, what service, I'd never had this before.

As we arrived in New Zealand I was flooded with positive thoughts. The very sign at the start of the village signalled this was going to be a happy hour. It was tempting to ring Mark in Melbourne and say I'd made it home.

Lush fields, birds singing, pheasants flying from the trees, cows lying in the fields; this felt just like home but for the temperature. The sun may have been shining and the sky the bluest I had seen in England but −1 °C told me that I'd be tuning the guitar more than once today. I warmed up by singing to the cows who proved to be a good attentive audience, but not the most generous. RAF planes buzzed overhead to Lynham Airfield as I dodged horse shit and walked over dead leaves. The smell of horse crap and sheep shit made me homesick.

Beaming in the sunlight was my New Zealand sticker. Surely locals would see the connection? Surely they'd see the relevance of a Kiwi visiting his country's namesake? How could I lose? I'd had a good sleep, I was feather-free and I was ready for entertaining. Could be a record day.

'Hi, I'm from New Zealand and I'm a door-to-door busker!' I said to my first lady of the day.

Her dull, uninterested face was overwhelming. A face of boredom quickly turned to fear, as if she'd spotted a sledgehammer in my duffel coat. She couldn't end the conversation quickly enough; the door was hurriedly closed, locked and bolted.

That's OK, I reassured myself, she was old and worried, I wouldn't have listened either.

No problem, New Zealand, I still like you and I still feel confident.

'I would listen to you, but I don't actually live here,' the old lady next door informed me.

This I found hard to believe. You don't live here? Dossing are you? No, don't tell me, you're just staying here till you get a more permanent job closer to town? You're 70!

I don't actually live here.

I still didn't understand why that meant you couldn't listen to a song. I wasn't aware you had to have a mortgage to listen to a busker.

'I'm just looking after the house,' she finally said.

'I'm from New Zealand as well, see?' I pointed to my New Zealand sticker.

'Yes, but I'm only looking after the house.'

'But I'm from New Zealand,' I persisted.

'Yes, but I'm *only* looking after the house.'

'But I'm from New Zealand!'

And so on and so on; she was old and I was unemployed, we could have been there all day.

Some houses have that ability to make you really nervous. The one now standing in front of me seemed haunted: paint falling off, curtains drawn, rusty unwanted cars on the lawn. A tractor and old tables sat in knee-high weeds along with a smashed birdbath and a second-hand fridge. This place looked like a bomb had hit it.

But, as had happened so many times before, it's at the houses you don't want to go to that something happens. Kind of like the nights you don't want to go out but you do and end up having a ripper.

I finally got the guts to do it, walked up to a door that upon inspection had no handle! I stood there in disbelief. There was no way to get into this house via traditional means, which, I'm sure you'd agree, makes life very hard for a door-to-door busker.

After such excitement and anticipation, New Zealand was fast becoming a wet fish. Everyone was grumpy or not interested; not so much as a smirk. Did they not know the effort I'd gone to? I had to make some leeway; this was embarrassing. My ride would soon be here to take me to Devizes. What was I going to tell Craig after initially being so excited about the village?

Down the end of a very long driveway a sign read, *No views of the airfield, please respect our privacy*.

Obviously, this was the sort of area where excitable trainspotters ventured into backyards they shouldn't, hoping for an elusive view of a Hercules getting its wing nuts changed. I suppose this sign should have been a deterrent, but in my opinion I didn't need any more encouragement.

It's funny, the longer a driveway the harder it becomes; at least if someone's house is on the street you can make a quick getaway. You can run into the neighbour's house. You can run across the road and hug a cat. If you're stranded down a mile-long driveway, evil thoughts and hallucinations take over. Big, fiery creatures and *Star Wars* freaks jump from the bushes and chase you down the driveway.

A negative response awaited me. 'No, not interested, thanks.'

'Come on!' I was losing my patience and had to start using other tactics. 'Do you know, no one, not a soul, has listened to my song in your whole village. I've come especially here, to New Zealand, because *I'm* from New Zealand, see?' again, pointing to the sticker on the guitar. '*Please*, just listen.'

'Oh, all right then, but I haven't got that long.'

YIPPEE! Begging is good, begging works! Try it at home, kids.

Typically, my poor victim seemed to do the old 'When's this song going to end?' look, closely followed by the 'Where's my bloody wallet?' look. I suppose it is hard to enjoy the moment when there's a stranger singing in your space. It's just very rare to see someone enjoy the moment and not look stressed.

Such trivial matters were washed away in minutes because, now, I had my first shiny gold coin from New Zealand.

She had even warmed up. 'Hope you make it,' she said with a half smile.

See? As soon as they see you're not going to steal the telly they act differently.

Planes continued to buzz overhead. If I were a plane spotter I'd be able to inform you of makes and models, but to me they were just a noisy piece of machinery landing next to your clothesline. I asked my new friend what it was like living next to a landing strip with Hercules and Tiger Moths.

'I've lived here for such a long time I don't notice it.'

'Really, that's interesting,' I said.

Bollocks, I thought.

Considering New Zealand was more a hamlet than a village, and I had exhausted most avenues in sight (that is, houses), my only option now was to follow a sign, *Country fresh eggs*. Honestly, turkey farms and egg farms; what bizarre occupations I was discovering in Ol' Blighty. I wondered whether the egg counters should get together with the China Reject managers from Canterbury.

But I was learning that being a door-to-door busker had a funny way of making you simplify things; the egg place would have people and ears and money. That's all I needed to know.

Country fresh eggs consisted of a concrete shed, a lone bike leaning against the front door and an *Opening Hours* sign suggesting they were never open.

Fortunately they were.

A scraggly old man who looked like Worzel Gummage very kindly said I would be allowed to perform. And I'm proud to say, my latest audience consisted not of turkey pluckers or builders or even Engelbert fans, but grown men counting eggs. Later I would find out they would count and sort 9,000 that day. Once again, 'Kentucky Fried Kitten' seemed appropriate, especially as the family cat made an appearance, rubbing against my leg while I sung of his brothers and sisters becoming part of a quarter pack. He didn't seem to care, along with the egg counters who weren't even listening. I could have been singing 'Stuttering Sadie from Stuttgart' and they wouldn't have batted an eyelid. Eventually, silence helped them with the decision that the song was over, although even then only eggs were on their mind. Thankfully, they stopped counting and passed me a quid.

'So, where have you been on your travels?' a man who I assumed was the boss asked.

'All over the place, mate. I was plucking turkeys yesterday. Did two in two hours,' I said, proudly.

'I wouldn't be doing that. Got to know what you're doing to do that.'

'Tell me about it,' I said.

OK, so I wasn't exactly setting the place on fire, but at least I had something to show for my busking in New Zealand. And even though in *this* New Zealand, there was a distinct lack of beer, barbecues and girls in bikinis, it did have its own charm. It was quiet and rural and there were lots of eggs.

True to form, my hands were now blue and I'd given up re-tuning the guitar. I'd just wander through the tree-laden roads practising out of key, which wasn't too hard. I heard footsteps sloshing through the horse shit behind me. It was a jogger who was suffering from 'cycling shorts riding up the bum syndrome'.

'You practising out here so no one can hear you?' she asked.

'No, I'm a door-to-door busker from New Zealand,' I said, finding it hard to imagine she'd have any coinage up those orifices even if I could get a song in anyway.

'You can come around to my house after if you like!'

This would've held some merit, but for the fact she was running away from me at a brisk pace.

'Really, what's your address?' I yelled.

'BYE!'

And she was gone.

Cycling shorts, that's it! I could wear cycling shorts as I busk the streets. Maybe not; my starved mind was up to its old tricks. I needed a manager who I could bounce ideas off. Should I wear cycling shorts? Should I busk even though I have a TRI? Could anything be more bizarre than singing to men sorting 9,000 eggs?

Well, yes, and it came at the next house.

A postman was talking to a plump lady at the doorstep of

what looked like an old chapel. It looked like a nice chat between friends and initially I wasn't going to interrupt their routine, but I'd had such a lousy hour I needed to know someone was at least home. Plus, you don't feel such a freak or intruder when there's more than one person at the doorstep.

So I scared the postie off and sung to the lady.

Actually, that's a lie. For this woman didn't quite understand the concept of door-to-door busking.

'Yes, that would be great!' she gleamed. 'You start singing and I'll go to the kitchen to see what money I've got.'

Um, that wasn't quite what I was thinking of. I could hear her rummaging through drawers, slamming doors and whistling in the heart of the house. Meanwhile, I was standing at a stranger's door singing to a Raggedy Anne doll hanging up next to Jesus on the cross. What have I become?

A painter in overalls joined her as she returned with a £5 note. I could barely contain my excitement at seeing a note instead of coins, so asked if she could take a photo of Overalls Man and myself in front of the chapel.

'Yes, I'd love to!' she sparkled.

Her enthusiasm was contagious. This was one happy woman and I was one happy man until she dropped my camera on the concrete driveway.

I didn't feel bad taking the £5.

GLAD TO REPORT, when Craig picked me up I had £7 in my pocket and I was sitting in a warm car. But I'm sorry New Zealand of Wiltshire, I can't hand you all the glory for Overalls Man and nimbly fingered plump woman, as they were actually based *outside* the village. I can only credit your village with £2. The first I got because I basically begged the woman by the airfield and the other £1 was from middle-aged men who counted eggs for a living.

Well done, for like my favourite lady in Reading, you saved your village's sorry arse reputation.

My hands never left the heater the entire journey. My digits slowly thawed and my toes slowly felt like they were mine again. Craig the journalist was going to some press conference in Devizes about child abuse; I figured gate crashing and singing to a bunch of cops wouldn't do much for his future.

It's amazing what five minutes in a normal, humane atmosphere can do for you. You feel, well, normal. You don't feel like a poodle or a puppet or a travelling gypsy. (Speaking of which, where *did* those gypsies live? I'd have to see them this afternoon.) I suppose the real luxury of taking a break was the fact that every time Craig spoke to me I didn't have to say, 'Oh, come on, just one song! What do you mean "no"? I don't care if you don't live here!'

As much as I would have liked to sing to the Wiltshire Police, Craig dropped me at a roundabout near the press conference. It was here that I would stand on the corner having an 'Engelbert' moment. What had only occurred to me in the last couple of minutes was the relevance of the name Devizes (as in the song 'Delilah'), or was that Tom Jones? Anyway, with the tune 'Why, why, why, Devizes' ringing in my ears I hit the street; the only thing I knew about the town being that its name fitted nicely into a song. How *I* would fit into *it* was anybody's guess.

I needn't have worried. The people in Why, why, why, Devizes were just great, starting with the mum pushing a pram in the main street. I approached her from the side and just started singing, the same tactic I had used with no success on the lady with the broken collarbone in

Canterbury. Fortunately there would be more luck here. She tried to get away from me, but I just walked faster, knowing that her baby would need a seatbelt and airbags if this nonsense continued. She eventually gave in.

'You're the guy off the radio?' she said. 'I heard about you in Reading.'

'That's me,' I said, acting as if it wasn't the first time someone had miraculously not only listened to my dribble on the wireless but also taken the time to tell me. I wanted to cover her in roses. Course, the only problem with my complimentary mother of one was that she didn't realise I wasn't a charity – I didn't walk up and down streets, freezing my buns off and singing for the hell of it.

'Got any coins then?' I asked, reluctantly.

'Yep,' she said and kept walking.

'Well?'

'Oh, you *want* some?'

So, the first pound in Why, why, why, Devizes came from a mother of one who was given no choice. The next four came from a woman with a blue tongue. She answered the door of her comfortable-looking house complete with attractive garden, asking me to excuse her as she was in the middle of icing a cake.

'But how did you get a blue tongue?' I asked.

'From licking the spoon,' she said matter-of-factly.

Wondering why the hell she was making blue icing in the first place, I eventually got round to telling her why I was in Devizes. But not before I was nearly savaged by two friendly golden retrievers.

'So, in effect you've been gambling?' she asked.

'Not exactly –'

'But you did have a bet and now you're paying the consequences?'

'Yeah, but –'

'Come and meet my husband,' she said, telling the dogs to stay inside.

Mrs Bluetongue's husband was banging away in the garden shed. A picture framer with a baritone voice, I liked him immediately. He very kindly invited me to sing among the latest frames where he and his wife became a most attentive and intrigued audience. They were happy, creative people. She with her cakes and dogs, he with his singing and art work. But what set this couple apart from everyone else I had met in England was that they were the first people to actually let me into their house (apart from the New Zealanders).

It was Mr Bluetongue's boat: he wanted to show it off. A 40-foot houseboat where they spent every summer made the old boy light up even more than his framing work. I was intrigued to think we couldn't have been further inland if we tried, and yet a canal yielding houseboats stretched for miles.

'A lot of Brits know nothing about these canals.' He pointed downstream: 'Forty miles that way to Bristol,' then pointing upstream, 'and eighty miles that way to London. In fact if you really wanted to, you could walk all the way along this river and end up in London.'

I stepped in dog shit on the way out but didn't care; I'd just met Devizes' finest.

More luck came my way in the form of a dad celebrating his fortieth birthday with his kids. I'm sure the kids answered the door hoping it would be Grandma with gifts for Dad and chocolates for them. Instead, a door-to-door busker smelling of golden retriever dung, grimacing in the cold, asked if he could ruin their day. I figured the kids would go for the Harry Potter song and felt quite proud every time they smiled when I mentioned his name but, in a moment of weakness, completely forgot that the third verse talked about Harry covering his magic wand when he met the local blonde.

The kids still smiled; Dad didn't.

A rousing reception ended with the eldest son passing me £5.

Shooting fish, this was easy in Why, why, why, Devizes.

I had learnt no matter how cold or grumpy or out of form you are, you have to strike while the iron's hot. Knowing Craig wouldn't be too far away I followed a sign that read *Jump Farm.* An old Irish woman sweeping her driveway pointed me in the right direction, adding, 'Oh, yes, the Jump Farm. You'll like that.'

I got all excited! Jump Farm, what the hell could it be, I thought. Maybe a frog enclosure or boarding school for pre-pubescent tadpoles? Or a place where French farmers hung out? I had visions of lily pads and swamps and Kermit singing 'Rainbow Connection'. I mean, what could possibly be around the corner that made the old lady so excited? I walked and walked and walked, not once seeing a sign pointing to the Jump Farm. After about ten minutes I figured I'd gone too far so returned to the old lady who had now discarded the scarf from her head and was weeding the front porch.

'What did you think of the Jump Farm?' she asked, still smiling.

'I didn't see it. All I saw was a bunch of new houses.'

'Nice, aren't they?'

'Is that the Jump Farm?' I asked.

'Yes.'

'The Jump Farm is a bunch of new houses?'

'Lovely, don't you think?' she said.

I didn't get it. That one's gone right over my head, Devizes.

I owed my Irish friend a song. I sang as a Kenny Rogers lookalike walked past and the old duck whipped inside to see what change she had. When she returned I informed her that she and the rest of the town had made Devizes the most successful place where one could door-to-door busk. In the last hour I'd made £10 and, amazingly, had a 100 per cent strike rate.

Not one rejection; I love you, Devizes.

If New Zealand was my 'Tuesday night, we have to get up for work in the morning' audience then Devizes was definitely my 'Let's get pissed, have a good time and forget about tomorrow' crowd. A rather weary-looking Craig emerged from a heavy press conference expecting me to tell him that Devizes had been no better than my country's namesake.

'I'm not surprised,' he said when my enthusiasm for the place confirmed my success. 'Loads of buskers in Devizes.'

'Are you going straight back to the station?' I asked.

'Yep, gotta get this story back so we can cut it up and put it on the news.'

'So, you're in a bit of a hurry?'

'Yep, why?' he said, swerving through a roundabout.

'Don't suppose you know where gypsies might live around here?'

The problem we were about to face was one of relativity. I didn't need to be anywhere at anytime; Craig had to be somewhere now. Time meant nothing to me; time meant a brown envelope to him. To make matters worse, I had no idea in hell where the gypsies lived: no address, no landmarks; in fact, I'd be surprised if they were even in the same bloody country. Craig checked his watch while I tuned my guitar. He rang the radio station while I scraped dog shit from my shoes.

Eventually, we saw smoke and the horses – bingo.

I told Craig I owed him my life as he sped off. I had found the gypsies, now all I had to do was find Dave.

Chickens, ducks, kids and puppies ran around home-made caravans and open fires. Horses and carriages sat in the long, rent-free grass. They even had a Christmas tree. I smelt the fire and thought to myself, these guys have got it sorted: no bills, appointments or Monday mornings. No car, no TV, no Sky Sport, no stereo, no money … AAAGGHH!

Take that back.

'Hi,' I said, walking up to the first caravan I saw. A dog proudly sat at the front door, while three other people, two well dressed and one, in more gypsy-like clothing, sat inside. It was obvious the two in more formal attire were visiting for the day, the real giveaway being the brand new Range Rover parked next to chopped wood and dead pheasants.

'I was told Dave would be here,' I said.

'Dave's my dad,' a young boy said, trying to saw firewood in half. That's the spirit, son, get them working for their money round here. Wouldn't see a four-year-old city kid sacrificing his fingers for a night's warmth. That's commitment, my son, good lad.

'Dave's still flat on his back,' the girl in the caravan said. 'We texted him this morning.'

Texted him? You're gypsies for Christ's sake! Gypsies don't text. Whatever happened to living off the land without power or water or food? What happened to living off the smell of an oily rag and brushing your teeth on rubber trees? Text messaging? That's uncouth, that's not normal, that's just … *modern*.

'How do you know Dave?' she asked.

'Oh, we met turkey plucking yesterday.'

The very words leaving my mouth made me feel ill. Was that only *yesterday*? God, so much had happened since I was standing in that shed singing Van Morrison songs and ripping feathers off a supermarket-bound bird. To think those workers were still there.

'We've got a dead pheasant over there if you want to pluck it for us!'

Careful, love, you're talking to a scarred man here.

Dave's relations gave me £3.50 for my song. I was stoked; things were going extremely well. I did, however, find it a little nerve-wracking walking around what was effectively their home, but the rest of the gypsies welcomed me with open arms and loved what I was doing. The fact that I did so well in Devizes was no surprise to them either, John the gypsy telling me they had a record busking day there themselves only three weeks ago: £197 in one afternoon.

'We can't give you any money, but if you sing a song we'll make you a coffee, won't we?' Jan my new gypsy friend said, motioning John to pass over some cups.

'Take milk?' she asked.

'Sure,' I said. 'This is great.'

And it really was. Even though we were freezing our tits off, we were sitting in the fields of Calne, singing songs and making a brew. Life was simple. Chickens pecked around us, dogs searched for fleas. A new arrival walked out from a caravan yielding at least five dogs. He had the best Mohican I'd ever seen. Darn right, I had Mohican envy. I don't know whether he'd just slept on one side for four days then the other side for five or whether he styled it specifically, but this thing was an award-winning piece of hair styling.

'You wanna buy a puppy?' he asked, sitting on a log next to me.

'Um, I do like dogs but I can't see it working that well. A door-to-door busker with a dog.'

It made me wonder what animals I could have saved on the way: a turkey, 9,000 eggs and a puppy. I figured life was difficult enough for a door-to-door busker without owning half of Noah's ark.

It was their caravans that intrigued me: no mod cons, no electricity, no kitchen sink or shower, just the bare minimum, like the old carriages in Westerns. How cool that people can still live like this, I thought.

No Sky TV, hmm.

'Did you build these caravans yourself?' I asked.

'Yeah.'

'And do you go all over the country?'

'Yeah, we've taken them to Scotland, everywhere.'

I couldn't stop watching his Mohican. It had a mind of its own.

'Do you ever get stressed?' I asked. 'Because it looks like you have nothing to stress over. No bills, no rent, no … Sky TV,' I mumbled.

'I get really nervous when we have to move,' said Jan.

'And don't you get cold in there, at night I mean?' I asked Mohican man who was patting his fat puppy.

'Breath keeps you warm,' he said.

Might keep *you* warm, pal, but I'm freezing my goolies off here just talking about the cold. I finished my cuppa and wished them well for winter solstice, leaving the puppy right where he was.

Luckily, the friendly couple with the Range Rover offered me a ride; I was so far off in gypsy land that I really didn't care how or when I got to the next place. The reality check they gave me was welcome.

'Would you like a ride into Calne?' they asked.

'That would be brilliant,' I said.

Sky TV and Range Rovers. Shallow, me?

AS THE FOUR-wheel drive glided along the road I struggled to stay awake. It had been a big day, halfway round the world to New Zealand, blue tongues and Jump Farms in Devizes, free puppies and busking gypsies in Calne.

'So, what did you think of that?' the lady in the passenger seat asked me.

'They were great. Good life, I reckon. They've got it sorted. Bloody cold, though.'

'And I don't know if you noticed … but … they don't *smell*.'

I looked out the window.

'They really don't smell,' she repeated.

12

Efail Isaf and Llantwit Fardre

Earnings to date: £230.50

THREE WEEKS OF door-to-door busking had produced £230. Now, that may seem a lot of money and true, it's £230 I didn't have before, but considering I'd been on the streets every day, rain, hail and shine and received more rejections than a third former at a disco, it still didn't feel good. My Midlands Bank bag was also starting to feel the strain with copious amounts of gold and silver shrapnel threatening to burst it at any minute. I suppose I could cash the coins in for notes, but that would be too logical.

In my darker moments I would worry that I wasn't even halfway to the magic number: £497.

Thankfully, the next part of my journey wouldn't see me having to act the fool. My mate Pete was heading to his home village in Wales for Christmas and had offered to pick me up from Swindon that night.

Perfect timing.

Pete had reassured me Wales would be a hit. I'm sure he also felt a little apprehensive as to whether his hometown would come through with the goods. After all, this *was* door-to-door busking and these days anything could happen.

The hometown in question was called Llantwit Fardre, which can be found by looking north-north-west from Cardiff and driving straight up and over the nearest large mountain (Garth). Not only was Garth Mountain a rather lovely piece of hill, it's also famous. You might remember never wanting to see Hugh Grant fumble his way through the movie *The Englishman Who Went Up a Hill but Came Down a Mountain*, that mountain being the one and only Garth.

I just hoped that Pete was right about his friendly country folk; I didn't want to become *The New Zealander who went to Wales but came back a casualty.*

'They'll love you here,' Pete reassured me. 'You're a Kiwi. The Welsh love the All Blacks. Just don't forget, you're in the land of Neil Jenkins.'

'Neil Jenkins,' I said. 'Heard the name, who is he again?'

'Only the top points scorer in international rugby.'

'You're joking, a Welshman! Sure he's not a Kiwi?'

'Welsh through and through, my man. Neil Jenkins is the master.'

Pete was right. Neil Jenkins was everywhere, although mostly in Pete's bedroom all over the walls. There were signed footballs, Pontypridd shirts and Neil Jenkins figurines.

Quite touching, really, although Pete was nearly 30.

My official tour of Wales started the next day. I'd decided to take the morning off and see stuff that, as a busker, I normally walked straight past. Sad that most of the time I was more concerned about the busking kitty rather than taking in the historical treats the UK had to offer.

It wasn't long before I knew where Neil Jenkins was born, where he went to school, where he played his rugby and where he drank. Pontypridd (meaning 'bridge over mud hut') was where Mr Jenkins used to spend a lot of his time. I say *used* to because now the leading points scorer in international rugby played for Cardiff (Ponty's main rivals) or the big money boys. Due to this, Jenkins now gets booed regularly at Sardis Road (Ponty's ground) for 'selling out'.

Tough crowd, the Welsh; things didn't bode well for the Kiwi busker.

There's another reason I was in an extremely good mood in Wales – for the first time in three weeks I had clean washing. Any backpacker or traveller will tell you this is a feeling of absolute pleasure. At the time, it seems too good to be true. There has to be some kind of mistake, you keep repeating. Waking up to a choice of three pairs of clean socks, not to mention underpants, almost sends one into an uncontrollable state of delirium.

Wales felt raw, on the edge, rustic, boasting places like Caerphilly Castle where teenage mothers walked past with babies, not realising the history that surrounded them. Maybe they did, maybe they didn't care? Something that was built in 1268 they see every day. Just because it was built in 1268 doesn't stop my baby crying. Just because people come from all over the country to see it doesn't stop my boyfriend being unemployed. Whatever was going through their heads didn't bother me: I loved that castle.

And things were so cheap in Wales. Where in England could you park for two hours for 40p? Where in England could you buy two chicken rolls and a drink for £2.90?

Even a busker could afford these prices.

There were some very special guests I wanted to sing to on Garth Mountain, so we headed there next. Being in the fresh air, dripping nose and wind whistling past your ears confirmed we were climbing a mountain on a day most normal people would only watch from the safety of their living rooms. Although we were hardly the oldest to grace it that day; an old man with wobbly knees was descending with his Labrador. The dog looked pissed off.

'For God's sake, your knees are worse than mine, yet you insist that we climb this bloody mountain every day. Look at the people watching from their living rooms, drinking hot tea next to the fire. Why can't we do that?'

'Shut up and walk, otherwise you get no dinner.'

Dogs have no idea, do they? I remember a famous quote: Have you ever wandered into a room and forgotten why you went in there? That's how dogs spend their lives.

I love them, especially the way they walk sideways. Seriously, if you look at a dog from behind when it's walking, they actually walk on an angle, as if they're pissed. You try to get them to walk in a straight line, impossible. It's like they've continually got their indicator on, veering onto a motorway off-ramp. I'm sure this is the reason our Labrador friend was so miffed at traversing the mountain every day; with all his zigzagging, angular walking and frustration at being two foot tall, he was probably covering twice the distance as his old master.

Nevertheless, they both continued, in silence, to hobble and wobble down the mountain.

The wind cut us in two as we reached the summit. A clear but freezing morning, we looked south over Cardiff, over the sea and to Minehead (in Somerset) and north up the valleys to the Brecon National Park. It was here I decided to get the guitar out and sing to my very special guests: the sheep of Garth Mountain. Much like the cows in New Zealand a couple of days ago, I was sure these woolly buggers wouldn't exactly be loaded, but it was worth a go. And seeing as I came from the land of 45 million sheep, it would be rude not to do a quick number.

Initially I was put off by what I saw – tails. The sheep had tails! I nearly fainted. Some had grey heads and white bodies. Some had black heads and white bodies. Long strings of wool resembling curtains hung from the fence. These sheep looked more like Afghan dogs. Their wool wasn't ... woolly.

It was more lank and lifeless, like they were all having a bad hair day. Did Catherine Zeta Jones suffer from the same problem?

Surely she wouldn't have scored that old ram if she did?

'Any requests?' I asked my lank-haired friends, tuning my guitar at the top of the mountain. One was trying to bleat something, although I couldn't understand him. Maybe it was the wind ripping through my ears or it could have been his indecipherable Welsh accent. If I'd known the chords, I would have sung the Elvis Presley number, 'I can't help falling in love with a ewe'.

Unfortunately I didn't, so the sheep would have to settle for 'Harry Potter'.

After a less than enthusiastic response from the sheep, we left and Pete dropped me off in the small village of Efail Isaf, saying it should be good for busking.

'Friendly people, nice community,' he reassured me.

As soon as he left and I'd approached my first house, I didn't feel convinced.

No buying or selling. You may be asked for identification read the sign.

An old lady greeted me, followed by her husband who loped down the stairs. Either she forgot to ask for identification or the sticker was only there as decoration. Regardless, she didn't seem to have a nasty bone in her body.

'Are you going to sing a Christmas carol then?' she smiled.

'Don't you want "Harry Potter"?'

'No, we want a Christmas carol.'

'But I don't know a Christmas carol,' I said.

'You must know a Christmas carol!'

I really should have thought about this before I left home. Chances are that, at Christmas, people like to hear Christmas songs. They took the time to ask about where I was from in

New Zealand, then passed me a shiny pound for my average performance.

One house, one coin; things were looking up. Maybe Pete was right about Wales.

During a lovely meal of haggis at Pete's mum's house last night (haggis in Wales? I know, it was bloody lovely, though), I discovered that one of the Welsh traits is to name people after what they do for a living. For example, if your name is John and you're a baker, you'd be known as John the Bread. I might be Justin the Song. Pat's a doctor? He'd be Pat the Death. Even less fortunate would be if Pat was a vet, then he'd be Pat the Dog.

Translation problems continued to plague me, even in Wales. Thankfully most people understood the bulk of my sentences, just the odd *bet* coming out as *bit*. The next abode in Efail Isaf provided me with a grandma who could not understand one word leaving my lips. I may as well have been speaking Swahili as I stood at the door, freezing, trying to explain a bet to a ginger-haired lady with no teeth. I tried speaking slower. I tried hand signals. If there were a car horn handy, I would have attempted Morse code.

I wasn't getting through. Of course, now the problem I faced was, would I just leave without saying another word? After taking up three minutes of her precious time, I now felt I had to justify not only why I was standing at her front door with a guitar, but also why I was acting like some brainless, Neanderthal chimp attempting amateur charades.

Younger woman baking wedding cake to the rescue!

'Oh, bless, what a lovely idea,' she said when I finally explained my reason for being. 'Sorry, I haven't got time to listen, I'm making a wedding cake for my cousin. Bless,' she said running to the kitchen. Old woman continued to stare at me. The younger woman returned with five gold coins. After only ten minutes of being in the cold, I was already desperate to retreat to a warm house so offered to help her with the wedding cake. (Yeah, like how? Your vast experience with wedding cakes and all!)

'Oh, bless,' she said. 'No, I think I can manage by myself.'

'Are you sure? I mean, I'm not doing anything apart from roaming the streets.'

'Oh, bless,' she repeated, looking at the old lady, who was still not smiling, looking more confused than ever. I thanked them for their time and put the money in my duffel coat pocket. As the door closed, I heard the old woman ask, 'But what did he *want*?'

I crossed the road and heard some loud Bob Dylan coming from the house on the hill. I had to knock loudly, which I never felt comfortable with. You have to feel pretty confident that whatever you're going to offer at their doorstep is going to be a damn sight better than them having a shit or watching a good film inside.

Course, it never was, but how many times in your life have you been met at the door by an idiot holding a guitar? Bob Dylan was muted and a rather nervous man with a hair-free, lily-white chest opened the door and looked at me as if to say, '*This* is what I turned Bob Dylan off for?'

Hi, I'm a door-to-door busker. I hope you weren't taking a shit or watching a good film inside.

'Is this for real?' he asked, when I told him about my misfortune.

'Sure is, I've been busking all around the UK.'

He wandered off to the kitchen while I sang, turned the music up again and passed me a pound.

'Good luck,' he mumbled.

Even grumpy people were giving money today; this was indeed a great place to busk. It was like I was on a slot machine and just kept winning. Nerves weren't taking over like they normally did.

I felt good. I felt confident. This was a happy village.

A woman had caught my eye as I was surveying which house next to choose. My attraction to her was unbridled by the fact I didn't even have to knock on a door; she was smoking in her carport. Just like the Bob Dylan fan across the road, she was pretty nonplussed at hearing a song but I gave her no choice. She leaned against the garage, inhaling. Unlike other people, who didn't know where to look when I sang, normally opting for nervous, fidgety movements, she just looked straight through me with piercing blue eyes. She made *me* nervous.

'So, are you a student?' she asked at the completion of my performance.

'I lost a bet.'

'Are you working?'

'No, you're not listening, I lost a bet.'

'Oh, you lost a *bet*, I thought you said *bit*.'

Damn Kiwi accent. I want a refund.

A puppy nearly bowled me over when the next neighbour's door was opened. A man on the phone covered the talk piece and asked, 'Are you a carol singer?'

'Sort of,' I had to admit. Some people didn't have time to hear my whole sob story. This man not only had to deal with someone on the phone, he also had to rescue his puppy before he sprinted onto the road. I grabbed the puppy, was asked not to sing, twice, and was handed a pound for my efforts. The door was closed before the puppy could repeat the manoeuvre.

The conversations I *really* wished I could hear were the ones behind closed doors. Such as when Mum walks back to the lounge and her husband asks, 'Who was that, dear?'

'Some Kiwi in a duffel coat attempting to sing.'

It was no different at this house; when the door was closed and puppy contained, I heard the guy on the phone say, 'What? Oh, I don't know. Some door-to-door busker. Anyway, what were you saying?'

Efail Isaf felt like a gold mine. I loved it. You could smell the history. Lush fields and winding roads contained dwellings with content people. Houses bore signs with exotic names like Bromebyd and Penllwyn. Only in Devizes had I encountered a 100 per cent strike rate.

Regardless of my success here, it still didn't stop the fact that I was too bloody stupid to wear gloves. I had been busking for an hour; my hands were once again blue, quickly turning purple.

I should have learnt by now.

I heard someone bolt down the stairs at the next house, saying, 'Whose coat is that jacket? By there over here now?'

What the hell did they just say? Was that *English*? Did I hear that right? 'Who's coat is that *jacket*?'

I was to find out later that afternoon from Pete that that was typical 'Welsh speak'. It made me sympathise with the old, confused woman ten doors down who couldn't understand a word I'd said. I was surprised more people in the street hadn't suffered the same problem when I opened my mouth.

An exhausted-looking mother opened the door, followed by two girls, followed by two more, then two more. Having a young, enthusiastic audience made me completely forget about my frozen digits. I launched into 'Harry Potter' to six young girls who stood there wide eyed and open mouthed. Huge cheers followed.

What an audience, I thought, what a change!

Then the girls were away: 'Did you see *Harry Potter*?' one asked.

'Who was your favourite character?' her friend erupted.

'Do you think it was too long?' said another.

'Have you seen *Lord of the Rings*?'

'Did you think it was too long?'

This was a happy, noisy house. The father passed me some warm coins, adding, 'Must get down to New Zealand one day. Good fishing apparently.'

He was closing the door, but I could tell they all wanted more; pity I didn't have anything appropriate.

I'd made £13 in an hour. It was time to warm the hands and lie on the couch. Pete and his mum were out for the afternoon so I made the most of lying on the couch doing nothing. I lay in peace, thinking about Garth Mountain and the 'Bad Hair Day' sheep and the kind village of Efail Isaf. I almost nodded off. I was almost in a slumber. That was, until an upstart little shit rang the doorbell, again and again and again. He started singing, yelling: 'JINGLE BELLS! JINGLE BELLS!'

'WE WISH YOU A MERRY CHRISTMAS, WE WISH –'

I was unaware that door-to-door carol singers actually sang before you opened the door – a technique maybe I should adopt? He sang and yelled until I could take no more. He made my pregnant seagull singing voice sound like a soprano. Who am I trying to kid? He wasn't actually singing at all. He was cashing in. He knew people were weak and vulnerable at Christmas and if he recited two, just two lines from some of the worst songs ever to hit the planet, he could buy a Walkman.

Bloody genius.

The next day Pete suggested I gatecrash the Reynolds family who lived in Cheltenham. He told me he knew them well and they'd be well up for a mad Kiwi knocking on the door.

'Even on Christmas Eve?' I asked.

'*Especially* on Christmas Eve,' he said.

13

Cheltenham

Earnings to date: £243

CHELTENHAM WAS REALLY into the swing of Christmas. It looked beautiful. Grand houses, nice cars, expensive shops; all signals that, if Chelsea was anything to go by, said, 'We have no money for door-to-door buskers.'

It was a crisp, clear evening when I knocked on the Reynolds' door. Even though seeing presents, a Christmas tree and copious amounts of food, booze and relatives made me homesick, the Reynolds family made me feel welcome immediately. A meal, bed and hospitality were on the way, but before the onslaught of whisky and all-night singing could commence, I had a small job to do.

One of their mates who lived down the road was always playing practical jokes on them – they all agreed a door-to-door busker would really piss him off. Tired and travel weary, the sacrificial lamb tuned his guitar and knocked on the door of No. 10.

The rest of the Reynolds hid behind parked cars on the street, which didn't look conspicuous at all! Indeed the recipient did look a little flustered when I asked if I could serenade on his doorstep. He was in the middle of painting his hallway. I kept talking so he couldn't refuse.

'Well, you sing and I'll go see what I've got,' he said.

I sang 'Harry Potter' to an older bloke, Jeff, who was also painting, standing on a ladder, sniggering. The practical joker came back from the living room with some coins and a small bottle.

'Surprise!' half a dozen weirdos yelled, jumping out from behind frost-bitten cars.

'You bastards,' he muttered.

Meanwhile, in my grubby mitt lay a £2 coin and a small bottle of port.

How inventive to give a busker alcohol; better than a filthy look any day.

I played songs till three in the morning at the Reynolds' home. My whisky glass just kept getting refilled. Did I complain? Did I buffalo! I also had a warm bed to look forward to *and* I still had clean washing. I was in paradise. Maybe I could just ring Mark and tell him I wanted to stay? How long would £240 last?

'You keep playing, son, we'll keep pouring,' Bruce (Mr Reynolds) said.

'Do you have to live on this money as well?' Jane (Mrs Reynolds) asked.

'Yep.' Burp, slur, sway. Bloody hell, whisky, strong.

'You're very honourable keeping the bet,' Bruce said, filling my glass again, as well as his.

'Yeash, that'sh what people ... (bugger, hiccups had arrived) ... say.'

'Do you have to pay expenses as well?'

'Too bloody right I do – that's why I'm trying to get home as quickly as posshible. Have you seen the state of the Kiwi dollar?' I thought this was *hilarious*. Is that my glass?

'Why are you doing it then?'

Is that you, Mrs Reynolds? Have you moved? Somehow my hands were still coordinating with my brain and chords were still reverberating from the guitar. After a minute or so, I remembered that someone had asked a question. But *who* was it and *what* did they ask?

'Hmm?' I asked no one in particular, hoping the person who did ask the question remembered they'd asked the question. With a bit of luck, they'd remember what the question was.

'Why are you doing it, this bet I mean?'

Mrs Reynolds! That's the one. You asked the question! I remember now. Back on track, here we go. Answer coming up any minute. Ears, brain, mouth, answer. Face Mrs Reynolds ... and speak.

"Cos it's a bet,' I said, 'and it's fun ... and I looove meeting people.'

There, not too hard, was it? Perfectly acceptable answer and well within the restraints of a civilised conversation. Now, where's that whisky? Bruce, someone's emptied my glass again. To be honest, it's been happening all night. Have one yourself. Don't mind if I do.

'How are you getting around?' Jane asked.

'Trains and busshhess mostly,' I slurred.

'Isn't that expensive?'

'Hell, yep. 'Spensive, mainly money wise.'

Bruce and Jane looked at each other, then resumed conversation. Something in their eyes told me they had some news that I would look forward to. Meantime, I needed a room that wasn't spinning.

I wouldn't recommend having a hangover at the house of someone you've just met. All you really want to do is drink coffee, read the paper, spend an hour in the shower, an hour on the bog and go back to bed. And it's unfair because your hosts aren't seeing the real you.

The *real* you doesn't salivate when you're offered a glass

of cold water.

The *real* you doesn't have four Panadol for breakfast.

The *real* you doesn't forget what happened last night.

I'm sure the Reynolds understood; to be fair, most were in the same condition, so at least we had a support network going. We were strong, we were tight and if anyone was stupid enough to walk past and say, 'Well, it *was* self-inflicted, you know,' we thumped them.

Then took more Panadol.

I DON'T KNOW if it was dedication or sheer stupidity that forced me to try busking that next morning. Maybe I was scared it would be my only chance in Cheltenham? True, I already had £2 and a bottle of port, but that was through semi-organised busking, not raw, door-to-door busking.

After spending an hour in the shower, I found the Reynolds family sitting around their beautiful big kitchen table, drinking coffee, reading the paper and resuming hangovers. They couldn't believe I was going outside, let alone planning singing door to door. It was Christmas Day, I reasoned, I had a hangover from hell and there was no time like the present.

Straightaway I had problems in Cheltenham and it was nothing to do with my headache. Most flats along the main street had buzzers. This created huge obstacles.

'Hello, who is it?' they'd ask.

'Hi, I'm a door-to-door busker. I look like death warmed up. I drank three quarters of a bottle of whisky last night. I smell like a brewery. Do you have a toilet I can throw up in? Fancy a song?'

At least face to face, you have a small glimmer of hope.

You can smile and wink and use your guitar as a weapon. Convincing someone via an intercom is not even worth the effort.

It was a bitterly cold morning. I walked past a flash clothes shop and saw my reflection. An unshaven man wearing a second-hand duffel coat, smelling of booze, with bloodshot eyes and blue hands faced me. If there ever was an opposite of Santa, I was it.

For the next half-hour, no one answered doors, people unloading their cars with booze and food told me they weren't interested. Mothers and fathers carrying huge presents unlocked their mansions, turned alarms off and walked into warm houses where eggnog and jolly music would greet them. They would ignore me on the way through. I felt like a nuisance. I missed home. Bugger the songs, I thought, I was now considering knocking on doors and asking for paracetamol.

In fact, the busking was going so badly, I was very tempted to find a quiet spot and start some normal street busking. But I'd never done it before. What songs would I sing? Where would I stand? Once again I needed Obi-Don Kenobi; he would see me right. It was weird that singing on the street seemed more nerve-wracking than door to door. Regardless, I had to stick to the bloody rules of the bloody bet, didn't I, and singing on the bloody street wasn't in the bloody rules.

Bloody All Blacks. Bloody John Eales. Bloody Mark.

As I crossed Montpellier Spa Road, I was nearly hit by a dickhead on a motorbike. Making my way through the hordes of happy families, I spied a homeless guy on the street selling *The Big Issue*.

'Got any spare change, mate?' he asked.

'Not bloody likely,' I said.

He said his parents lived overseas, his girlfriend had just left him and he was put in jail for selling illegal PlayStation CDs – pirating. His eyes were red and puffy, a cigarette butt hanging from his lips.

'I wish I could play guitar,' he said. 'Give something to the people.'

I was about to ask him whether I could sing next to him, maybe even do a double act, when he suddenly asked the time, grabbed his mat, his coffee, spare change, ran off to a bin and threw something in. He then got in a car and sped off.

Even homeless people didn't have time for me today.

I was too embarrassed to go back to the Reynolds and tell them I had received nothing from their hometown. The Carlton Hotel for a quiet orange juice seemed a fine idea. And did this place *swing?*

I walked into the foyer and smelt gravy, boiled cabbage and overcooked roast turkey. Awful Christmas music blared from the tinny speaker and leftover brandy and wine glasses sat next to used ashtrays. A selection of guests resembling the entire cast from *Cocoon* sat, eating their lunch and clinking glasses.

Bless them, they'd been waiting for this day all year, or had they? Did they despise it just as much as their sons and daughters did, having to bring them to some stale old hotel for a set-menu lunch?

I *think* I was becoming the Grinch who stole Christmas.

'Happy Christmas,' I said to the lady at reception.

'And to you, sir,' she smiled.

'What have you got planned for your guests today?' I asked, maybe deep down wishing I could also open Christmas crackers and drink sherry with the oldies.

'First of all they have to guess the weight of the Christmas cake,' she said, pointing to a box labelled *Christmas Cake Competition.*

'Can I enter? What do you win?' I asked.

'Christmas cake.'

'Oh, maybe I'll leave it.'

'And then the guests are brought into the lounge and we have a special Christmas quiz and then we all make Christmas hats!'

Poor buggers. I don't want to get old.

'And *then*,' she continued, 'later on tonight they will all watch what has become a British institution over the years. Because I can tell *you're* not from around here.'

'That's right, I'm from New Zealand. So what's the British institution?'

'Christmas episode of *Only Fools and Horses.*'

I LIKE CHRISTMAS in the cold better. Sure, it's great having a BBQ on the beach, wearing shorts, playing cricket and swimming, but when it comes to a *feeling* of Christmas, it somehow seems more appropriate being in a place where you freeze your nads off. Santa Claus in all the Coke ads is in the snow, all the Christmas movies are in the snow. Christmas shopping is wearing a scarf, walking the dog, stopping off for a mulled wine and a chat with a friendly neighbour.

I think I was starting to lose it, so I decided to swallow my pride and head back to the Reynolds. I needed water, warmth and sympathy. On the way back I saw the homeless guy who'd so quickly sped off when I was trying to talk to him earlier. He was with a girl (could have been his girlfriend), who was carrying a Gap bag. They jumped into a relatively new Fiat and drove off.

I was stunned. How can people do that? Do they not have a conscience? Then it dawned on me; what I've learnt from busking is that if you ask, you get. Sure, you have to handle rejection on a daily basis and your confidence takes a huge dent, but you can do it.

If you ask, you get.

OK, so a beggar still needs to buy presents for their family, but isn't it sad to think they have to sit on the streets and lie to do it?

I headed back to the house, hung over and needing water. Jane met me at the door and offered me fresh coffee and a ham sandwich at the kitchen table. I felt right at home; Jane and Bruce had an amazing way of making you feel like one of theirs. And along with a hot coffee that arrived in front of me came seven words from Jane that would change my life: 'Would you like to borrow our car?'

– 14 –

Oxford

Earnings to date: £245, a bottle of port and a car

www.doortodoorbusker.com

Before we get to Oxford, I have to tell you: during my travels people had been able to keep in touch with me via my website, www.doortodoorbusker.com. Here is a smattering of the messages left:

Hi there,
You poor thing, losing a bet to an Aussie – but thumbs up to you for not reneging on your bet. Not sure what your plans are but I could possibly put you up for a few days.
Location = Belsize Park (North-west London).
Philippa

Well Justin,
I've heard you 'play' and 'sing' in Swindon and I think it'll take you a loooooooong time to get enough money! People will only give you money for one of the following reasons:
1. To get rid of you
2. Out of sympathy
3. Because they are mad. Note, there is no mention of musical appreciation in the list.
Good luck and don't ask me for any more money.
Tony

If you need a place to crash, our door is open to you.
– Jack and Kate

I am an ex Pom living in New Zealand. I often hear about this 'good old Kiwi ingenuity' but I never see anyone actually putting it into practice. Good to see!
Damon, Auckland

HOPE YOU GET BACK HOME BEFORE I RETIRE.
REGARDS,
CHIPPY

Justin
I have actually been planning a bit of an overseas experience myself, although I think I'm at the wrong end of the age scale. You've inspired me to just get on with it and not to worry too much about the money.
Sandra

I don't think you will ever put Robbie Williams out of a job but stick with it, son.
Doreen, Southampton

When you've been travelling by yourself, it's messages like these that keep you alive. To think people actually took time to write just because I'd made a stupid bet filled me with pride. Some messages, such as Jack and Kate's, didn't even leave an address. Others such as Philippa's in North London had arrived a bit late.

Most messages were positive: go for it, we're thinking of you, you show them, etc. My favourite, though, had to be one that simply read, 'What a load of rubbish.'

Couldn't agree more. Next time, leave your name.

Unfortunately, the next guy did:

How's the busking going, sheep-shagger?
Just thought I'd let you know it's been a great summer
so far. We're just having a few beers and watching the
cricket. Loads of chicks, great weather. My mates really
want to meet this Kiwi mate of mine who lost the bet.
Maybe you can swing via Oz on the way home.
Hope you're freezing your balls off!
Mark

Oxford

Having spent days doing nothing at the Reynolds', I realised
I was fast becoming the world's only door-to-door bludger.
I had to get back to work or at least stop raiding their pantry,
so decided to head to Oxford for a few days as the car
wouldn't be back from London till then. I'd told Jane I
would then come back to Cheltenham and pick it up. I still
couldn't believe that I wouldn't have to drag my bags and
guitar around various railway stations and worry about train
timetables.

It was an old car that they always kept out the back. Even
so, I felt bad saying yes. The only condition was that I drop
it off in Glasgow for a member of their family at the
conclusion of my trip. I said that would be no problem.
Course, they didn't know I'd also like to go via Nottingham,
Sheffield and York.

Hope they hadn't checked the speedo.

Just before I left Cheltenham I asked the Reynolds where
a sad loner might like to spend New Year's Eve. Oxford was
suggested, purely for its student life and interesting history.
This sounded like a fine idea and would fill in a couple of
days nicely. Till then, I could only watch maniac drivers
from the bus window. Normally I was jealous of the man
driving next to us in his brand new BMW, able to stop at
will for countless toilet breaks and food stops. But now,

things would be different. Now I had a quiet confidence, a crooked smile and a bursting bladder, knowing one day soon I'd be joining them. I also made sure I bought a return bus ticket as it was cheaper and this was the busy time of year. I wouldn't want to be in Oxford for longer than need be; not when there was a car waiting for me in Cheltenham.

Travelling light was my New Year's resolution. All I took on the bus to Oxford was a guitar, some deodorant, a wallet and some toothpicks. (Dental hygiene: very important when dealing with the public.)

No towel, no clean clothes, this was art in its purest form. Unfortunately for the people of Oxford, this busker felt so strongly about his craft he may well craft an eventual strong smell of his own that could force the odd homeowner to pass him soap and a towel at the doorstep.

EXPECTATIONS VERSUS REALITY is one of the best things about travel. What you expect and what you end up seeing are often completely different. For example, someone might absolutely hate Cape Town because they arrived on a miserable day, had their wallet stolen and choked on a chicken bone. On the other hand, someone else may have drunk G and Ts in the sun, been shouted dinner and met the love of their life cruising up Table Mountain on the gondola.

Travel is so personal, like music and movies and books.

'I can't believe you've never been to New York!'

'You haven't read *The Grapes of Wrath*?'

'Oh my God! Have you never seen *The Breakfast Club*?'

Yeah, well I've been to Melbourne, read *The World According to Garp* and I've seen *Asterix in Spain* six times, so screw you.

It was no different in Oxford. What I expected was to run into loads of students and busk in wealthy areas to rich entrepreneurs who would take me under their wing, sit me by the fire and exchange stories about *The Grapes of Wrath* and *The Breakfast Club*. In reality, I ended up sharing a room with 16 others in an Oxford backpackers' hostel where I sang for half an hour (my longest performance to date), yet didn't make one penny.

I arrived at the hostel early afternoon and asked the girl behind the front desk if there was a place I could leave my deodorant and toothpicks while I hit the streets. Very kindly, she let me leave them in reception.

I felt like the new kid at school. Backpackers from all over hung out in the lounge, drinking beer and playing pool. They all seemed great mates. A guy who seemed to be the ringleader slouched in a comfy chair in the corner, sipping on a dark drink. This was just a phase, I reassured myself, I had been in these situations before; by the end of the night we'd *all* be great mates.

'All right! Got a guitar, sing us a song,' the makeshift barman yelled as I was walking to my sleeping quarters.

'Later, mate,' I said, realising I'd have to busk before it got too dark. There'd be plenty of time for drinking and shenanigans later on; in the meantime I had to see whether the people of Oxford would give more than Cheltenham.

Typically I didn't take a map and was lost within minutes. I walked aimlessly around the city in the freezing cold. With nowhere in particular to go and no one in particular to see, I ambled along, hopelessly scouring anything that resembled a residential doorway. My only saving grace was the sheer beauty of the buildings and the feeling of wonder standing beneath them. A posh girl came out of one of them wearing knee-high boots, an elegant coat and the latest MP3 player Walkman.

The first thing I noticed was how nice she smelt.

Then again, maybe I stunk.

Expecting her to either brush me off or hide her Walkman in anticipation of some dodgy busker lightening her load, I was surprised she helped with directions. Man, she really did smell nice. She informed me I was in completely the wrong end of town if I was looking for residential housing.

'This is the main city centre,' she smelled, I mean said.

'It's mostly shops, churches and students around this area,' she continued. 'What you want to do is head straight down that street, go past the traffic lights, over the roundabout and past the shops.'

This may have been what she said, but what I *heard* was another story: 'It's mostly baby talc, apple shampoo and freshly cut lawns around here. What you want to do is go straight past the coconut lotion, over the woman's neck and past the clean sheets.'

Unfortunately the parking warden I met on the next corner (I wouldn't have had to talk to him if I'd actually listened to directions) didn't smell so good. He had bad teeth and his mate was giving someone a ticket. He wasn't interested in a song but was intrigued by my predicament.

'A door-to-door busker; that's pretty rare, isn't it?' he said to his mate.

'Rare? Bloody unheard of!' he replied in a Scottish accent. 'Do you let people try before they buy?'

'What do you mean?' I asked.

'You know, give people a bit of a taster like, "Hey Ju…", "Let it …!"'

'No, hadn't really thought of that, to be honest.'

'You should, might make more money. Are you heading up to Scotland as well?'

'Not if he wants any bloody money!' his mate said.

It was clear I wasn't getting anywhere talking to parking wardens and sweet-smelling girls. Eventually, I found residential housing; after a street of blank stares and closed doors, an old man said, 'It's just after Christmas. I'm feeling very convalescent.'

Woo, wee, spot the Oxford graduate! He closed the door and opened it just as I was walking away.

'You've picked the worst time of year,' he said. 'Most students are away.'

'You think I *chose* to come over here?'

'Well, the average age on this street is sixty. You won't get any money.'

This was all I needed to hear; door-to-door busking was a great way to break stereotypes.

I saw a house with a Christmas tree in the front room. This was a good sign and gave me confidence. At least they were into festive spirit; I somehow translated this to meaning they'd be keen to listen and give money. The fact the woman saw me from the lounge window didn't help. As you know, a lot of people take this opportunity to hide. I thought this woman had too, as she took a while to surface, eventually coming through the garage door. She was wearing a dressing gown and slippers at three in the afternoon.

'You have a lovely voice,' she said. 'Let me go and get some money.'

And she's under 60, you convalescent git.

She apologised for only having £3.50 but quickly took 50p back when she realised it was her husband's special coin.

'Take care, my love, you have a lovely voice,' she said again as I left.

A JAMAICAN GUY on saxophone was busking outside Waitrose. I heard a man next to me say to his wife as we went past, 'Bloody awful, isn't he?'

His wife couldn't really hear her hubby's complaints as she was wincing, with index fingers in her ears. I didn't think the musician was that bad but it made me realise that sort of comment was what I was up against. Even a saxophonist with musical talent couldn't please the public; what chance did I have?

Of course, in between these times of something actually happening at doorsteps were times of no one answering, dogs scaring me off the properties, shivering, coughing, humming to myself and trying hard not to look like a homeless person.

Mind you, maybe I should take that up; at least I could drive a Fiat and shop at Gap.

Yes, I felt like a loner. Yes, I sometimes felt desperate. No, I wasn't going to give up. That was, until I got back to the hostel. I was exhausted and all sung out. An hour and a half of busking had produced £3. The last area I tried, Jericho, I may have even appeared a little too desperate. I followed a young couple for about a hundred yards, threatening a serenade most of the way. I tried to convince them, much like a bad telemarketer, that they *really* needed the Harry Potter song in their lives.

Then I realised how stupid I must have looked.

HAVE YOU EVER spent a New Year's Eve with complete strangers? I was initially looking forward to it; new people, new stories, from all over the world in my case. Problem was, I was missing the Reynolds' kitchen table already, not to mention their fresh coffee, shower and upstairs toilet. I had been spoilt last night, now I had to share my room, shower and toilet with 14 blokes and a t'ai chi expert. I have nothing against t'ai chi, it's just that in a room not big enough to start an ant farm, having a guy standing on one leg facing you can make life a little uneasy. Bunk beds dominated the room like chunky skyscrapers, each housing dirty laundry and leftover pizza. I could have easily stayed in the room but for that very word: room; i.e. none *of* it.

So I went back into the lounge where people continued to drink. I ordered water and sat listening to 'Lonesome Town', wondering how I was going to make it to midnight. It was 4.52 p.m. and people were getting ready to go out. I only had the clothes on my back.

Eventually it happened. Eventually I had to bite the bullet and make a fool of myself; someone asked me to sing a song. I suppose from their point of view it was fair enough: guy walks in with guitar, he must want to show off and sing. This couldn't have been further from the truth.

As buggered as I was, a feeling of optimism shattered my lethargy; I worked out how many potential coins I could make from the less than sober audience. I started with 'Kentucky Fried Kitten' and received a less than enthusiastic response. Halfway through 'Harry Potter', the ringleader, still drinking rum in the comfy chair, said, 'Na, forget those songs, play covers.'

If you've ever played piano or guitar at a party, you'll know people can get very demanding when they're pissed: 'Play this, do that. Come on then. Don't play that, that's shit!'

Realising the big boss in the big chair didn't like my originals I adapted and started playing other songs, still thinking that I could make some good busking money from the room. Miraculously I remembered most of the chords to those songs I learnt in my bedroom when I first started playing guitar. I squeezed out 'Hotel California', 'Proud Mary', 'Stuck in the Middle with You', 'Crazy Little Thing Called Love', 'No Woman No Cry', and 'American Pie' with some authority. I'll admit, I wasn't really enjoying it, but it was like I had to do this to be accepted; these were the hard yards, better to achieve them early in the night, then we could party.

At the end of the performance my fingers ached and my throat was dry. People were clapping and drinking. I had done it. I had managed to blag my way through some pretty average party songs.

Despite this, not one person in the crowd gave money, not even 50p. Maybe they didn't understand my problem? They were backpackers after all; I know from experience, when you're backpacking, money is literally gold, but even so. £3 from the streets of Oxford, nothing from the backpackers.

Eventually a guy at the bar bought me a beer. Six hours to go till midnight.

People continued to drink, play pool and dress up for the big night. I was feeling a little flat, missing mates and home, but was cheered up by three guys who were touring Europe. When they heard about what I was here to do, they said, 'You've got some bastard friends.'

A guy from Melbourne wearing a bandanna, singlet and shorts (on 31 December in the northern hemisphere!) was doing his best to charm some Japanese girls at the table next to me. His main problem seemed to be one of communication, which unless you're going to jump on the table and screw, can be quite a sizeable one. He was obviously in a real quandary; three beautiful Japanese girls sat opposite him and he hadn't said a word in the last five minutes. Suddenly his eyes lit up, he grabbed one of the Japanese girl's hands and said, proudly, 'Kingashinnen!'

Now, my Japanese is about as good as my guitar tuning so I had no idea what he just said. So too the Japanese girl, who looked at her friends. She looked confused, as did they.

'Kingashinnen!' he repeated. I'm in here, he was thinking.

Unfortunately, it was lost on our Japanese girl who, in the thickest Birmingham accent, asked one of her friends, 'What did he just say?'

Bandanna Boy's heart sank.

WHEN EVERYONE APPEARED to be ready (even I put fresh deodorant on), we left for the first pub. I wished it was 11 p.m. Instead it was just before seven. Still five hours to go before I could even think about bed. Drinks flowed and jokes circulated while everyone waited for midnight.

It was 9.45 p.m. and I was hungry. I found a food caravan in the main street and somehow digested a three-day-old kebab and soggy cheeseburger. I'd like to say I then took a lovely stroll around the buildings of Oxford, soaked up the history and marvelled at the timelessness of it all. Unfortunately, as I didn't have a map I just ended up getting lost.

Really lost.

Not only did I not recognise buildings or streets, I realised all too late that I didn't even know the name of the hostel where I was staying. I had achieved a similar feat in Barcelona four years previously. Whenever I arrive in a new city, providing it's not too cold, I like to go for a run. I don't know why; I never run at home, it's just somehow more romantic discovering a new city on foot, bursting your guts, sweating over the pavement. Maybe it's an ego thing. Maybe you're secretly trying to set a good example for your country's counterparts.

'Hola, yes I'm a Kiwi and all Kiwis run! Forget your siesta and get off your fat, lazy arse.'

So, like Forrest Gump, I started running and running and

running. I didn't know the name of our hotel, what street it was on; the only Spanish word I knew was *Coke*. After half an hour of running I eventually ended up at Barcelona Zoo. I was miffed to discover two locals couldn't point me in the way of the nameless hotel on the nameless street, although they did point me in the direction of *Coke*.

It felt the same in Oxford; just like Barcelona, all the streets looked the same. The beauty is mesmerising, you just keep walking, thinking in some warped way that the city will look after you and you'll end up where you started. After all, how could you get lost in a beautiful city?

Sure, Calcutta you could get lost, but Oxford and Barcelona – no chance.

That was until the non-map-reading Kiwi arrived.

Not only was I lost, I was also cold. I wanted my bed. And despite not knowing anyone at the hostel, I still had to be back by midnight so I could at least acknowledge 2002. A police car stopped as I crossed at some lights. This could be my only opportunity. I knocked on the window and a cop looked at me. He wound down the window.

'Hey, guys,' I said.

'Evening,' said the driver. He looked about 17, clean-shaven and baby-faced. Looked like he was still at high school.

'Where are you guys going?' I asked, expecting a 'None of your bloody business, on your way, son.'

'Nowhere in particular,' he said.

I decided to chance my arm. 'Do you know where the backpackers' hostel is?'

He looked at his partner who shrugged. 'I think so, why?'

'Is it close?' I asked.

'Miles away,' he smiled. 'Get in, we'll take you there.'

Bingo. Free ride with the cops. Although something told

me this fresh-faced Babycop was just trying to avoid the big jobs, the nasty jobs. If he picks up the stray Kiwi he won't have to go to the homicides.

'This is great, guys,' I said, playing with the electric windows. 'It's freezing out there.'

'Well, it's just nice not to have to deal with someone who's been mugged or raped.'

Yep, definitely avoiding the big jobs. Not only that but, like myself, they were both very good at getting lost. Three times in fact. One tried his best to make the map unreadable, turning it upside down and peering at it too closely.

Meanwhile on the RT we heard, 'Incident involving a man and a shopping trolley. Car badly damaged.'

I wanted to stay with them all night. Unfortunately, they found the hostel.

With only an hour to go till 2002, a Welsh guy with a girlfriend who looked like Anna Kournikova joined me, holding two beers and six shooters.

'I used to sell door to door,' he told me, downing his third shooter. 'Ten per cent of people will buy anything. You sell them a plastic dog turd? They'll buy it. It's the other eighty per cent you've got to convince. When I used to sell door to door, I'd sometimes find I needed a morale booster, just because it was such a depressing and degrading job. I used to wear a suit, knock on the door and say, "Hi, I'm from the UFO society, just wondering whether you've seen anything strange in the last half hour."'

We drank and discussed best rejection stories.

It was now only five minutes to go before midnight. My lonely New Year's Eve was nearly over. I couldn't wait. A bunch of Spanish guys did something very strange before Big Ben struck 12. They delved into their backpacks and produced a sizeable bunch of grapes. They gave 12 grapes to each Spaniard and informed me that every time Big Ben struck, they would eat a grape. Spanish tradition, they said.

I tried the same with pints but it didn't work.

And then it finally happened, we all watched TV, Big Ben dinged and donged and the Spanish boys ate grapes. It was 2002; what a bizarre feeling to look around the room and not know a soul. I stood there like a spare prick at a wedding. Only one New Year's tradition to complete; problem was, I didn't know who to kiss.

So I kissed everyone!

Finally, it was time for bed. From backpacking experience I knew if you got more than three hours' sleep in a room full of farting males, you're doing well. Throughout the night, various males in various degrees of drunkenness stumbled in, the last arriving at 9.46 a.m. Then you get the 'sneaker inners' who are quite happy to sleep on a mattress, if only for a few hours just so they can avoid paying £10. The two sneaker inners I encountered arrived at 3 a.m. and lay down fully clothed. By now, let me tell you, this room smelt of one prolonged fart.

The sneaker inners left about two hours later. The girl struggled to get up; she was wearing a crop top and I could see her pierced belly button. She was wearing only a T-shirt and I could see the outline of her breasts. The boyfriend saw that I was awake, put his finger to his lips and they shuffled away. Within minutes someone else was in the bed. Perfectly executed; a backpacker tag team with experience.

And I'll tell you what: if bedrooms could drive, this one would have been well over the legal limit. Farts, beer, bad breath and socks; this room was rank and getting worse by the minute. I wondered whether the ladies in the next room had to suffer the same fragrances. As you can tell, I hadn't acquired my three hours' sleep yet. Keeping me awake was the uncertainty of who would be sleeping above me on the top bunk. It was the only bed vacant.

Wonder no more. Within minutes a guy blasted in, crashing through the door unaware that members of his own sex were also blind drunk and in need of shut-eye. He banged into the door, into the wall and tripped over at least three pairs of shoes. He was breathing heavily. Concentration was obviously absent but something he was desperately trying to hang on to. The real test came when he tried to pull his jeans off. Balance and coordination were obviously hanging out with concentration somewhere in the Greek islands, because he made a right spectacle of himself, slipping on his own socks and crashing into the bunk bed. The manoeuvre was complete when he yanked himself onto the top bunk, nearly tipping the entire structure over in the process, still breathing heavily, swaggering to the correct end of the bed and farting three times.

'Hi, honey, I'm home.'

'You could have called.'

'SORRY, SIR, NO buses on New Year's Day.'

This was news I didn't need. I had a bus ticket burning a hole in my back pocket and I wanted to get back to Cheltenham so I could start my new life with the old car. I looked a fucking mess. Three hours' sleep would have been a blessing; I don't think I managed one. The first day of 2002 I was unshaven, had a rooster head (caused by not showering and waking up in the morning with a hairstyle that resembles a rooster's head) and was hung over. Not a good start to the year.

The last thing I wanted to do was hang around spending money in Oxford but it looked as if there was no other option. I could have taken the train via Worcester and paid

£25 or spent the next two hours eating cold burgers in Burger King listening to 'She Bangs' by Ricky Martin. That was a low point. I felt like shit. Half of my chicken burger dribbled down my sweatshirt. I didn't care any more. This was not getting any easier. As well as the cardboard fries, I realised I'd also have to bite the bullet and pay for accommodation if there were no buses to Cheltenham today.

The lady at the hotel booking office took one look at my rooster head and ungroomed stubble and said, 'Here's the list of hotels in the area, but I think a lot of them will be too expensive for you.'

Happy New Year to you as well.

She was right, though. The YHA, flooded with Germans, was the only thing in my price range. Unfortunately, I had not renewed my membership (as if I ever had one!) so couldn't rest my head there. The only other option was to walk. And walk. And walk.

Three miles and over two hours later I'd had enough. I didn't care any more. I needed a bed, a shower and a room with less than 16 people. I considered busking along the way to help pay for B&Bs that were charging £35 for a tiny room, but had no energy. Plus, anyone in their right mind would run a mile with me looking like this.

'How much for a room?' I asked the old lady with more stubble than me.

'Fifty pounds,' she said.

Fuck.

Oh, fuck it.

This can be my Christmas present. Look out Visa.

I ran a bath, sat on the toilet forever and watched the BBC's *The Wonder of Animals*. I had a simply marvellous time. I jumped on the bed. I spread my coins all over the floor.

I tried not to think of the money.

I thought of the money.

I tried not to think of the money.

I thought of the money.

That night, as I tried to nod off, not thinking about the money, the shower seemed to come alive. Along with it going drip, drip, drip, the bedside clock went tick, tick, tick and the wall heater went clunk, clunk, clunk. Sometimes they held an amazing rhythm and, in a moment of complete symphony, all went at once. It annoyed the hell out of me, but even more frustrating was that just as I was about to get up and belt the hell out of anything electrical, I found myself click, click, clicking my fingers and tap, tap, tapping my feet.

Then I remembered why it was I was lying in bed.

I woke up thinking about the money. I made the most out of my bedroom telly and watched another movie on the 14-inch screen. A sign just by the main control panel puzzled me: *Please after 11 p.m. Moderate volume.*

It's a 14-inch telly for God's sake, not a boom box. What damage can it do?

Then I remembered if I wanted breakfast, I had to be downstairs by nine. I tried not to think about the money (£50 in New Zealand could buy a second-hand Honda), and reassured myself breakfast would be well worth it. Cardboard hash browns, eggs rolled in fat and bacon that tasted like it was straight from the pig's arse told me otherwise. For the second day in a row I had a rooster head. I'm sure the two Japanese girls in the corner were making chicken noises as I ate.

DON'T LOSE YOUR ticket, don't lose your ticket, I kept saying to myself. I'd checked it once an hour for the past three days. I could just imagine myself losing it and having to fork out another for my bus ride to Cheltenham. It's there, it's there, I kept telling myself. My back pocket proudly held the bus ticket. It was an hour till the bus would be leaving. Finally, my hell in Oxford would be over. Don't get me wrong: lovely place, shit time.

I have the ticket. I have the ticket. Need a hot chocolate. Why am I wearing thin socks when it's −2 °C?

The bus finally arrived, I put my hand in my pocket and … my fucking ticket had gone! Unbelievable! Between the time I'd gotten a hot chocolate and complained about freezing feet my bus ticket had pissed off. But where? And how? And when?

I found myself now giving £10 to the bus driver, in a foul mood with a rooster head.

'You haven't got a 50p, have you?' he asked, trying to give the correct change.

'I had a bloody ticket up until ten minutes ago!'

I reluctantly handed him my new money for a new ticket.

'Well?' he asked.

'Well what?' I replied.

'Where are you going?'

This is like when someone's driving you home, but they've never been to your house before. Just because *you* drive to your house every night and you know where to go, you automatically presume the person driving will also know. Then they drive past your street and you yell, 'Oi, where the hell you going, idiot? My street's back there! Jesus.'

This bus driver should have known I was in a bad mood and he should have known where I was going before I lost that sodding ticket.

'What a stroppy little door-to-door busker you've turned out to be,' I could hear my mother say.

– 15 –

Rugby

Earnings to date: £248, a bottle of port (half drunk) and a car

RUGBY GOT ME into this mess. Rugby can get me out of it.

Funny, the only thing Poms could really tell me about the place was it was hard to get to.

'Have you been to Rugby?' I'd ask.

'No, it's really hard to get to. I think you turn right at Coventry.'

They were dead right; Rugby *was* hard to get to, even in my brand new, old car. God knows how I would have got there by train. Of course, what I forgot about driving was that I would have to concentrate. I was a little surprised to see the car didn't come with its very own co-driver who could have told me not to head towards Birmingham; or Bristol for that matter.

Getting the car was everything I'd hoped for. I would never have to cart those bloody bags around another train or bus station. A car could go where I want when I want. Everything I owned was in it: my guitar, my moneybag, my backpack, my deodorant and toothpicks. Only thing I didn't have was clean washing and a map. I'd managed to get this far without one but to continue on a map-less journey through the UK, now that I was a responsible citizen on the road, would be a tad optimistic, not to mention bloody stupid.

I felt like I was 16 again. Wow, you're gonna let me drive *your* car, out *there*? I was sure the cops would sooner rather than later figure out I was just a low-life busker stalking poor British people and stealing car parks from people who really needed them. People with jobs and mortgages and a proper life to lead. And, oh, how I howled when I drove past some poor bugger who had obviously run out of windscreen cleaner and was piling big clumps of snow onto his windshield. How I laughed, how I sniggered, how I quietly took the piss out of that idiot, until the same thing happened to me about an hour later and I had to think of something as cunningly genius.

Except I was too much of a pansy to stand outside in the snow.

AFTER TAKING numerous wrong turns and lengthy diversions via incorrect off-ramps (slip roads) I finally ended up in Rugby late afternoon. I suppose when everyone arrives in this town they have a good laugh at the names of things: Rugby School (do they ever get any work done?), Rugby Chiropractor (what about cricket injuries?) and Rugby Police (like there's not enough security at the ground to stop streakers like Mark).

As it happened, my first challenge in Rugby was not to find nice, wealthy punters, but where the hell I was going to stay. I may have made the ingenious move of purchasing a map, but not so ingenious was failing to pile snow on my own windscreen, hence having to look through a gap the size of a golf ball most of the journey. What I *didn't* have was a hostel/hotel guide.

Oh, well, B&Bs will be easy to find, I thought.

They didn't have flashing neon lights saying *Cheap winter*

rates for lost Kiwis, however. Again, I was tired and still in search of a co-driver who tonight could also double as my masseuse and tea lady. I parked outside a four-star hotel just to see what it felt like. I looked up at the rooms, then I looked at my beaten, scarred Visa card. Then I saw the lights; but why is the bar the only part of a hotel that has a neon light? How degrading, how belittling to think people who drink booze would be stupid enough to be attracted to a neon sign just because it says *Happy Hour – Two for One*.

I was there in a beat.

I had no money, though. I just needed information. Instead of asking the lady at reception for a list of hotels *way* cheaper than this dump, I befriended a well-dressed Indian enjoying a gin and tonic. His beige jacket and striped tie were perfectly cut. His hair was gelled and seamless; not one out of place. He emitted a calm and wonderful aura, quite the opposite to me who was just after a quick bargain.

'Go to the Seven Stars across the road, you'll pay no more than ten pounds,' he said.

Yippee! Screw your £35 I wanted to say to the receptionist, but she was gone. It wouldn't have made any difference anyway. The Seven Stars was deserted, no one in sight, not one light on. I'd have to keep looking.

I found a pub with music blaring, loud enough to accommodate at least two hundred people, providing they were yelling at the top of their lungs; only difference was, there were only three guys leaning against the bar. Is this a ploy by publicans? Play music deafeningly loud so that people on the street think they're missing out on the biggest party ever, when in reality the people inside wouldn't be able to hear if a rhino just fell through the roof into the lounge bar?

The bar in question was Checkers Bar where I'd hopefully get a good sleep. I walked up five flights of stairs with heavy bags to my room. The heater didn't work, there was a shower but no toilet and the kettle seemed like it hadn't been cleaned since 1946. But it was only fifteen quid, so I couldn't complain.

What I desperately needed, however, was good food. I walked around in minus temperatures for half an hour, eventually having to settle for McDonald's. Service is not what it used to be in this fine establishment. A girl was in mid-conversation with her co-worker, obviously unaware I was at the counter waiting for food that never quite looked the same as it did on the poster.

'Yeah, well that's nothing,' she yelled. 'I was up till fucking six on New Year's!'

Then she saw me. 'Ahem … Hi, welcome to McDonald's, can I take your order?'

I WAS HOPING the guys back in the bar who couldn't hear anything over the Backstreet Boys and Gabrielle would give me some tips on where to go in Rugby the following day. As Don Partridge said, a pub is the best place to meet people and gauge the feeling of a town. Only thing was, I was feeling antisocial and my slowly going deaf friends were obviously feeling the same. Their circle was a closed one, so I climbed the five flights of stairs with cold burgers and dry chips in my stomach.

After a fantastic sleep I was ready to attack the day. I knew nothing about Rugby other than it was where the game actually started all those years ago. After such an unsuccessful attempt at finding good food last night I wasn't that optimistic finding any this morning. After only five minutes outside it soon became apparent I wouldn't be able to busk for long without having to find the warmth and comfort of a café.

And that's exactly what I did.

'What's the temperature this morning, do you know?' I asked the waitress who handed me a menu.

'I heard on the radio it was minus one. Do you want breakfast?'

I rubbed my hands together, cursing my dumb-arse brain. Why … don't … I … just … buy … gloves?

'You won't have a lot of luck in Rugby, people are very cliquey,' the smiling waitress informed me. 'If you get through to them they'll be all right, but I don't rate your chances. Go further north, it's great.'

But she would say that seeing as she was studying in Newcastle. Like many other Brits I'd met on this trip, she too had been to New Zealand and loved it. There was hardly a door where someone didn't know of someone who had an uncle, or who had just been or had always wanted to. This often kept me going, knowing that home was still there. It was still alive.

'It's weird,' she continued. 'You say that in New Zealand people don't really tip? Sometimes really rich people put their American Express card on the counter and never tip here. Yet other times you get poor people who will leave you a couple of quid.'

'I find the same door to door,' I said.

Soon a huge plate of scrambled eggs, mushrooms, toast and edible (!) hash browns arrived in front of me along with a glass of orange juice, which would be my first since that pub in Canterbury.

'Enjoy your breakfast,' she said. And it was those three words, said so nicely and accompanied by such a nice meal, which convinced me I would have to leave her a tip.

I felt guilty even before I started eating; I had no money, how was I supposed to leave a tip? I decided I would sing to her as my tip. I became nervous, suddenly hoping no one else would come into the restaurant. What would I sing? I tuned my guitar in the corner. My eggs got cold.

Guitar now tuned and ready to go, I completed the best breakfast I'd had in England. Ten other customers had since arrived as I made my way to the main counter to pay.

'Did you enjoy your breakfast?' another waitress asked.

'It was great, thanks. In fact, so good that I want to sing to your friend as a tip,' I said proudly.

'You want to what?' she asked, keying in the amount on the till.

'I want to sing to her, as my tip.'

'I'm sorry … but restaurant policy dictates we can't have you singing in here.'

'You're joking, right?' I was fishing around in my pocket for coins to pay.

'No, not joking. Restaurant policy says you're not allowed to sing in here.'

'Just let me sing to this lady and the chef,' I said. The waitress had since arrived back in the room. She looked confused. 'I want to thank them for my breakfast,' I insisted. Bloody hell, did I have to apply for a visa?

'Not possible, I'm afraid,' said the manager.

'OK, well, I'll sing to you outside,' I said to the waitress.

'No, I don't think so,' she said.

I walked outside and waited. She was making coffee. Both were serving customers, trying to avoid eye contact. After five minutes she finally came out. Folding her arms was essential in the cold; she was only wearing a blouse. I sang a song (with a guitar once again badly out of tune – will this thing ever sound good?) and was on my way.

She thanked me and got back to work. Everyone in the restaurant was now looking, wondering what was going on and what they'd missed out on. You talk to the manager, I wanted to say, if *she* opened her eyes to new experiences instead of hanging on to red tape, you too could be listening to my shite singing.

You won't have a lot of luck in Rugby, people are very cliquey.

Once again, this was all the motivation I needed. Once again, no one knew how Rugby would fare in the door-to-door busking stakes. As I've talked about before, it's not the sort of question you can ask a local: 'How do you think I'll do as a door-to-door busker here?'

'Never heard of it. Get a life, I'm busy.'

'Right, cheers then.'

I decided a good time to start would be while I still had feeling in both hands. Moultrie Road presented me with comfortable, middle-class housing, big lawns and a good feeling. The first dwelling I wandered up to was, what I thought, a massive house. The garage door was open and there was a sign on the lawn: *Keep off the grass except for in emergencies.*

But what would constitute an emergency? A last game of cricket before your grandfather had a heart attack? A rugby scrum with an ambulance driver?

I knocked at the door and was greeted by a woman who didn't seem keen. She fetched another woman, who said, 'You'd better come in then.'

All I could smell was boiled food, mainly cabbage.

'Would you like a coffee, my Babs?' a lady asked from what seemed like one of many kitchens. I was led down a corridor. Why could I smell cabbage and only cabbage?

Where the hell was I? Where were they taking me? I started to get concerned. Then I walked into the lounge and found ten old people seated backs to the wall, around the periphery of the room.

Oh my God.

Of course, the boiled food!

The overbearing smell of *cabbage* now made complete and utter sense.

I had gatecrashed a rest home!

I would soon discover the absolute beauty of busking in rest homes: captive audiences. Well, it's not as if they're about to go anywhere now, is it? Perfect for a door-to-door busker who had too much time on his hands. It was warm, no one would be in a hurry to complain or tell you to bugger off, and as long as you could tolerate the smell of boiled cabbage, a gold mine was just around the corner.

My audience consisted of ten old ladies who knitted, slept, stared into space and occasionally dribbled. In fact, very reminiscent of the Engelbert audience I played to in Wellington, but for the knitting.

Deciding which song to play wouldn't be a major concern either as most of the poor lasses couldn't hear a word I said. Some expected me to change their commode, others thought I was there to turn the heating down while others thought I was there to 'fix the venetian blind in my room that goes clank, clank, clank in the night when I'm trying to sleep'.

But the best was to come – meeting Doris.

Doris with dementia. Doris who couldn't stop laughing. Doris who became my best friend.

She was perched in the corner, crying with laughter the minute I walked in. We're not talking giggle laughter, we're talking howling, God-I'm-drunk-and-I've-heard-the-funniest-joke-ever laughter. Continuously, not stopping, crying, tears rolling down her cheeks laughter.

'I know what you're thinking,' she said, winking. 'I *know* what you're thinking.'

'What?' I asked, not able to stop laughing myself.

'I know what you're thinking,' she repeated and howled, literally *howled* with laughter.

The other oldies in the room were unimpressed, they looked tired and bored with Doris's party tricks. Some rolled their eyes, others tried to sleep; others reminded me I still hadn't done anything about 'the blind in their room that was going clank, clank, clank'.

Meanwhile, Doris continued to laugh.

And laugh. And laugh.

I tried to play a song but was interrupted.

'Look at him,' she said, poking the poor lady to her left, who was just concentrating on being old. 'He can't play for laughing, look, he can't sing for laughing!'

It's fair to say a group of half-pissed, half-stoned cockatoos could not have made more noise than this one mad old bat in the corner.

'I know what you're thinking,' she repeated, laughing when she caught her breath. 'I know what you're thinking.'

Let me tell you, by this stage I felt I was letting the rest of the room down and focusing too much on Doris. I really was trying to sing something. Unfortunately, though, Doris had transformed herself into the most savvy, career-ending heckler I had ever encountered.

I couldn't concentrate. I couldn't play. I laughed. I cried. I needed the toilet.

Thankfully, that's when Charlie arrived. The only man lucky enough (or unlucky enough, depending on which way you look at it) to make it to the age of the rest of the room.

'All right, mate?' he said, sitting two chairs down from the giggler.

'Can you make a living out of this?' he asked when I told him what I was doing in the UK. 'Must be nice travelling around.'

A semi-normal conversation with Charlie brought me back to life and for this I was grateful. I tried to avoid eye contact with Doris but I could hear sniggers, smirks and nasal spasms coming from her corner. After a minute or so I made the fatal mistake of looking at her. I couldn't help it, she was like a child that needed attention. And sure enough, when I looked at her, she erupted into the king of all laughing fits. I seriously thought this latest bout would require medical attention.

I turned around to Charlie again who asked me more questions about travel. He looked sad, like he wanted to be young, freezing his balls off like me and knocking on doors. He looked confused, then smiled as if my being here had sparked memories of his own travelling days.

Poor Charlie, I wanted to take him to the rugby, drink beer and talk cars.

Doris, you can come next week.

'My sister moved to Oz twenty years ago,' he said. 'She married an Aussie guy and never came back.'

'Sorry about that, Charlie. Oh well, suppose you can't have everything.'

Again he looked confused, then winked and pointed at me when it registered.

'Do you ever get hungry?' he asked.

'On the road you mean?'

'Mm, do you ever get hungry?'

'Yeah.'

'What do you eat?'

'I normally have some eggs,' I said.

'What kind?'

'Scrambled.'

'How many, three or four?'

'Just two.'

'Yep.'

Satisfied that Charlie now knew my daily intake I finally sang 'Harry Potter' to the room. The nurses and the rest of the ladies clapped. And guess what, Doris laughed all the way through.

'Have you got a girlfriend?' She winked again. A lady next to her got the giggles.

'I know what you're thinking.' Oh, come on, Doris, this is getting boring.

'What! What am I thinking?' I was now intrigued. What *was* I thinking?

'You,' she said mid-giggle, 'you want to marry me!'

Um, that's not quite what I was thinking, Doris, but nice guess. What I was actually thinking was, how you can laugh all day without any of these other poor bastards doing you some serious damage.

All right, I'll be honest, Doris made my day. Three pounds found its way into my pocket along with a banana a lady who'd been asleep during the entire performance passed me as I was leaving.

This was getting ridiculous.

Capitalising on my success, I asked a nurse whether there were any other rest homes in the immediate area.

'Sure, there's one just across the road,' she said, showing me to the front door.

'Hey, thanks for letting me sing. Tell me. Doris, is she always like that?' I asked.

'Yep.'

'Twenty-four hours a day?'

'Yep.'

'How do the others put up with her?'

'They don't,' she said. 'It's a terrible thing, dementia.'

I didn't know what to say.

'Can you thank them again for me? I had a great time. And tell Charlie I'll eat my eggs.'

'Sure, no problem. And good luck!' she said, closing the door.

I don't want to get old.

Sure enough, there was a rest home across the road but the same success didn't await me. A nurse on her break answered the door and, although keen to listen, wasn't about to invite me in. Very kindly she gave me £1.70 to go with my banana. Unfortunately that seemed to be the last rest home in sight; I'd have to go back to more conventional means.

Rugby people are very cliquey; you won't get money around here.

This urban myth fed to me by the same girl who fed me breakfast was about to be cracked in a big way. The people of Rugby were brilliant. Inviting, charming and friendly. While saying that, not all of them had what I wanted – loose change. The first door I knocked on bore the sort of sign I'd grown accustomed to in the last month:

We do not buy or sell to callers at the door.

It may be necessary for you to make an appointment at a time that is convenient to us.

You may be required to show an official identity card.

In other words, fuck off. Of course, I knocked – love a challenge.

The door opened to reveal an elegant, well-dressed woman who embarrassingly listened but admitted to having no money.

'Looking at all the art you'd think we were loaded,' she said, pointing to the staircase behind her. Antiques and brilliant artwork wound their way up to the top floor. Watercolours, oils, portraits and landscapes covered the walls.

'My husband works on the telly, on the *Antiques Roadshow*,' she said proudly, scouring her purse for anything that was round and could be used as legal tender. She was very embarrassed.

'Don't worry about it,' I said, seeing nothing with any of the above characteristics was anywhere to be seen. 'So what's it like living in Rugby?' I asked.

'Rugby? Oh, it's lovely,' her eyes lit up. 'And it's a great pleasure when the All Blacks play here. We always get to meet them.'

'Have you always lived here?'

'Yes, we grew up in Rugby, our parents grew up here and so did our grandparents.'

'It's amazing the number of accents in the UK for such a small geographical area. For a country only the size of New Zealand, the difference in accents is astounding. Obviously you have over sixty million people and we have only three, but still.'

'Well, as a rule, we Brits don't move around a lot. We're not like you Kiwis gallivanting around the world. Of course, that is a bit of a generalisation, but as a rule we don't move. We tend to stay in the same place, and that's how accents develop.'

Clever, I'd never thought of it like that.

'You have to go to Rugby School,' she yelled as I walked away empty-handed. 'They love Kiwis!'

I WAS OFTEN asked what the lowest amount I'd ever been given was. Generally, if people were prepared to listen, they would give at least a pound, but never much more. At the next house in Rugby I was about to record a new low. The house was a veritable mansion of a place. A long, sweeping driveway led to a three-storey, very old, historic-looking family home. A man greeted me and while he didn't exactly show hostility, I would have preferred he told me from the outset that he was in an extreme hurry and wouldn't be hanging around. It would have saved us both the hassle. Instead, at the end of my spiel, he turned and yelled up the stairs, 'Sue, you come and cope with this, I'm leaving.'

Sue would have been 15 or 16 with long, red hair and a freckly face. She looked awkward as I sang and, like most people, was relieved when the event was over. At the conclusion she handed me what felt like four or five coins. I never count at the door; that would be rude, so I thanked her and made my way down the long driveway. When I knew she'd closed the door and retreated to safety (probably on the phone as soon as possible to warn her friends of some stalker dude wandering the streets), I unclenched my fist and discovered what I'd earlier predicted: four coins.

Four coins with a grand total of 10p!

I suppose you're wondering how the hell I could be so impressed with the people of Rugby considering the last two houses had given me such a small amount. Well, it all happened after that. Twelve pounds came my way with relative ease, one house after another, keen to listen, keen to give. A lot of people in Rugby were keen to hear how my travels had gone and keen to tell me how many members of their family had been to New Zealand.

On that note I decided to follow the advice of our antiques collector and try busking at Rugby School. My confidence was riding high by this stage. Plus it seemed apt to let the School of Rugby get me out of the mess the game had gotten me into.

The story goes that, back in 1823, William Webb Ellis was so bored playing football he decided, mid-game, to pick up the ball and run with it to the other end of the field. You can imagine he would have been pretty bloody unpopular with the other players on the field that day, but what was an obvious 'hand ball' then has now become the game of rugby as we know it today. And here I was, at the very school where William Webb Ellis was probably beaten up in the penalty box, staring at the very field where it all happened.

But would Rugby School entertain a door-to-door busker? Or would I have to change the rules like William Webb himself?

I walked up to some grandly beautiful doors with a sign pointing towards the Headmaster's Office. A lady cleaning the window saw me bolt up the stairs so she opened the door. What am I doing here, I asked myself for the two-hundredth time.

'Come on, my darling, in you come, you must be freezing!'

Her concern was genuine, like your mum's when you came home late.

'How can we help you?' she asked, with puppy dog eyes.

'It's … a long story,' I replied, rubbing my hands together, hoping the school's heating was on. 'It's all John Eales's fault,' I continued. 'John Eales and Jonah Lomu.'

Her face was blank. I may as well have said, 'It's all Basil Brush's fault,' for it was plain to see she had no idea who

Lomu *or* Eales were. Then again, why should she? Just because she cleans the floor of the Rugby School doesn't mean she has to know what position Basil Brush played.

'I don't think you'll get a good response here, it's very quiet,' she said when I told her about the bet.

'Good, a challenge then,' I said.

She took off her gloves and swept the remainder of dirt into the corner. She seemed in two minds. She could just as easily have showed me the back of the door as quickly as she showed me the front, but she seemed too adventurous for that. She took a breath, paused, then said, 'Who shall I get for you?'

'Anyone, I'll sing to anyone,' I said, remembering that if I didn't tune the guitar quickly a pregnant seagull may soon be doing the rounds in Rugby School.

'Someone important?'

'Someone fun. No, bugger it! Someone important.'

A few minutes later she came back with a woman in a trendy tracksuit and a man in a grey suit, who looked at me like I'd just slept with his wife. All three were looking at me through a glass door at the bottom of a stairwell. The cleaner motioned to me to come through, holding her index finger over her lips at the same time.

'Can't do it out there, the headmaster's in a meeting!' she whispered.

'Oh, right,' I said, wondering why that would be a problem.

Serious Man looked ready to give me the cane. Looking over his shoulder every ten seconds, it seemed like he was worried the big Rugby God in the sky would see him taking five minutes off. He folded his arms and frowned at me. Shit, I hope my guitar is in tune, I thought.

Then, I sang, very quietly, like I was in a library. Every

time I raised the volume a bit, trying to emphasise a funny line in the song, Serious Man would put his finger to his lips. When I'd finished, the two ladies quietly laughed and clapped while Serious Man said, 'Right, very good,' and walked off.

My female listeners scraped together £2 and wished me luck.

I love crushing myths, Rugby: a warm heart.

16

Nottingham

Earnings to date: £266.80, a bottle of port (half drunk), a car and a banana

'DON'T GO TO Nottingham, it's boring.'

'Nottingham? There's nothing there.'

'Why would you want to go there?'

'It's just a city.'

Again, expectations versus reality. What I was told about Nottingham and what I actually experienced were worlds apart. Before I left Rugby I checked my emails and was blown away to discover that both *The New Zealand Truth* and *South Wales Echo* wanted to do a story on my busking adventures so far. There was also one from Susanna (my housemate from Swindon who bought £40 worth of junk from the charming door-to-door pedlar), saying that Mark from 96 Trent FM in Nottingham was keen to get me into their studio for a chat. She also said there'd be a chance of a meal and a bed.

I was there in a flash.

When I arrived in Nottingham, exhausted and delirious after having to read maps and follow directions (again, if I actually listened to people instead of looking at spinach in their teeth, I would get to places with a lot more ease), Mark met me at the reception of Trent FM.

'Welcome to Nottingham! Have we got a day planned for you!' he said. 'Grab a coffee, then we're off.'

I felt humbled that people wanted to help out like this. What was to follow was a dream day, playing to a potential 60,000 people and falling on my arse a dozen times or more.

First stop was City Ground, a place steeped in history and Nottingham Forest's home ground. Now, my football knowledge is limited at the best of times but it didn't stop me going straight to the boardroom, sitting in director Eric Barnes's chair and, unbeknown to the board, signing up 12 New Zealand players for next year's FA Cup.

I then spirited to the middle of the pitch and sang to 35,000 empty seats and four bemused groundsmen. Steve, one of the bemused, couldn't offer me any coins for my seagull squawking, but said I could take a tractor and a bag of sand for my efforts.

'Maybe another time, Steve. Trying to keep luggage to a minimum.'

I'm sure it's the same for most people: football stadiums, or any stadium for that matter, do something to you. The hairs on the back of your neck rise, an air of expectation follows. You get the feeling, sometime soon, *something* will happen. I've always wanted to have a flat right inside the Melbourne Cricket Ground. Imagine, waking up on match day, pulling back the curtains, taking a leak and opening the fridge. Sorted.

What fool isn't going to come around and watch the game?

'That's not such a stupid idea,' Steve told us when I asked about flatting at City Ground. 'We've got one Forest fan here who wants us to spread his ashes over the pitch. I said to him, "But you're not dead yet." He says, "Well, I'm just preparing for when I do"!'

While Steve was telling us about booking deaths in

advance, I quietly started fantasising about the offer of that tractor. I'm sure he wasn't serious. In fact I know he wasn't, but wouldn't it look fucking brilliant if the door-to-door busker turned up to each town on a sodding tractor!

You'd sure know he was coming.

I admit, my guitar may have been many things on this trip: personal friend, prop, possible weapon but never, as far as I know, had it been used as a cricket bat. That was until now. For the next item on Mark's Tour of Nottingham was to take me to Trent Bridge, the home of Nottingham Cricket. On an outfield completely covered in snow, where Sir Richard Hadlee himself enjoyed huge success in the eighties, I swept, cut and drove my way to a personal milestone: the highest total by a door-to-door busker away from home.

'Oh, what a shot! That has raced away! Did you see the way Brown effortlessly stroked that piece of snow to the boundary. He moves onto two hundred and thirty-six and New Zealand win the game by eight wickets. Absolutely sensational start to what has been a tour of two halves. In fact –'

'Justin, can we go now? There are other places to see,' Mark hollered from the boundary.

'Yeah, sure. I'll just sign a few autographs,' I said.

'Travis have played here, Craig David has played here, Blink 182 have played here and now Justin Brown has played here,' Mark said as we walked into the National Ice Centre in Nottingham. Unfortunately, just staying upright and off my arse was more on my mind than strumming chords and after such a long innings at Trent Bridge, I'd definitely need a massage later from the team physio. Two old people skated past me, making it look easy, while I tried to work out how many people I'd actually sung to today.

Let me see: 35,000 at City Ground, 20,000 at Trent Bridge and now 12,000 at the ice rink. Of course, if you were talking actual *people*, not empty seats, there would be fewer than ten.

But that's not the point now, is it?

MARK LIVED IN a place called Bottesford and, just to make things easier, informed me that his housemate had also changed his name to Mark for the evening.

'That's very kind of you,' I said. 'So what's his real name?'

'Mark,' he said.

'Oh, well, that worked out nicely then.'

What Mark told me next indicated it was going to be a messy night.

'Don't forget, your interview is at six-thirty tomorrow. We'll leave the house about six.'

Oh no, not this again, I thought. Flashbacks of Reading came back to haunt me, the whisky, the late night, the abuse by the woman at 6 a.m. Sitting in the kitchen, eyeing a bleary-looking brew called Cripple Cock Farmyard Scrumpy, I said, 'Best I stay off that then.'

The two Marks decided to take me to their local for a quiet one. Unfortunately, and yes, you know exactly how this story goes, that quiet little unobtrusive ale slowly becomes a demonic, gate-crashing mother of all hangovers. But God, did we have a good time achieving it.

In a serene moment by the fireplace, I suggested to the table that we play the 'Movie Star game'. Simple game really, you just go around the table and have to name an actor who would play that person if they had a movie written about them. If your best mate looks like Sean Penn, that's who would play him in a movie.

I've played this game numerous times before and, like

most drinking games, it normally fades off into obscurity as soon as the next beers arrive. But not this time. And it was all to do with the talent at our table.

Lofty from *Coronation Street*, Beaker from the *Muppets*, Roger Moore and Macaulay Culkin. It wasn't just our table either. Somehow, this little pub in Bottesford had become a smorgasbord of celebrities. Bruce Lee was at the bar and Anthony Hopkins was at the cigarette machine.

The only problem with the movie star game is when everyone's had a few drinks. It's then that they start scouring the pub, bored with their already 'discovered' stars. We need new lookalikes, they scream. This is when fights can start, especially if everyone gets the answer at the same time. For example, if someone walks in and looks like the Fat Bastard off *Austin Powers*, everyone laughs at him in unison and at least one member of the table is stupid enough to yell, 'I know this one! I know this one! It's ... Fat Bastard!'

THUMP!

I was surprisingly chirpy the next morning despite helping the local brewery reach record high profits and eating fish and chips at closing time. Another Mark (bloody hell, do you have to be called Mark to live in Nottingham?) welcomed me into the studio at 6.30 a.m. and we got straight into it.

'You're listening to Trent FM. Now, we did mention earlier that we'd have a busker with a difference in the studio this morning. I know it's that time of year where you have no money but we need you to dig deep, go into deeper debt. Justin, welcome, I take it you're not from Nottinghamshire?' Mark said.

'No, I'm from Auckland, New Zealand.'

'Oh well, you can't have everything in life. How much have you made so far?'

'Two hundred and sixty-six pounds and eighty pence, a bottle of port –'

'That's an unwanted Christmas present! That's not allowed.'

'And a banana from a rest home in Rugby.'

'You went to a rest home!'

'Two actually. Strange, this old woman passes you a banana and three quid, I didn't know what to do.'

Mark couldn't control himself; rest homes, bananas, idiotic buskers, it was all too much.

'So where have you been exactly?'

'All through the south, although now I want to see if the *north* is friendlier.'

'Well, that's a foregone conclusion, isn't it? Let me just get this straight. You're not allowed to sing on a street corner and earn money that way?'

'Definitely not.'

'Because we have an old guy here in Nottingham, who I'm convinced is an accountant by day, who sits outside WH Smith with a xylophone playing 'Come all ye faithful' in April. Funnily enough he disappears at this time of year – the time that would be most lucrative. We have our own buskers here, but you're not allowed to do that, are you?'

'No, Mark, it has to be door to door. That's what makes it so difficult. It's funny, a lot of men in particular get scared I'm going to sing them a love song. It's a very strange feeling, you must understand, serenading a man on his doorstep. Poor bugger never knows where to look.'

'It's the year 2002 after all,' Mark said. 'And what kind of songs do you do?'

'Oh, "Harry Potter", "Kentucky Fried Kitten".'

'What, Kentucky Fried?'

'Kitten.'

'I'm enjoying my last show today,' he grimaced. 'OK then, listen up Nottingham, we want your money. Give us a call if you'd like a door-to-door busker personally delivered to your door.'

'I'd just like to add, Mark, in today's unstable financial climate, I'd like to let the people of Nottingham know … that I accept the euro.'

'You'd be the only person in the country who does!'

After gathering numerous addresses from keen Nottingham listeners, we then hit the streets to see how much I could raise in the great white north. And it really was white, snow everywhere and a temperature of, get ready for it, –8 °C!

That's right, minus eight!

It may not seem like the sort of problem you can bring up at the dinner table, but I'm sure as soon as we hit the streets, my strings had shrunk. There, I've admitted it. Don't mention it again.

First up, we went to Beverly's house. 'I'd like a busker to brighten up our road. It's really quite miserable down our street,' she'd said on the radio.

Beverly was waiting at the front door by the time we arrived. It was pitch black and ice prevented us from running up the driveway to match her enthusiasm. She was leaning on a walking stick, a woman of about 50 with a few missing teeth but a warm smile. Having listened to us whingeing about how bad the traffic had been, she replied, 'I love the traffic. I used to be disabled. Now I'm just happy to be back at work, in amongst it again.'

She loved the song and handed me £10. You can stay anytime, Beverly.

If I thought £10 was worth getting out of bed for (despite the fact we were now seriously in danger of losing all ten digits; it had now dropped to −10 °C!), then I wasn't at all prepared for what the next house was about to offer. We were going near Sherwood Forest to see 'Anne's daughter' who was celebrating her birthday. Anne had told Mark on air that she would give the door-to-door busker a pound for every year of her daughter's life. The cynics in all of us thought, yeah right, she's probably just turned three.

Luckily that wasn't to be the case.

Not only did Anne come through with the goods, she also had a sense of humour. The two signs on the front door read: *Sod the dog, beware of the kids* and *No Jehovah's witnesses. No salespersons or market researchers.*

When she answered I said, 'Hi, we're from the Jehovah's Witness Sales Research Company.'

Anne's daughter made her way to the front door and couldn't quite work out why a man, blue in colour, was shivering his way through 'Happy Birthday'. Upon hearing the birthday girl was a devout vegetarian, I felt a quick dose of 'Kentucky Fried Kitten' was in order as well.

'Well,' Anne said at the conclusion of the song, 'I promised I'd give you a pound for every year of my daughter's life. How old are you honey?' she asked her girl.

Please say 57, please say 57.

'I'm twenty-two today,' she said quietly.

Twenty-two pounds from one door step.

I think I fainted.

Just to top off the day, to put an end to my superb time in Nottingham, it was only fitting that I tried a brand new place to busk. As we were driving through Radcliffe on Trent we passed the local funeral home. The woman (who was over the moon we'd stopped to say hello, 'No one ever comes to see me,' she complained; I wonder why!) listened as I tuned my guitar in the freezing cold.

When she was ready, I started strumming two songs that I felt fitted the occasion perfectly: 'I Just Died in Your Arms Tonight' and 'Knockin' on Heaven's Door'.

17

Sheffield

Earnings to date: £298.80, a bottle of port (just the bottle now), a car and a banana (slightly squashed)

ALL I COULD think about when driving into Sheffield was the film *The Full Monty*. The empty steel mills, the long depressing days, the unemployment, the stripping; ah, sounds just like home.

I'd never been this far north in the UK before, so had no idea what to expect, but if it was to be anything like Rugby and Nottingham I'd be in for a bloody good time. I was also extremely proud of myself for finally purchasing a hostel/hotel guide. Along with my recently acquired map, I was turning into quite the well-equipped traveller.

I drove into Sheffield at 9 p.m. with no clue of where I was going to sleep. It seemed empty. There were no cars to speak of. Roundabouts were car-less; worst thing about that was having no one to follow. It's a common male rule, follow the car in front. Keep following them. Even if they lead you to London via Oslo and Bombay, it doesn't matter. You hold on to that glimmer of hope that they *may* know what they're doing. They *may* know where they're going.

God help people that followed me for the same reason.

'Why's that idiot going up the one-way street … in reverse? More to the point, why are we following him!'

One vital piece of information I'd read from my coffee-stained *Sheffield Accommodation* page was that I'd have to head towards Ecclesall Road. Oh, bloody great, easy name to remember when driving in the dark. The E Road, the E Road, I kept telling myself. Surely there can't be too many Ecclesalls?

Unfortunately my UK map only showed main motorways and not inner city streets.

It was entirely up to me to find the E Street.

Suddenly the *Mission Impossible* theme kicked off in my head. I turned the heater down from High so I could think. I even put down my pie and drink; this was serious. But how could I find Ecclesall Road without getting out of the car, without asking for directions?

Wait for a bus to turn up with the E Road written on the front of it.

And that's exactly what I did. Just as I was about to enter a roundabout for the tenth time, a bus came past with the neon sign in the window, *Ecclesall Road*. Genius! What a bloody genius! Follow that bus, don't take your beady eyes off it and for God's sake put down the pie and drink.

What was to follow wasn't exactly a high-speed chase; I'd prepared myself for a full on *Dukes of Hazzard*, smash up anything in sight, two-wheeled kind of adventure. Instead, the bus tootled along at 20 miles an hour and stopped every 200 metres to pick up more assassins, I mean customers.

'Come on, come on,' I yelled. 'Do something exciting, speed up, plant a bomb, anything.'

The driver indicated, pulled out, indicated, pulled over; this went on for half an hour. It wasn't really an action movie at all, more an instructional video of how to drive a bus like an old man.

Still, I should be grateful. It got me to Ecclesall Road and from there I could find a place to rest my head.

I found a phone box and called the first B&B I could find in the book. Of course, if I was a local I could have just driven all over town and found out first hand if there were spare beds.

But I wasn't; I was a fumbling tourist with pie down my shirt.

'Three – five – zero – two?' a voice belonging to an old lady asked.

'Hi, do you have accommodation for tonight?'

'I'm ever so sorry, love, we're all booked up tonight. Have you tried Mrs Whitehead?'

'Mrs … Whitehead?' I asked, having no idea what she was talking about.

'Yes, Mrs Whitehead. Have you tried ringing her?'

'No, I haven't.'

She gave me a number and again apologised for having no beds. I rang it.

'Four – two – zero – seven?'

I thought Sheffield was a big city, what's with the four numbers?

'Hi, is that Mrs Whitehead?' I asked.

'Yes, love.'

'Do you have accommodation for this evening?'

'I'm afraid we're all booked up. I'm ever so sorry, have you tried Mrs Thornton?'

'Pardon, Mrs who?' This was getting ridiculous.

'Mrs Thornton. Two ticks, I'll get the number for you.'

Fingers crossed, I hoped I wouldn't be forwarded to Mrs Stanley, Mrs Crosbie, Mrs Chapman or anyone else for that matter. Was it just me or did everyone seem to be unaware I had just been involved in a slow-speed bus chase and needed a lie down?

'Five – four – three – six?'

How sweet, the four-number thing again.

'Hello, is that Mrs Thornton?'

'Yes, dear.'

'Do you have a bed for tonight?'

'We have accommodation, yes.'

Hallelujah.

DAVE AND JOAN ran a bed and breakfast from their home in Millhouses, an obviously more upmarket area in Sheffield. Joan reassured me it was easy to find. What she didn't know was who she was dealing with: a flightless, directionless Kiwi who had just driven up and down the E Road more than nine times.

It was close to 10 p.m. as Joan opened the front door to welcome me. For someone who was more used to skungy backpacker hostels and washing my laundry in the shower while I was having one, I was very impressed with my comfy bed and little digital clock by it.

Joan came halfway up the stairs and asked, 'Will you have a cup of tea?'

'Don't mind if I do, Joan, that'll be lovely.'

There were three other bedrooms upstairs. One door had *Rupert's room* written on it and the other *David and Joan, please knock if you require assistance.*

Don't give the busker an inch, Dave, he'll take a mile. Expect a song at 3 a.m.

Even though it was after ten, Dave and Joan were in full swing taking down Christmas decorations. They were both pretty swift in their seventies, climbing on boxes and pulling down Christmas lights. Meanwhile, my cup of tea was sitting next to the sofa in the lounge. There was a little tray with a little teapot, cup, bowl of sugar and couple of shortbread biscuits. How cosy; how I felt at home.

'Do you have decorations at home?' Joan asked, taking some streamers off a photo of what I presumed were her kids.

'No, not really. Mum and Dad do.'

'I don't know why we bother, taking them down takes all night, doesn't it, David?'

'Yes, dear,' he said from atop a ladder in the hallway.

I knew why they did it. They loved it. It felt like they really celebrated Christmas plus it gave them something to do for two months of the year. Dave came out to the lounge and plonked himself on his favourite chair. He brushed the dust off his slippers and flicked on the TV.

Rock 'n' roll, Saturday night in Sheffield watching *You've Been Framed* …

Dave and Joan were really enjoying *You've Been Framed* so I didn't talk during the programme, but as soon as the ads came on I asked them how they thought I'd get on in Millhouses the next morning.

'You won't get much money around here,' Dave said, after telling me he'd lived in the area 25 years after spending 41 in London.

'Yes you will, people are very friendly around here,' Joan argued.

'No you won't,' Dave said.

'Yes you will,' Joan said.

And so on.

After hearing about my exploits at the Nottingham funeral parlour, David told me he too dealt with dead bodies on a daily basis.

'You're a funeral director? What's it like, really?' I asked.

'People die at the most inconvenient times, Justin, and have you noticed when you read the paper,' he said, tapping his nose, 'most people die in alphabetical order.'

I suppose people ask that question all the time; that seems to be the stock answer. Much as if you were a doctor, 'People are dying to get my job', or a hairdresser, 'There are loads of fringe benefits'.

But what I really wanted to know was how they deal with dead bodies all day, come home, read the paper and eat mince on toast as if they were bank tellers.

'It's much like any job, you have to learn to switch off,' he said, pouring himself another cup of tea.

'And do you have busy times of the year? Christmas rush?'

'Well, we're very busy this week. Thirty-four funerals before Thursday.'

I had more questions on the ready but *You've Been Framed* came back on.

A SENSATIONAL, MUCH needed sleep put me in a grand mood for the next day's busking. I didn't need to drive anywhere, didn't need to read maps, just had to throw the guitar on my back and walk down Dave and Joan's street. There was one small hiccup, however; they planned to head out for the morning and wanted money for the room before I left.

'But I'm just about to go busking, Joan, I'll have your money in less than an hour.'

She looked at David who wanted nothing to do with it.

'We'd just rather have the money before you left,' she said.

'I'm not about to go anywhere. My bags are inside,' I said. 'I'll see you back at the house in a couple of hours and I'll have your money, I promise.'

'Why don't you go and get the money now? Then it's all done,' she persisted.

'I'm going to go and busk to get your money.'

'But what if you don't get it?'

'No chance of that, Joan, Sheffield on a Sunday? You yourself said you live on a friendly street,' I smiled.

'Why don't you just drive down to Tescos and get the money?'

Cut me some slack here, you've got to trust me, Joan. Where's the trust gone? Look, I haven't got the bloody money but I'll get it. You're pissing me off, Joan. I was fuming. OK, fair enough, I owed them money and Joan ran a business. She was also old and veering away from her daily routine was not part of her routine. I accept that. But what pissed me off more than anything was that she didn't believe I could get the money from her street.

There was only one thing to do – show her I could.

Such a silly thing to put me in such a bad mood, I know, but I'd been door-to-door busking for over a month now; maybe it was starting to show. I drove to Tescos, got some money out (again, I didn't want to dip into the busking fund), and gave it to Joan just as she and David were leaving.

I felt like I'd just had an argument with my parents.

Despite the setback of upsetting Mum and Dad, I trudged along to the first house directly across the road.

Not since Devizes had I met a family that was so keen to let the busker into their home. If you'll remember Devizes, the picture framer and his blue-tongued wife who invited me out the back to view their houseboat. Well, this family in Millhouses went one step further, inviting me into their lounge and asking me to sing 'Wheels on the Bus' to their three kids, who in turn chipped in with renditions on the piano, recorder and violin. It sounded a right royal mess, we were all off key, but that didn't matter; what was important was that despite the argument with Mum, my first house in Sheffield had been successful. I had made £3 in as many minutes.

'Got any more songs?' the father of the house asked.

'Yeah, but they're all rude.'

'Maybe not.'

Funny that the next house would be one of the only ones in the street that would reject me. A man wearing a tatty jersey and who hadn't brushed his teeth since 1955 said to me, 'Sounds interesting, but I think I'll leave it.'

'You sure? I can give you a taster,' I said, taking the parking warden's advice in Oxford.

'No thanks. In fact, I've been thinking about putting a notice up saying we don't do anything at the door. You've inspired me to get it done today.'

Urban foxes skipped over black ice further down the road. David had told me last night a lot of foxes live in the area. Not exactly tame, he said, but some people feed them on their lawns. BMWs parked outside two-storey brick houses, once again parading pristine lawns and gardens. Ice was all over the road and footpath this morning. I nearly slipped on some as I tried to make out a sign further down the road: *Humped Zebra Crossing.*

I had an image stuck in my mind of some Quasimodo zebra running down the street yelling, 'The bells! The bells!'

A man who must have been three metres tall answered the next door. Amazingly, he also invited me into the house. I couldn't believe it. A month of freezing my buns off at the door, now I was being invited into lounges. It was a Sunday as well, which I think made a huge difference; kids in pyjamas lounged around watching cartoons, mums and dads were in good moods, well rested and slurping coffee. I was *hoping* Three Metre Man was going to accept the offer of a song. I had seen numerous musical instruments in the front room as I approached the doorstep. I was sure a man so into music wouldn't be able to resist a private performance.

Halfway through the song he invited me into the music room where he picked up an instrument called the strovile. I'd never heard of it before; it looked like some sort of African violin made from tin. What was it about this street, everyone seemed to be musicians. Not such a surprise to the people of Sheffield, I suppose; common knowledge that loads of British bands come from the north.

The kids clapped at the end of my song and Three Metre Man's wife went to the kitchen momentarily.

'Why don't you do a *Lord of the Rings* song for next year?' one of the kids asked.

Not only attentive, creative as well. You guys can stay on.

Mum came back from the kitchen with a couple of quid and a kiwi fruit. Did I look hungry or something, was I looking on the skinny side? First port, then bananas, now this. Although I wasn't about to look a gift-horse in the mouth, or call her one either for that matter. Not in front of her husband anyway.

'What you need is one of these,' she said, passing me the kiwi fruit. The kids waved at the front door and Three Metre Man, still holding his strange African instrument, stood on the veranda in his socks and said, 'See you next year!'

People were big on door signs in England, I decided. In New Zealand I'm sure there aren't as many *Keep away if you are selling* sort of signs. Maybe we just don't have as many pushy salespeople interrupting our dinner every second night. We do have our fair share of Jehovah's Witnesses but they normally amble around on a Sunday. I've found as long as you answer the door in a priest's gown and scream, 'Jesus saved us so we could sleep in!' while offering bread and cask wine, they don't seem to bother you too much.

Have your identification card ready which will be verified with your depot was what I found stuck to the next house. The whole depot thing grabbed my interest: imagine a central warehouse where all door-to-door buskers met to discuss their day and compared earnings. Can't see it happening myself, since there's only one gambling fool prepared to do it.

I knocked on the door for the third and last time. All of a sudden two people jumped out of the car parked right next to me in the driveway. They scared the shit out of me. The fact they had been just chatting in the car while I knocked on their door for the last couple of minutes was kind of eerie.

'How long have you been in the car? Have you been there the whole time?' I asked.

'Yes, we've been watching you,' the older girl, probably the daughter, said.

'Oh … right,' I said.

'We were just talking about our cousins in New Zealand and here you are,' one said.

I sang a song to the mum and her teenage kids. The two kids walked off at the end without uttering a word.

'Did they not like it?' I asked the mother, who was looking in her purse.

'No, they didn't like the song at all. Here's £2. Have a good day.'

Even though I was in a relatively well-to-do area of Sheffield, it didn't stop most doors having three deadlocks, padlocks and a couple of latches. Obviously burglary was a common occurrence in this neck of the woods. A man wearing a white Puma shirt and matching Puma shorts took at least three minutes to unlock his front door while

I waited, eyeing up my kiwi fruit. It had been a good day so far.

'What do you want?' Puma Man asked, peering through a half-open door.

I gave him my spiel.

'Anyone ever thumped you?' he asked.

'No, not yet, why?'

'Just thought they might have. Why did you pick this area?'

'I don't know. It's quite nice, I suppose, friendly.'

'Let me tell you, go to some other areas in Sheffield and you'll get thumped.'

'Best I avoid those areas then, eh?'

'Look, I really don't want a song, I'll just get some money, then you can leave.'

'Come on, I really want to play "Kentucky Fried Kitten" to you.'

He laughed, 'All right, all right, I'll get my daughter.'

A confused teenager, also in her pyjamas, wandered down the stairs and wondered what the hell Dad was doing at the door. Both looked at me sideways when they heard the lyrics. I guess a song about a cat ending up in a fillet burger is not everyone's cup of tea on a Sunday morning.

'Good luck at squash,' he said, trying to get rid of me.

'Yeah, well I'm fired up now.'

Much like walking through Wales and Devizes, in Sheffield I felt like I was on the poker machine and just kept winning. Nothing could dampen your spirits on these days. Doors were not obstacles. On a bad day, a stupid piece of wood with a handle could play havoc with your heart rate. The key is to just keep going, often the worst days bring reward.

I spotted a couple of milk bottles sitting on a porch. Greenpeace stickers filled most of the front door. A man who wouldn't look out of place on a Cadbury's ad as the 'loving grandfather' answered. He had kind eyes. His bright multi-coloured jersey looked like it was from Nepal, his pants from the same place. His wife, dressed in similar clothing (these funky oldies were obviously modern-day hippie types who popped off to places like Kathmandu), soon joined him on the porch. Upon seeing my New Zealand sticker she remarked that her cousin had just been there for a month.

'Look!' she said, pulling a New Zealand key ring from her pocket.

Once again it was nice to know home was still there; two hundred quid to go.

'Would you like to hear a song?' I asked.

'That would be lovely,' said the lady.

'What would you like, "Harry Potter"?'

'Oh, wow, could you maybe sing something else?' the husband asked.

'You don't like "Harry Potter"?'

'It's just that we've got a very sick daughter and, well, it's all about spirits and things, isn't it? We'd let you in normally, but you shouldn't come in now, she's very poorly and won't want a stranger in the house.'

Everyone's facing their own battle; you never know what people are going through behind closed doors.

I didn't want this day to end, the busking was just too damn good. But once again, my fingers were freezing and slipping on black ice was becoming second nature. David and Joan were home by the time I returned. David was reading the paper and Joan was fussing around in the kitchen whistling to Frank Sinatra on the radio. Old people really know how to do entertainment. We need PlayStation and the Internet and DVD players. They just choose a radio station they like and stick with it. Plus they never have to buy CDs.

The house was warm and I felt proud I had raised enough money for my room.

'Hi, Joan,' I said at the kitchen door. David put his paper down and joined us.

'How'd you get on?' he asked excitedly.

'Twenty-two pounds ... and a kiwi fruit,' I said, smiling.

'Is that all from our street?' Joan asked, nearly dropping her teacup.

'Certainly is.'

'Only ten more of those mornings and you'll be back home,' David said, reaching into his pocket. 'Here, this is for your trip,' passing me a shiny £1 coin.

Joan made me a cup of tea before I left and while she baked muffins, still whistling to Frank Sinatra, David watered the plants. I sat down to read the latest *Hello!* magazine: Michael Caine was showing people through his home and talking about his latest movie. I couldn't help but look at David and compare the two Brits.

Michael Caine, a womanising, very rich, very famous man, married to Miss Guyana.

David, a funeral director, married to Joan for 40 years and never more at home than wearing his slippers and reading the paper.

Same age; worlds apart.

SHEFFIELD HAD BEEN good to me. Throughout my travels I'd heard that York, especially in the summertime (a time I wouldn't be there!), was the 'busking capital' of Britain, with many students choosing to hit the streets and sing for their supper. For this very reason, I had to get there. Now the time had come to visit the busking capital of Britain.

18

> **York**

Earnings to date: £321.80, a port bottle, a banana skin, a kiwi fruit and a car

I HAVE A question: Why in God's name would you live in Sheffield when York's just down the road?

Wouldn't you want to live in the city that boasts York Minster (the largest medieval church in northern Europe) and The Bar Walls (the finest remaining circuit of medieval walls in England, built during the thirteenth and fourteenth centuries and standing two miles in length)?

Or was I being an idealistic dreamer? I guess it's all about money. My point is, I was genuinely blown away arriving in York. I had no idea a place like this even existed. How many Brits had *not* been there? I'm sure most Southerners prefer to pop on the Chunnel and opt for cheap booze in France when a medieval city you'd normally only find in a Lego set awaits them on their doorstep.

I was keen on seeing the city centre of York, not just the suburbs like Sheffield. Another thing that simply astounded me about Britain was the amount of distance you could cover in such a short time. One minute I was at David and Joan's, the next I was standing outside a B&B in York. As it was the middle of winter, I had a choice of which room I'd like. I'd hate to see this place in summer; the owner told me it was crazy.

'Worst time of the year. Best time of the year, but worst time of the year if you get my drift,' he told me. 'The place is full of Americans. We don't take them any more. They're too demanding and they break the beds because of their weight.'

For the first time on this busking adventure I actually felt like a tourist. I had a bed for the night and it was too dark to hit the streets singing; the only thing left to do was wander around, map in hand, passport on money belt, and wait to get mugged. My host did give me a map before I left for the afternoon, but if he knew what I was really like with directions he wouldn't have bothered. A map of York, Barcelona or Oxford; it didn't seem to matter. To me it may as well have been written in Arabic. I can understand the *You are here* bit, but as soon as I leave that exact spot I'm stuffed.

Why don't they have GPS tracking for door-to-door buskers?

Just like a tourist, I gawked, poked and prodded my way through the inner city. York may be a historic city filled with medieval monuments and old buildings, but that didn't stop it from having the mighty essentials, like a bingo hall. A dozen or so three-wheeled scooters, complete with carrier baskets and designer cushions, were parked outside. I guess this is the old-age equivalent of parking your Harley outside the pub. Bernie and Beryl probably come out pissed after bingo, poor and grumpy, do a few doughnuts on the footpath and ride off into the sunset.

So how *did* I spend my time in York? Was it spent walking through the Shambles (one of the most well preserved medieval streets in Europe)? Or did I visit Clifford's Tower (a thirteenth-century stone tower erected by William the Conqueror)? Or was it spent in Borders drinking free coffee refills and managing to polish off Bono's autobiography in one sitting without buying it?

Sad to say the last.

Call me uncultured, call me uncouth; that didn't stop me finding a pub called Ye Olde Starre Inne, supposedly the oldest in all of York. I sat down, desperate for company, nursing warm ale, hoping out of nowhere my mates were going to jump from behind the bar and join me. Realising that wasn't going to happen, I headed over to a table where I saw a couple of middle-aged Australians. Nothing quite like hearing Aussie accents in the middle of a Yorkshire pub; be akin to hearing a cat meow in a Korean takeaway. Just as I was about to make a fool of myself by saying, 'Fancy that, I'm also from the arse end of the world,' they decided to split.

So I bought another Speckled Hen and found a cosy corner, suddenly thinking how much I'd fancy a spot of Korean right now. Two guys walked in and sat down two tables away. One of them was really pissed off about something.

'Yeah, well, at the moment I'm just looking for a Welshman to kill,' he said.

'Easy mate, this is a nice pub,' his mate offered.

'They threw bottles on the pitch and everything. Fucking Welsh …'

'Take it *easy*,' his mate whispered.

This continued for a few minutes while they polished off their pint. One continued to curse the Welsh while the other, his support network, told him not to worry, 'There's always next week.'

'Fucking Welsh,' he mumbled.

I had to ask, 'Who lost?'

'Leeds,' he smiled.

'To who?'

'Cardiff City,' his mate said.

'Is that bad?' I asked.

His mate spat his beer back into his glass, half went over his shirt. Their names were Dallan and David, they'd just been watching Leeds play Cardiff in the White Swan pub down the road. Leeds had lost 1–2. This, I gathered, was bad.

'They're a nothing team, mate,' David told me. 'We've [meaning Leeds] been winning everything, they're not even in the same league, they were playing eighties football, boring, predictable …'

'Why don't you just say they played well?' Dallan asked.

'Because they *didn't* fucking play well. How can you play well when your father's your uncle? That's what it's like over there, your sister's also your mother.'

'Why can't you be gracious in defeat? You're gracious in victory.'

He said nothing, then looked at me: 'Where are you from, mate?'

When David found out where I was from and what I was doing in his country, he said, 'You got balls doing that. What are you drinking, I'll get the beers in.'

While David was waiting at the bar, Dallan informed me he was glad I was here. 'It'll be good for David not to talk about football for a while,' he said. 'He needs new friends that aren't interested in it,' he reassured me.

A mobile rang as soon as David returned with fresh beer. He picked it up. More animated conversation followed as he moaned about the game, the Welsh, the weather and the Welsh to whoever was on the other end of the line.

'Yeah, well, I'll see you soon, love. Bye,' he said. 'That was the bitch,' he said to both of us.

'You'd never say that if she were here,' said Dallan.

'I fucking love my son!' he said thrashing his heart. 'Got two kids. I'll put some music on!'

A couple of minutes later U2's 'Beautiful Day' came bursting on.

'This is a cracking song,' he nodded, playing air guitar at the same time. 'Reminds me of football, they always play it at the start of the Premiership on ITV.'

'Why didn't you go to the game?' I asked. 'Instead of watching it down the road?'

'Too expensive,' Dallan said. 'Thirty quid to go to a football game now. Most Brits can't afford it. It's killing the game.'

'You play a lot of rugby in New Zealand, don't you?' David asked.

'Yeah.'

'I just don't understand rugby. All you do is run around after an egg all day. Egg chasing, that's what it is. Only the upper class play it here.'

'What about football?' I asked. 'All you guys do is run up and down a pitch all day chasing a ball.'

'But why don't they score more in rugby? They have all that line to score but they never do. All we have is a tiny goal.'

'Good point,' I had to admit. 'Why don't they?'

'Don't say good point,' Dallan whispered. 'You'll just get him going.'

'I'll get the beers in!' David said.

'Beautiful Day' came on again; the second time in as many minutes. David had indeed secured fresh lagers and kept looking at his watch, informing us he'd have to be home soon.

'Suppose the bitch will want me to get some food on the way home?'

'You wouldn't say that if she were here,' said Dallan.

'You know the two best-ever sportsmen to come out of Australia?' David asked, excitedly.

'Well,' I said, 'that would have to be Don Bradman and –'

'No, no, no … Don who? Mark Viduka and Harry, Harry, Harry Kewell!'

'Verruca and who?'

Dallan laughed. 'Verruca! Why has no one ever called him Verruca before?'

'Harry Kewell is the best player to ever grace the planet,' David continued. 'Saw him score a goal the other day, right shoulder onto left knee, onto left shoulder, onto right knee and BANG! Nearly took the back of the net off. Harry Kewell, he's a fucking awesome player, like last week when –'

'So how long have you been away from New Zealand for?' Dallan interrupted.

While David did his best to include Harry, Harry Kewell in every conversation, I marvelled at the fact that people had been drinking in this very pub some two hundred years before New Zealand was even discovered by the Europeans. Dallan and I tried to imagine dwarves with a life expectancy of 35, banging into the tiny doors as they waddled to the bar for more booze.

'Did you hear that, David?' Dallan asked. 'People were drinking in this pub two hundred years before New Zealand was even discovered.'

'Really? Shall I get the beers in for our New Zealand friend?'

Unbelievably, U2's 'Beautiful Day' came on for the third time. New beers were on the table and I was starting to sway. 'You like this song, don't you?' I asked David.

'Oh, it's a cracker, reminds me of Harry, Harry, Harry Kewell!' he said.

'Do you ever wonder how U2 have still done it after all these years?' I asked, hoping Harry Kewell wouldn't come into this conversation.

'It's like when I was a kid and I listened to U2 and I thought they were the duck's nuts. But then Oasis came along and they came at just the right time. It was a timing thing and they blew it, they had the world at their feet but they blew it. Like, when you support Leeds, you really love it as a kid and go to every game, you have a few years off and now I fucking love it again. Leeds are like U2.'

Only a Pom could use football as an analogy for anything.

I LIKED YORK already. I had no idea how the busking would go, but that didn't matter; being shouted beers by two hooligan Leeds supporters suited me to the ground.

'You Aussies travel a lot, don't you?' David asked.

'New Zealand, David, he's a Kiwi,' Dallan corrected him.

'No worries, yeah, we do like to travel,' I said, quite used to the misunderstanding and no longer keen to fight it.

''Cos I've met loads of Kiwis and I've been down under as well,' David continued. 'It's weird, you Kiwis and Aussies are so relaxed when you're over here, until you go to somewhere like Sydney, where the same blokes you met here are now home. When you meet them over there they're all stuck up and arrogant.'

I'd had too many beers to stick up for the Aussies.

'So what's it like growing up, living in Britain?' I asked.

'Britain's the best place to live in the world,' said David with unbridled enthusiasm, although now we were entering uncharted waters in the form of what was happening in places like Bradford and Afghanistan.

'The biggest problem in somewhere like Bradford is all these Pakis who earn British pounds and share our land. These same guys are now going to kill our guys over there,' he said, referring to Afghanistan.

Maybe we should go back to that Aussie issue; could be less work.

The guys couldn't leave without buying me one last beer.

'Have to feed the family, otherwise we'll be in the dog box. What say we get a curry, Dallan?'

'Whatever, I'm easy,' he said.

As they put their jackets on, David handed me a £20 note.

'What the hell's that for?' I asked.

'To get the beers in, we have to leave.'

'No way, give me a call tomorrow. I'll bring some busking money.'

I had told them where I was staying, hoping we could hook up for a drink tomorrow night. Just like trading addresses with someone you've met on a bus, we all knew we wouldn't write or call; it's just a polite way to end an evening. The alternative was an awkward, fumbly hug or kiss, which would not have been pretty.

'Top lad, you're a top lad, you. Don't forget, Harry, Harry, Harry!'

They swayed arm in arm through York's oldest pub's front door and waved at the entrance.

'Oh, and guys,' I said, and they turned around. 'You played like shit tonight.'

If I was Welsh and said that two hours ago, I wouldn't have been here to tell the story.

Unlike a couple of hours ago when I felt like a sad loner, now I felt quietly pissed and quietly content. I was even singing to the Eurythmics on the jukebox; obviously that beer was stronger than I thought.

Don Partridge was right; buskers always end up in pubs. The Leeds boys may have been late for tea but it was still only 9 p.m. I still had two beers in front of me; plainly the Poms had far superior gullets. I sat back in the big old pub chair and found a great local magazine called :*here*, which was billed as York's free-est magazine. A very cool, very lively music scene was evident in this part of England; I'd learnt that from the 'musical street' in Sheffield. For such a small-budget magazine I was blown away by the depth of its lead stories: I wish old people would stop assuming I'm on drugs, says young criminal.

And: Unemployed man said to be disappointed in types of jobs coming to York.

My elderly drinking buddies from the pub in Harlington would have enjoyed the phone survey as well:

Snooker rocks – 01904 333 333

Snooker sucks – 01904 333 444

Snooker ate my brain – 01904 333 555

It was plain to see York had a sense of humour, but would it have one tomorrow when I really needed it?

A GREASY SPOON breakfast awaited me the next morning. Of course, after the six cups of coffee at Borders do you think I could sleep? Would I in fact ever sleep again was more the question. Only two other people were in the room as I awaited my eggs. They had their backs to me and were scouring maps and guides, deciding how they would spend the day. I wouldn't have that luxury; I knew exactly what I had to do and wasn't looking forward to it. The transistor in the corner of the room was blurting out Terry Wogan on Radio Two, talking about bad Christmas presents. The owner of the B&B gave me another map along with my bacon and eggs. Maybe he'd forgotten he gave me one yesterday; or maybe he knew I was entirely useless and had lost it already. After discussing the bet and telling him some of the more unfortunate busking tales, he wished me well for the day.

'Good luck,' he said. 'I don't know how you'll get along here, but good luck.'

'That's the thing, mate, no one ever does. And thank you.'

The woman who'd been facing the wall up until now turned her chair around and faced me. Her husband also looked at me. I knew they must have been listening, looking at maps can't have been that interesting.

'OK, I'm too curious now, what is it you're doing?' she asked.

I explained the bet while slurping my tea.

'Did you make the bet here or in New Zealand?'

'New Zealand, last August,' I said.

'Do you have to live off this money as well?'

'Yes.'

'Do you think your mate would have streaked if he had lost?'

'No.'

'Is New Zealand better than Australia?'

'Course it is.' What was I supposed to say? I couldn't believe an adult asked that question. I remember when Bill Clinton came to New Zealand and a boy made the front page of the paper asking him, 'Is New Zealand better than America?' I think Clinton wormed his way out of it by saying something like, 'They're both very different.' My point being the question *then* came from an eight-year-old. This was a grown lady. Unfortunately, her questions only got worse.

'Do the pubs still close at six in New Zealand?'

'Yes, all of them,' I said hurrying the last of my coffee.

That toast could stay on the plate.

'And my great-aunt told me that everyone in New Zealand is in bed by nine?'

'Really?'

Where's my key? Must leave, is that my jacket?

'And there are no birds left.'

'Uh huh, really? Lovely, bye now, you have a good day.'

I didn't really know what to expect from the streets of York. To be honest, I suppose I was either expecting very rich people or very tight people. Regardless, I was confident due to the huge success in Sheffield only two days earlier. I looked forward to continuing that good run of form.

I love the buzz of walking through a new town, especially a town as beautiful as York. I wandered past York City Fire Station and saw a fireman smoking. Now there's something you don't see every day.

It was so cold the river had completely frozen over, which provided hilarious viewing in the form of ducks walking around on an icy river. They looked like Africans on ice skates. As they came in to land on the solid surface they couldn't stop. Panic on their face was evident: 'Shit, this is not normal! The river, it's … not watery, it's all hard and SHIT! Is … that … the bank already!'

Donk!

Oh how I laughed and laughed and laughed.

Until I stepped in duck shit.

Confidence turned to despair within minutes. I had indeed been too spoilt in Sheffield on Sunday. Was it really any surprise that no one was home on a Tuesday morning in York? Do you really expect these people to just wait around till the busker calls at their house? These are busy people, Brown, with busy lives.

I'm even talking to myself now.

It's freezing cold and it's not even as if I'm *getting* rejections. No one's even opening the door to tell me to fuck off. Sandringham Street provides glimmers of hope with the odd house still bearing Christmas decorations. This is almost enough to give you hope in a moment of darkness; at least if they have decorations they'll be nice people, I reason.

That's if they were bloody home! Why is nobody home today?

Ducks' revenge, that's what it is. They're all probably watching me from the riverbank, bruised and battered, laughing at the very man who was laughing at them as they tried to land. Karma, I deeply believe in karma today. I will have to watch my step. It could be the day I finally quack.

After a joke like that I think I already have.

The first person to answer the door lived in a veritable mansion of a place.

'No, I don't really want a song thank you, goodbye.'

A ginger cat followed me down the driveway, trying to rub against my leg. I hate cats. I wanted to kick it; karma, Brown, karma. A builder with really bad acne was working on the next house. I didn't have the balls to walk up to him so just whistled and walked on. I often wondered what people were thinking in instances like this; a guy with blue fingers walking door to door with a guitar.

'Maybe he's selling guitars?'

Melbourne Street awaited me around the corner. Karma, this has got to be the street. Everything's making so much sense now, Mark's from Melbourne, you didn't kick the cat; this *has* to be the street. Isn't that how karma works: you don't kick cats and good things happen? Unfortunately, Melbourne Street was a fizzer. Every apartment had an intercom. As you know the chance of someone in my position getting past an intercom is like trying to get a meeting with a CEO without sending in a CV.

A guy who looked exactly like Adolf Hitler rode past as I spotted another ginger cat. What is it about York and ginger cats, this was starting to scare me. Maybe the cats were scheming something with the offended ducks on the riverbank? Or maybe, as I thought before, I had really been doing this for far too long.

Somehow I had to scrape together another £170 or thereabouts if I was even to think about getting home.

Another ginger cat! Ah, they're really onto me now. I'm sure the third ginger cat I'd seen in five minutes was wearing some sort of headset as well. And was that a stun gun in his pocket? But where are the ducks? I quickly looked around, figuring they were probably in a getaway car just around the corner. Ginger cats and York; I was beginning to wonder whether it was some sort of prerequisite to living in the town.

'We'd like to move to Yorkshire.'

'Do you own a ginger cat?'

'No sir, I'm afraid we don't.'

'Sorry, no can do.'

I had to move quickly if I was to get away from the ducks and cats. They're smarter than you think, you know. A perfect team; the ducks fly overhead like police choppers, while the cats sneak around and under buildings with the swiftness and ease of a mongoose.

I still had no money and I was still cold. Most houses had no lights on. A man crossing the road, wearing a black beanie, yanked on a lead, as two pitbulls by his side slobbered and showed their teeth. He looked like a real hard bastard, I decided to let him resume his day without a personal serenade.

The two ladies pushing prams behind him, however,

wouldn't be so lucky. They were perfect fodder for the penniless busker desperately trying to escape the ducks and ginger cats of Yorkshire. Sure, all three kids cried when I sang and sure, Mum looked at me like I was some sort of bad clown, but I made 40p; I was on my way.

My first coin from an actual door came at the next house; a bunch of flats down a long driveway. An old lady, who'd lived in York for 40 years, kept the door latch on while I sang, and then passed me £1. She also pointed me in the direction of student housing where I was over the moon to sing to someone attractive, coherent and under the age of 70; a rarity busking in the middle of the day. A blonde girl holding a huge cup of coffee, knocking around in a sloppy T-shirt and track pants, told me she was about to sit her psych exam. Things were looking up; maybe this was to be the street?

Just when I thought normality had been restored I spied another one; his ginger fur sparkled in the sun. He was cleaning his paws and skulking underneath a fence in the neighbour's property. Not only was he wearing a headset, he was also whispering into a walkie-talkie and writing notes.

Damn you, damn you all.

'Hi, I'm a door-to-door busker from New Zealand,' I said to a woman painting her front door.

'No, no, we don't have those around here,' she said.

'I know, I'm the world's first.'

'No, not interested, you won't get anything out of me. Try next door, it's her birthday.'

Excellent, I thought, a person who doesn't know me from a bar of soap is about to have a song sung to them. They'll probably think a nice friend has set the whole thing up and sent me round. Should get a good tip for this one. The front door was answered by an old woman wearing far too much make-up. Astonished, surprised, she called another younger, brunette woman to the door. I had no idea whose birthday it was or even what her name was, so just started to sing.

'Hi, I'm a door-to-door busker and I heard it's someone's birthday today,' I smiled.

They both looked like they were going to faint. I took a punt, guessing it was the younger woman's birthday and started singing, 'Happy birthday to …?'

'Beth!' she prompted me.

'BETH!' I added. 'Happy birthday to you.'

Both were still in shock, probably wondering who had stitched them up. Meantime, I wanted money, a concept they hadn't quite grabbed as I froze on the doorstep. Trying not to ruin the magic, I said that along with being a Surprise Birthday Busker, I was also desperately trying to make enough to fly home. Beth handed me a £2 coin. Suddenly another older lady sprinted out from the kitchen screaming, 'Shut the door, shut the door! The canary's loose in the kitchen!'

Ah, door-to-door busking, you really do meet the most interesting people.

Soon I was singing 'Harry Potter' to two girlie students next door. Thankfully they were pissing themselves. Mid-song we saw Beth get into her car across the street.

'Happy birthday, Beth!' I yelled.

Poor Beth, she still looked confused, as did the girls on the doorstep. 'It's her birthday,' I said.

Next door again I was also made welcome. Another girl, who seemed to be in the middle of study, papers and coffee cups everywhere, told me, 'Sorry, but I've got no money.'

'No worries,' I said, 'I'll sing anyway,' hoping she'd either have fruit or beer or ginger cat poison as possible payment. At the conclusion of the song she said she felt guilty giving nothing so ventured inside. Which brings me to another point, which people (mostly blokes I'll admit) often asked about: 'The Horny Housewife'.

'Is it true?' they'd ask. 'Do they really exist? Did you come across any on your travels?'

Well, I wouldn't know, but if I was single and keen, I'm sure the odd girl who answered the door, wearing just a T-shirt or dressing gown, may have been quite happy to go down to the pub or stay for more than one song. Of course, she'd have to listen to a song about a dead cat. That may not go down quite so well. As far as an encore goes, I don't know, maybe she'd find out the last time I showered was in Wales.

This particular girl had now been rummaging around the house for five minutes; I was losing the feeling in my fingers. What the hell was she doing in there? She finally came out saying, 'Can you come back tomorrow? I'll have some money then.'

'Forget it,' I said.

One thing was blindingly obvious about door-to-door busking, which probably relates to a whole lot of things in life – perseverance. A morning that started off poorly was now going OK despite being chased by ducks and cats. I guess an advantage I had was preparation. I knew what to expect. I was *prepared*. The answer was either going to be 'Piss off' or 'Go ahead'. The person on the other side of the door, however, was about to experience something they'd never experienced; they were *unprepared*. One minute they're answering the phone or doing the washing, the next minute the doorbell goes, they answer it expecting it to be Uncle Brian with the car papers, instead it's an unshaven busker who speaks funny.

I only went to the next house because it seemed to have a

sense of humour. Gaudy flowers were painted all over the front porch and tacky half-smashed gnomes sat on the steps. A male my own age answered and it occurred to me that this was also very rare, which brings me to another point people often ask about: 'The Horny Househusband'.

Just joking.

'You want to sing me a song? Sounds innovative,' he said. 'Come in out of the cold.'

Maybe this guy *wasn't*.

I sang a song to him in the lounge of the flat. Cigarette butts decorated every available surface, leftover dinner grew in various places, *Pulp Fiction*, *Wonder Woman* and *Wombles* posters wove their way around the walls. Ah, flatting. I felt right at home. I counted 33 empty beer bottles in the lounge. Still, it smelt like it needed a bloody good mum.

'I can't give you that little for that fantastic tune,' he said, handing me a few coins.

He ran upstairs for the second time. This is always a strange time, sitting in a stranger's lounge waiting for money. Perched on the sofa, sitting on the edge, whistling, trying not to appear too comfortable.

'I'm so glad you came around,' he said. 'I'm up to my eyeballs, so stressed about an exam tomorrow.'

'What's with the flowers and gnomes at the front?' I asked.

'We've got a hippie for a landlord.'

It wasn't exactly a fortune, but over £15 had now found its way into my duffel coat pocket. I decided to try one more house before calling it a day, although I wished I hadn't.

A cross-eyed, hairy-chinned woman with yellow teeth wearing a tie-dyed shirt answered. I'm not being impolite, this woman would have scared a bulldog off a meat truck. She did in fact have a dog in her hands, just a small one, but big teeth nonetheless, which it flashed with regularity.

'He looks vicious but he doesn't bite,' he/she said.

Yeah right, I thought. I tried to speak.

'I'm a door –'

BARK!

'I'm a door-to-door bus–'

BARK! BARK! BARK!

'I'm a –'

BARK! BARK! BARK! SNARL! BARK!

'Look, I've only got copper but I'll give you copper if you go away,' he/she said.

'No, no, it's –'

BARK! BARK! BAAAAARRRRRK! HOWL!

All right, you yappy little fucker, I'm leaving. Go and sit with cross-eyed woman on the couch.

What an idiot, now I'm talking to dogs.

Only one thing worse than talking to dogs.

And that's seeing another ginger cat, the sixth one today.

OK, you little bastards, you win.

Now, leave me alone.

19

Whitby

Earnings to date: £337, a port bottle, a banana skin, a kiwi fruit and a car

'JULIE, I LOVE your tits.' This is the sign I remember most as I drove towards Whitby. It was handwritten on the side of the motorway. Along with the wonderful, touching message was a detailed drawing of two well-defined mammary glands. To the point, I thought, and no hidden meanings. No mind games here, Julie. I think you know exactly what the message is.

I've been lucky enough to visit three Whitbys in my life. This one, in the north-east of the UK, Whitby to the east of Toronto in Canada, and Whitby just north of Wellington back home. It'd be fair to assume this Whitby, in the UK, is the oldest, and was also the starting point of the maritime career of Captain James Cook. This is where he studied his craft and where he took off on his voyage of discovery. I suppose the bloke that charted New Zealand deserved a visit from a Kiwi like myself, but he's not the only famous fella from these parts; it was while he was staying in a B&B in Whitby that Bram Stoker wrote the story of *Dracula*.

So, in a place soaked in history, where Captain Cook once planned his global discoveries and Bram Stoker wrote one of the most famous stories ever, what was I doing in this inspirational town in North Yorkshire?

Washing my smalls in a Whitby launderette with three middle-aged women.

The three women in question were having a quiet cuppa in their lunch break. I was hoping I'd be able to busk for my laundry. It wasn't long before they figured I was a novice when it came to commercial washing machines but, then again, who isn't? Insert 40p here, 30p in there, put the powder in here, don't touch this, leave that there. I didn't know where to put what but three ladies had great pleasure in telling me.

'Better than watching telly, isn't it?' one said when I finally had it on the right cycle.

I was so excited watching that filth go around, it's gonna be so white, I thought. I'm going to have clean clothes again! They seemed a little lukewarm about the busking for laundry idea so I changed tack and asked which local streets would be good ones to hit.

'Well, if you go down to the main square there's heaps of buskers there in the summer.'

'No, Maz, he's not allowed to do it in the street, it has to be door to door,' the youngest of the three said.

'Oh, bloody hell, you'll spend a night in jail!' said Maz.

'Yeah, do you have some sort of licence?' another lady asked.

'What, as a door-to-door busker? I'm the only one I know of.'

'Well, I wouldn't open the door if you came around to my place. There are a lot of old ladies around here, they won't open their doors. Why don't you do it on the street?'

'Because, Maz,' I said, 'it's part of the bet. Where do *you* live?' I asked her.

'Like hell I'm telling you!'

I continued to watch my washing go around, loving every minute.

'Look how white they're getting, go my son!' I urged the machine.

'You can go somewhere if you've got something to do.'

'I've got nothing to do,' I said.

By the time the second spin was over, though, I was starting to get a little peckish so decided to get a good northern England feed of fish and chips, mushy peas and a pot of tea. One piece of bread, cutely cut into two triangles, also accompanied the meal. It reminded me of something your mum would do. A huge, robust-looking dude with a shaved head was also tucking into his lunch. He was covered in earrings and tattoos, parts not covered by tattoos were clad in black leather. It looked hilarious to see someone you definitely wouldn't like to cross in a dark alley delicately picking up his cup of tea like the Queen herself, and getting a special little plate for his one piece of bread, nicely cut in two.

Kind of killed the whole image he was striving for.

'Oi, Brutus, let's smack these fuckers over!'

'OK, Delboy, as soon as I've finished my cuppa. Any more bread, love? And can you cut it into triangles? You *know* that's my favourite.'

I COULD SEE why people raved about Whitby; it felt good to be here. Red brick houses spilled down a headland to a beautiful harbour and estuary. Shops down the medieval streets bore signs like *Arguments Yard*, *Harpooner Cottage* and *Bottom Shop*. I felt like I was in a Charles Dickens novel. The wind ripped straight off the North Sea – to think I was looking out across the ocean towards Denmark. A fishing rod would also have been handy with many shops boasting fresh bait for sale.

In the meantime, I had to check on my gruts and socks.

The ladies hadn't moved by the time I got back to the launderette. My washing, however, had. It had been loaded into one of the many dryers and was gloriously spinning around; I could almost hear its glee: 'You bastard, how could you leave it so long? We're not animals, you know! Never again, do you hear us? We won't tolerate being worn four days in a row ever again!'

I sat down to read a trashy magazine with a full stomach, happily knowing I'd have clean clothes for, hopefully, the rest of the trip. The magazine was crap so I spoke to the youngest lady (she still would have been 50), and it turned out her mother also worked there.

'You must see some sights in here,' I said to her, as she folded T-shirts.

'Do we ever,' she said.

'Do you ever wear gloves? You must get some disgusting laundry.'

'All the time. There's one man who comes in wearing a suit, he must work as a banker or solicitor. He's a well-dressed sort of chap. You have to wear gloves just to touch his smalls! I don't know how he can even wear them.'

Glad she hadn't seen mine.

'I mean,' she continued, 'if it was me, they'd be in the dustbin in no time. Honestly, it's only the elastic that's holding them together. Best of it is, it's only top show; lovely suit, disgusting underpants. You'd think he'd wear nice smalls as well.'

Jan had lived in Whitby all her life and worked in the launderette for many of those years. The more I talked to her the more I realised that staying in one place is quite commendable. There'd be no stress, you'd know everyone, your 70-year-old mum would come in for lunch. Course, it would drive me around the twist, probably yourself also, but if you can handle it, chances are you wouldn't die of a heart attack trying to get the budgets done or catching the next tube.

'Don't you ever feel like you're missing out?' I asked Jan, when the topic of travel came up. She had told me she'd never been on a plane; she'd been on a helicopter once, to visit her son in Cornwall.

'No, not really, it doesn't bother me,' she said.

'Have you been to Ireland?' I asked.

'No.'

'Wales?'

'No.'

'Scotland, surely.'

'Oh, yeah, been up to Scotland, just for a weekend, mind you.'

'What about London?'

'Yeah, been there for a show.'

'How long have you lived in Whitby?'

'Forty-two years.'

'What would you do if you won a trip to Thailand?'

'I wouldn't go.'

'Would you give it away?'

'Probably, yeah.'

I NEEDED A place to stay for the evening. I'd also have to get some busking in before it got too dark, although with that wind coming straight off the North Sea, I can't say I was looking forward to it. I had read in my ever-reliable, out-of-date guidebook that a backpackers' hostel lay just down the road. I've got to say this put me in an extremely good mood. I now had clean clothes and I was looking forward to meeting other backpackers, exchanging stories, maybe heading into town and who knows, could be a big night, have a few beers and see what happens.

But travel never works out like you expect.

The Swedish lady that ran the hostel said to me, 'People would just complain if you tried door-to-door busking around this area. We get loads of buskers in the summer, you should come then.'

Only one thing to do: just like in Sheffield, I had to prove her wrong.

However, as it turned out, *I* couldn't have been more wrong.

I didn't even look at the room Mrs Sweden had assigned me. I didn't have time. I wanted to hit the streets and earn some dosh before the sun retired. The first road I chose was called Greenlane; it was next to the sea and smelt of fish, with hundreds of seagulls swooping overhead. For some reason those first few dwellings scared the hell out of me. I chickened out.

A woman cleaning her lounge could see me walking up the drive from the front window. This was always a bad thing, it gave them time to prepare or run away. Surprise was the name of the game when you were door-to-door busking. Catching people off their guard is what I thrived on. As I figured, no response came when I knocked on the door. She was probably hiding in the basement or calling the police.

People must have been 'vacuuming' at the next six houses as well, as no reply came. The cold North Sea wind felt like it was cutting me in two. I spotted a girl in the front of a house watching TV. I rang the doorbell to no avail; the curtains were drawn quicker than I could retune my guitar.

Aha! A woman outside cleaning her window, no need even to knock, got to be a winner.

'No, I don't want a song,' she said. 'I've got to go to work in a couple of minutes.'

'Can I sing to you while you clean your window, no charge?'

'No, thanks.'

It was just a quiet village minding its own business and I was the village idiot.

Still, at least I would soon meet a multitude of backpackers from all over the world and get quietly trashed in the many bars that Whitby had to offer. Well, it may have been something like that had there been more than one occupant in the hostel. Ten rooms, each laden with ten double bunks, lay empty. It felt like a boarding school in the holidays. The upside was I could choose whatever room I liked. After all, not only did I have an eight-bed room to myself, I also had fresh washing. I was the only person in the place.

The plan of drinking and telling lies was swapped for lying in the huge lounge by myself and calling *The Mirror* on the available phone. The guy who interviewed me for the *South Wales Echo* had given me the number and recommended I call them. He believed it was a story they'd probably like to follow. I had no one else to call, so what the hell?

'Do you want to do a story?' I asked in my best journalist voice when I finally got through.

'What's it about?' the man said abruptly.

I explained my busking adventures, again in my best journalist voice, using big words like disestablishment-arianism at every available moment.

'No, we did an article on begging last week,' he said, sounding like he wanted to end the conversation as soon as possible.

'Begging!' I sat up. 'This isn't begging, it's door-to-door –'
'We did an article to see which town gave the most to a beggar we dressed up. He had a bowl in front of him on the street.'

'I'm not a beggar,' I said, flatly.

'People won't be interested in that story,' he said and hung up.

I WOKE UP with the flu. I blame the Norwegians and the Danish and South African backpackers for not providing body warmth when I needed it most. The room was so cold I couldn't get out of bed. But the bed was freezing as well. I couldn't move. I wanted to call Mrs Sweden: 'Please, Mrs Sweden, some cheese on toast and a hot-water bottle. Cancel all appointments.'

After the previous day's penniless effort in Whitby I wasn't exactly brimming with confidence to hit the streets again, especially as I had half of Niagara coming out my nose. Whatever happened, I had to get a move on. I wanted to be in Glasgow by the evening. Mrs Sweden had great delight in telling me I wouldn't make the 223 miles in one day. It didn't look that far on the map.

I had to eventually crawl out of bed and sprint to the toilet via the below freezing floor tiles. I really felt like shit, I wanted to be home today, I had no energy and I had made no money in Whitby. I just couldn't face knocking on someone's door, especially if they were going to tell me to bugger off.

First of all I had to revisit my favourite butcher shop that sold fresh buns with loads of moist, thick ham off the bone for 60p. In the space of only 24 hours, this had quickly become my favourite meal in Britain. I could get very used to these, I thought. We're creatures of habit, we find something we like and we never go anywhere else, hence I was passing £2 over the counter and I received breakfast and lunch in return. Things were definitely cheaper up here.

Glasgow was beckoning but I'd have to give Whitby one last chance to redeem itself.

There's nothing worse than hearing or reading about how bad people's flu symptoms are so I'll spare you the details. Let's just stick with 'death warmed up' and leave it at that.

I've always said that a town doesn't count as stingy if it's mostly older folk that don't answer the door. They're excused for that. They're taught not to open it, so it's fair enough that the first couple of houses in Whitby contained, let's say, *mature* womenfolk who refused to open up.

A small, wee man with tufty grey hair and a thick accent was more accommodating next door. He had sausage-like fingers, animated speech and a joke every sentence. Best of all, he listened with great enthusiasm.

'I suppose you want some money now, don't you?' he said, running inside.

He came back with five gold coins. I wanted to hug him. Not a bean yesterday; already today: £5.

An interesting sign awaited me at the top of the next driveway: *Beware of the dog. WAIT HERE.*

Was I supposed to ring for attention? Was I to be aware of the dog, then wait? Or was I to wait at the top of the driveway until the dog saw me? It was all a bit too much so I marched on.

A smart-looking, brand-new townhouse presented me with a lady who then in turn called out for her husband. Both stood on the doorstep, smiling while I sang. Afterwards we talked for ten minutes or more when, finally, the wife said to her man, 'You're looking for new ways to make money, here you go,' she said, pointing to my guitar.

It turns out he had a stroke six months ago. Yesterday was his first day back at work. He was now working 27 hours a week instead of 38. Used to work for a handicapped boy but didn't have the job any more.

'I used to be in a band myself, three-chord Charlie kinda band,' he smiled. 'Mostly waltzes and country music.'

He still had that sparkle in his eye, as if he still wanted to be playing himself.

'Course, you can't do any of that now,' he continued. 'It's all drum beats and mini discs. One singer, that's all they need. But there are some *really* good musicians in Whitby, although they keep to themselves, quite happy to go unnoticed. There's some major talent in the north. A guy called John Dory used to play in Whitby, sang songs about fish. Where were you busking yesterday?' he asked.

'The other side of town,' I said.

'I'm surprised you didn't get beaten up. We're not being snobs or anything, it's just that there's nicer houses here on the west side of Whitby. A lot of problems on the other side, mostly council housing. So, where are you heading next?' he asked.

'North,' I said.

'Not Newcastle and Middlesborough, I hope, you definitely *will* get beaten up. I used to have a job delivering ice creams in Scarborough. I remember a kid who came up and asked for a flake, no, make that two, he said. My sister's paying, he'd say, and he started eating his ice cream and then run off. Course, it wasn't his sister at all, was it?'

I decided to sing another song as their son had just turned up on the doorstep. The mother then passed me some money. To be honest, if they'd offered me a day in front of the telly in their warm living room, I would have taken it.

'Shall I grab my electric upstairs and we can go around

together as a duo?' he said pointing at my guitar.

'If I knew what I was doing I'd be following *you*, mate.'

I resumed my flu-like symptoms, put the loose change in my pocket and headed for Scotland.

> **Glasgow**

Earnings to date: £344, a port bottle, a banana skin, a kiwi fruit and a car

'THE MAIN DIFFERENCE between Scotland and England is, in England they're called woodlice, here they're called slaters.'

'*Right.*'

'What do you call them in New Zealand?'

'Slaters.'

'Ah, so we have a lot in common then!'

This was one of the more memorable exchanges I had with an old Scotsman, who felt it was his duty to point out that, despite differences in customs, political system, geography and accent, the most noticeable difference between the two countries was what each called that ugly little insect.

Mrs Sweden was right, Glasgow was a fair hike from Whitby, but I did manage to roll into Scotland at around 7 p.m. As soon as I arrived in the city, people beeped, cut in without indicating, abused loudly and waved fists. It made me homesick.

I passed places like Scotch Corner and Hartburn on my way and even spotted sheep donning tupping paste. If you're not aware of what tupping paste is, I believe, or I was *told* by reliable sources, that it is a paint of sorts that they spray on the ram's private parts so the farmer will know which lady sheep he's serviced in the paddock. No such thing as a private life when you're a sheep, I guess. You couldn't exactly lie, could you?

'Don't talk shit, Colin! Explain the red paint on her arse, then!'

A mate of mine always thought tupping paste would come in handy in nightclubs, so you would know which girls to go near and which to stay away from.

OK, it was me.

An endearing memory I have of arriving in wonderful Scotland was when I was about thirty miles shy of Glasgow itself. I had been busting for a leak for several hours but stupidly held on. In the end, I was about to explode. Even though a Welcome Break lay only miles away, I decided to pull off the main highway and find a quiet spot to shake a leg. And it was *really* quiet, lovely in fact; no cars, no noise, cows on the hill happily munched and mooed. I felt very confident that this was a fine place to piss.

Adding to my confidence was the fact that a car hadn't come past for at least five minutes, what would be the chances of one coming past now? And you know, you *just* know deep in your mind, this is a stupid thing to do, but you just have to go. You also know, reading this, that only one thing can happen; unfortunately it did. As I stood there, happily showering the fields of Scotland, I heard a car in the far distance. The low hum of the engine made me panic a little. I wondered how far away it was. It was getting closer. I was only half done. And closer. For God's sake, not now, let me pee in peace! The van was now changing gears and slowing down. I started to panic. It was now behind me, only doing about five miles an hour, turning into the road to my rear. I looked over my shoulder to see a vanload of teenage boys, egged on by a ginger-haired ringleader who leaned out the front window, screaming, 'Yeehah! Flop it out, big boy, Wohooh!'

Welcome to Scotland.

So, there I was in a sushi restaurant in Glasgow deciding a half-healthy meal was on the cards. Opposite me, a woman and her bald (by choice) boyfriend sat chatting away. He had obviously opted for no hair at all rather than sporting the traditional 'comb-over'. I miss the 'comb-over': those few wisps of hair, the last dying strands that a man flicks over his hairless forehead, all in a vain attempt to fool passers-by that he actually *has* hair. Will it make a comeback, I wonder, or will men continue to adopt the Andre Agassi shaved look?

I hope not.

Two well-dressed Japanese gentlemen sat at the table next to Bald by Choice Man and his girlfriend. I knew they were Japanese because they were speaking Japanese. Appearing to have finished their half-eaten meals, they then got up to leave, putting their jackets on and walking out. The woman could not believe what she was seeing. Looking across to their plates, she saw a huge mound of Japanese food untouched.

'Look,' she said to Bald by Choice Man. 'There's sushi, tempura, loads of stuff.'

He nodded at the table, as if to say, 'Well? Grab some.'

She said no, trying to concentrate on her menu. It's as if the rest of the restaurant, which was only a small room, was saying, 'Go on, get in there, you know you want to. You're *hungry*, it's only going to waste. It's perfectly good food, no boys' germs.'

Go my son, I said in my mind. Get into your work.

She looked at me. 'They're only going to throw it out,' I said.

She scratched her head. She looked as if she'd gotten herself into a situation she really didn't want to be in. But she really wanted the sushi; a dilemma which was only resolved by her finally reaching across and grabbing a huge plateful. She looked like the cat who got the cream. I gave her the thumbs up and she proudly passed some to Bald by Choice Man.

And bugger me if it wasn't like a movie script – minutes later, as if on cue, the two Japanese guys walked back in! They casually took their jackets off, then saw half their food gone. Thief woman went as red as Bald by Choice Man's head. The Japanese men looked confused. I pissed myself.

'Oh my God! I am *so* sorry ...' she said. 'I thought you'd left.'

She punched Bald by Choice Man in the arm: 'You *told* me they had left!'

'What? I ...' BBC Man was speechless. I was still laughing. The tempura was getting cold.

'I'll buy you some more,' she said, not knowing whether to spit out the contents or swallow it. 'We're just about to order,' she continued. 'Let me get you some.'

'No, no, it's OK,' said the Japanese man. 'Not hungry now. We just finish our beers.'

I think this made the lady feel worse. I bet the Japanese men were starving, just too polite to say anything.

Next to me other people had left, leaving a receipt and £20. I was going to point out to Thief Woman and Bald by Choice Man that maybe they could add to their tally by taking some dosh as well.

Bad move; she's probably a little sensitive right now.

West End, Glasgow

The morning was damp and overcast. Rain threatened, but at least it wasn't too cold. The first front door in Scotland, I was greeted by a well-dressed man in his early forties.

'Sorry, I'm on the phone, otherwise I'd listen,' he said.

I got the feeling he was telling the truth. This is not a brush off I tell myself. I still have the flu and feel like shit but have to soldier on. I have to make the most of Glasgow; I have a good feeling about it. So many people had told me I'd have to make it to Scotland so here I am.

That was to come true at the next house – a lovely old lady (why are old ladies always described as 'lovely'? It's never, 'She was hot,' or 'She's a fox, that old bird. Wouldn't mind giving her ...' OK, right, I guess I answered my own question).

After more than six weeks of busking, I now had a fair idea which people couldn't say no; this old lady was a case in point. Her warm eyes and effortless smile made me feel welcome right away. A quick-fire rejection was the last thing on her mind. Her husband, who stood hovering on the stairs, looked like he had other ideas, but I didn't give him a chance to say no, quickly bursting into song accompanied by a three year old at Nana's feet. Grandchild cried, Grandma laughed, Granddad looked confused. Grandchild continued to cry; shut up, kid, I've got the flu, you can cry when I leave.

While Nana ran to the kitchen, her husband left the comfort of the stairs and started chatting to me.

'So, how are your rugby team going to do this year?' he asked.

'How do you think I got into this mess in the first place?'

'Were you guys too scared to play the English this year?'

he said, alluding to the fact that the All Blacks had toured the UK but not played England. Nana then came out with a £1 coin and a plastic bag.

'What have you got in there?' I asked.

'To keep your energy up,' she smiled.

I delved into the plastic bag once they'd closed the door; two Tescos deep-filled Christmas mince pies, a pot of Devon custard and a yellow plastic spoon.

What a fox; I didn't have the heart to tell her I hated mince pies ...

Well, did I hit the jackpot at the next house or what? A lady with a nice disposition, who would also have difficulty saying no, said, 'You'd better come this way.'

Amazing, the first instinct in the north is to let you into houses. In the south, as you know, it never happened. Up here, it seems second nature.

I walked into the lounge to find ten women and numerous babies.

'You've got us at the right time of the month!' one howled.

'Speak for yourself,' the others laughed.

Turned out my timing was impeccable; I had gate-crashed a once-a-month mother's coffee group. Excellent, bloody excellent. I scoured the room: ten ladies, ten kids and counting. Some were guzzling breast milk, older ones were riding trikes around on the old wooden floors. Don't screw this up, I told myself, could be a very good little earner. I sang the song and, along with rapturous applause, received £13.50.

'We're always told not to let people into the house, but you can come anytime,' the jovial larger mum out of the group said to me. She was also hunting high and low for spare shrapnel.

Then they were away: 'Where have you been?' they asked.

'What's the most interesting place you've been to?'

'What happens if you forfeit the bet?'

The American lady in the room said I should copyright the Harry Potter song.

'Call again!' they yelled as I left via the front door.

Don't tempt me, I'll see you next month.

Drizzle continued to fall, although it was so mild I had to take my scarf off.

My day only got better; Frank the painter answered the next door, hailing, 'Entertain me, make my day.'

I needed no more encouragement to serenade a painter holding a cup of coffee and a paintbrush. Frank the painter had been self-employed for 26 years and had painted this very hallway he was now working on six years ago.

'I'd invite you in for a cuppa,' he said, 'but it's not my house.'

Frank was the sort of guy you'd love as a mate. You could tell he'd always be up for a laugh and a pint. He'd always lived in Glasgow although he wasn't too keen on the reputation it had acquired.

'Glasgow gets a bad name, mainly because fifty to one hundred years ago there was a lot of crime and a lot of poverty. A lot of people used to get beaten up. In the early seventies, the name Glasgow became synonymous with unemployment, economic depression and violence. My family was a classic example: we used to live in a tiny house, there was my mother and father and my two brothers. It was hard living; no hand basin, no toilet. And we weren't out of the ordinary, we were just your typical family. Now, to look at Glasgow you wouldn't know it. It's multicultural, great pubs, lively art scene, I love it.'

Frank passed me a couple of gold coins and a 'Frank the Painter' pen.

'I know it's a long commute to New Zealand,' he said, 'but if you ever need any odd jobs done around the house, give us a call.'

Not only did I have a painter's pen, some mince pies, a plastic spoon and some custard in my duffel coat from Glasgow, I also had a – you guessed it – rest home in my sights. As we know, rest homes are good.

Rest home = captive audience. Rest home = bananas.

I was let in by the head nurse who showed me the way to the lounge and said, 'I'll just go and get the rest of them for you.'

What, the *rest* of them? Oh, no, pressure. All the foxes were fast asleep in front of me. It was 11 in the morning. Crap morning telly polluted the room. I spied a woman who was upright and coherent, latching onto her immediately. I told her what I was doing in Scotland and that I was about to entertain the whole room.

'Oh, love, that sounds interesting,' she said, grabbing her pillow from a reclining chair.

'Where are you going?' I asked, panicking.

'Got to go up to my room,' she said.

'No, don't leave! Stay, no one else even knows I'm here!'

One by one the oldies filed in and were helped to their favourite chairs. The pressure was building. Shit, they probably thought this was going to be a full-on concert. Budgies in the corner of the room squawked and laughed at me. It was still raining outside. Where's Doris with dementia when I needed her?

I stood at the front of the lounge while the head nurse, whose introduction took longer than my entire performance was going to be, said to the sleeping crowd, 'Now, he's been through England on his trip and he's sung to many, many people. But we're gonna do better than England, aren't we, ladies?' she said, raising her voice.

A resounding 'Mmm?' from twenty old ladies and one dozing old man.

I sang, budgies shat, old ladies snored. The few alive at the end clapped. I waited for them to pass forward their wills. Come on, Beryl, give the lovely man your will, I wanted the nurse to say.

Unfortunately, not so much as a coffee bean, not so much as a three-month-old chocolate from under their pillow, not so much as an inner sole from a crusty old slipper found its way into my grubby little mitt.

I had made diddly squat from the Glasgow rest home. Zilch. Zero. Nothing. Squat.

I hung my head in shame and slipped through the side door before the others woke up. Obviously I wasn't quick enough. A lady who'd only woken up as I strummed the last bar said to me, 'Is that all we're gonna get?'

The budgies squawked. The orderly escorted me out. 'Thank you,' he said, closing the door.

It was now bucketing down with rain and my guitar was getting wet. A rain check was in order.

I had to concede I'd had a bloody good day in the West End of Glasgow. And even though the flu was making me grumpy and irritable, at least I had food and money in my sky rocket. However, I was still some £140 short of the magical number. I had to think outside the square; sure the busking had been profitable, but I needed the remaining money *quickly*. My patience was running out.

I booked into a hostel for the night and checked my emails. I was stoked to see more messages from people I'd never met, people who just wanted to see me finish. But even more satisfying than that was discovering that, in the next few hours, New Zealand were going to be playing Australia in the VB series in Melbourne. Chances of finding the cricket on a TV in Scotland were indeed remote. I accepted this, but could not resist a quick trip down to Ladbrokes where I discovered New Zealand was paying £5 for a win.

Deep down, I knew we had no chance, we hadn't beaten them for years.

Fuck it, I'll put seven quid on.

Hey, big spender!

Now, because of the time difference between Melbourne (which is where the game was played) and Glasgow (which is where I slept), the game wouldn't start until 4 a.m. GMT. I admit, I may be a sad bastard, but I'm not a complete loser, hence, I would not be sitting on the Internet all night watching cricket. And just to keep things well rounded, I have included details of the game for cricket lovers and non-cricket lovers. Word of advice: non-cricket lovers, don't read the first one.

Cricket lover's version

Before this crucial VB series match actually started, I think it's fair to point out the following: Australia had won 18 of its previous 21 one-day internationals; New Zealand only eight of its previous 28. As the match began, the form held true with Brett Lee snaring 3/43 and Glenn McGrath 2/47.

New Zealand was in real trouble at 94/7. They then went on to make 199/8 from their 50 overs. The Kiwis must have been worried when Australia didn't waste any time, blasting 95 off the first 15.

But New Zealand obviously had other ideas with Shane Bond and Chris Cairns bouncing back brilliantly. Both shattered the middle order, and after the disastrous run out of Steve Waugh, the Australians could only watch in horror as its middle order collapsed. Before New Zealand could complete their sensational 23-run win, regrettably, play was stopped for eight minutes as members of a noisy contingent in the Great Southern Stand decided to target members of the fielding team with a stream of projectiles.

Order was only restored when a vanload of police officers descended upon that part of the stadium to evict more than 200 offenders. It was a disappointing end to the match.

It is a gentleman's game after all and that, I'm afraid, is just not cricket.

Non-cricket lover's version

A bunch of guys turned up wearing silly clothing. Some hit sticks with balls, some didn't. Men in white coats made funny signals when the ball went into the crowd. There was no nudity and no good-looking guys. There was a lot of yelling and screaming and we all looked at a big TV for five minutes while they decided if the man wearing the motorcycle helmet was guilty. If he was, a new man came out wearing, *tragically*, the same clothes. Do these guys not liaise with each other before the game? Then they played with their balls for about three hours, swapped sides and did the same thing all over again. The only really interesting part of the day was when some really pissed guys next to us threw nectarines and Coke bottles at the Kiwis.

'Yes! You fucking beauty!' I screamed when I checked the scores in the morning. Thirty-five pounds would soon be coming my way. Thank you Australian cricket – I won't forget your generosity.

Victoria Circus, Glasgow

Instead of cashing up straight away, I hit an area called Victoria Circus to see if I could add to my tally. Strike while the iron's hot. Once again, Glasgow turned on the rain as I approached a man who owned two brand new Audis. He wanted nothing to do with the door-to-door busker. Unlike the French couple next door who had lived in Glasgow for 25 years and loved it because 'People say hello to you on the street.' They informed me their daughter lived in Auckland. Bingo. Two pounds.

Do you remember that ad on the telly that said, 'If you're a woman living alone, the last thing you should say to someone at the door is "I'm living alone".' For the obvious reasons.

Unfortunately, no one had bothered to tell this next lady in Glasgow.

'No, I'm not interested. I'm here by myself,' she said, when I asked if I could sing to her.

Now call me old-fashioned, but I would have thought that was the last thing you should say to a gambler wearing a second-hand duffel coat with a runny nose. I mean, you might as well just say, 'Hi there. Hey, nice balaclava. You'll be pleased to know I'm here *all* by myself. Please, have a look around. Help yourself to tea and coffee. If you need a hand with anything, give me a yell, although I probably won't hear you. I'll be down the back of the farm operating some *really* noisy machinery.'

I nearly chickened out when I read the next sign: *No hawkers or circulars*. Was I one of those, I thought to myself. Maybe a hawker, definitely not a circular. Sometimes you've just gotta do it, I decided. I didn't want to but had a feeling something special was about to happen.

I was right.

The door slowly opened. He was wearing a Tibetan hat with a guitar draped over his shoulders. Holy shit! Was I seeing things? An identity crisis I did not need. *Who* was the door-to-door busker here?

I must have been standing there for 30 seconds before I could say anything. The other door-to-door busker had an aura that immediately put me at ease. He was calm, almost Dalai Lama-like. A little old and wrinkly perhaps, and even a little green around the gills, but this magical figure before my very eyes emitted peace and well being. He must have been seventy-odd, his bloodshot eyes and strong smell nearly flooring me. I was overcome, almost transfixed in a state of delirium.

Then it clicked! Oh my God, I wanted to jump for joy. This was it! This was the moment Obi-Don Kenobi had talked about long ago in Seaford. After six weeks of busking around the UK I had reached my zenith.

I was looking at ... Yoda!

'What do you want?' he finally snapped.

I explained my pilgrimage and reason for being to the master.

'No, I don't want a song. I'm too hung over to do anything,' he moaned. Ah, so that would explain the smell (vodka), and the eyes (vodka), and green around the gills (vodka).

This was not Yoda and I was not well.

– 21 –

Edinburgh

Earnings to date: £397, a port (bottle), a banana skin, a kiwi fruit, a car, some Christmas mince pies, some custard, a plastic spoon and a Frank the Painter pen

UP UNTIL NOW, I'd only sung about him. Today, I found myself in the very city he came from. Not only that, in the next day or two I would also find myself trying to busk to the very author who discovered him.

In the meantime I had to get lost, which wasn't difficult in Edinburgh. Sure, the drive from Glasgow was easy enough, but once I actually got to Auld Reekie itself, I was completely disorientated. And it's all due to those bloody one-way streets, I tell you. How the hell is an ignorant tourist supposed to know their way round? Most of the time the only option was to head down a one-way street, then you'd get cops yelling, 'Hey, that's a one-way street!'

'No kidding, it's the only way to go!' I yelled back.

This is all part of the revelation I'd recently had about myself as traveller: I'm very good at getting lost, I'm not good at *being* lost.

I could go on and on about the sheer beauty of Edinburgh, but you've heard it all before. It is literally a city where you can't believe your own eyes. For some reason I had low expectations of the place. I didn't bank on the fact I would have to stop in the streets every two minutes to glare, gaze and gawk at medieval castles that overlooked the city like sleeping giants.

Once again I had timed my arrival perfectly for door-to-door busking, i.e. it was pitch black. I would have to rely on Don Partridge's advice and meet new friends on barstools. After a cheeky whisky and a read of the sports section at the Jolly Judge, I went past a swank hotel where I heard a pianist belting out numerous songs destined for elevators and department stores. In between numbers I asked him, 'Where can I go in Edinburgh where they play live music? I want to sit around a bar singing crappy old Billy Joel songs with complete strangers and make a right tit of myself.'

'I know the perfect place,' he said.

Fingers Bar was situated on Frederick Street. This was the place to go if you described the above symptoms. Apparently, a guy plays piano till three in the morning while everyone else sits around the ivories, slowly but very raucously getting pissed.

'Do you ever play there?' I had asked my friend, playing easy-listening favourites in the posh hotel.

'No, no, no, no,' he said. 'No way.' He brushed some dust off his dinner jacket.

'Why? Bit different to here, is it?' I asked while he sipped what appeared to be a Martini.

'Too hard a gig,' he said. 'You gotta really know what you're doing ... and the crowd gets abusive.'

This was sounding better all the time.

At 10 p.m., when I arrived at Fingers, there were only four other people in the pub. Two of those were working behind the bar. The others were a 50-year-old couple, snogging and playing footsie opposite my table. After such a build-up, I was fast preparing myself for an anti-climax.

Where were all the people? Where was the abusive crowd?

Just as I was putting my jacket on to leave, a man who could only be described as a seventies Elton John (bald head and all), stepped up to the piano in the dimly lit corner of the pub. It was 11.20 p.m.

'See what I can get away with here,' he told the small but attentive crowd, then started tinkling away at a jazz number. As soon as he started playing I had the 'we could be here a while' feeling.

Along with grabbing a fresh drink, I also decided to secure a seat around the piano. It may get busy, I told myself, when the other pubs close.

Word of warning; if you go to Fingers Bar you will end up singing Dan Hill's 'Sometimes when we touch' and think, what a fantastic song. You will wail away to 'Crocodile Rock' and 'Piano Man' and wonder why they don't write songs like that any more. You will forget the lyrics to 'Blue Suede Shoes', 'Sweet Caroline' and 'Who the Fuck is Alice' and think you are the best goddamn singer in the world.

However, before the crowds rolled in (proof that my early seating manoeuvre was a very timely one), there was a small altercation involving a man, 13 tequilas and a faulty eardrum. You see, the piano that 1970s Elton was playing had a very cool, clear Perspex lid; this meant you could see the black and white keys jump up and down as he played the notes.

Meanwhile our very pissed friend, who wasn't listening to a word poor Elton was saying, tried to show his appreciation by whacking the top of the piano as hard as humanly possible. Obviously this disturbed Elton a little, who was trying his darndest to sing 'Uptown Girl' with a straight face.

'Can you stop doing that, please?' he asked the drunk,

who was now struggling with gravity itself. He whacked the top of the piano again, harder than before.

'I said, can you stop doing that, please?' Elton asked.

'Yeah, sorry.'

He did it again.

'Can you stop doing that, please!'

'Sorry, won't do it again.'

He did it again.

'Stop it!'

'Sorry, it's just that … wow,' he said, looking at the keys in some detail. 'Looks like a bird, wow! Looks like a bird!' he laughed.

No, it looks like the inside of a piano.

He whacked it again, Elton called security and we had one less person in the pub.

That didn't matter, though. The swarm of drinkers after 11 was unbelievable. It was like the whole of Edinburgh had just woken up. Each time I looked up there were 20 more people. It was heaving. My seat was now prime real estate, confirmed by a woman who squeezed past to get to the Ladies, saying, 'You've got the best seat in Edinburgh tonight.'

I felt like the luckiest man in the world.

An Aussie guy sat next to me. I bought him a beer to celebrate the Kiwi's victory the day previous. His Scottish wife asked me what I was doing in these parts. When I told them, the Aussie said, 'Did you bring your guitar?'

'No, left it in the hostel,' I said.

'Bugger, 'cos if you did I would have thrown you up there!' he said, pointing to the top of the piano.

We drank together and sang. Meanwhile, 1970s Elton John continued to play the gig of his life. This was his moment; he had the crowd in the palm of his hands. Complete strangers clinked glasses and did their best to help him out with 'Angels', 'Don't Look Back in Anger', 'Proud Mary' and 'Your Song'.

Just after he had played numerous Elton John and Billy Joel numbers, a less than sober woman leant on the piano and asked, 'Do you take requests?'

'Sure, what would you like?'

'Something by Elton John or Billy Joel?'

We couldn't get enough of this guy. Don Partridge talked about this back in Seaford: the power a good musician could have over an entire room. He took us places, he made us reminisce, he made us buy more booze, he made us happy. What power, what a cool thing to be able to do.

He'd gone an hour and a half without a break, people continued to swarm around the piano as if he was Stevie Wonder. Eventually he had to stop; it was now our turn to repay the favour. The only thing we could come up with was 'Happy Birthday'. We felt pathetic, it wasn't even his birthday but it was the only a capella song we all knew.

'I need a piss so bad my back teeth are floating,' my Aussie mate said, excusing himself after our tuneless rendition for Elton.

This was my cue to meet the Three Ms from Scotland: Mickey, Mikey and Morris. They were all best mates and within minutes we had much in common; we were all very pissed and we were all about to be kicked out of Fingers Bar.

'Why don't you come back to my place for a night cap?' slurred Mikey. 'It's only a hundred yards down the road, it would be a real honour.'

'That'll be great,' I said.

I hope I don't throw up in your toilet, I thought.

TO SAY MIKEY'S house was impressive would be a gross understatement. The entrance itself was the size of an average lounge. Marble floors, a grand piano, antique furniture, funky sofas, expensive prints, along with state of the art stereos and DVD players, made me realise I could never live like the gypsies in Calne.

'Get a load of this story!' Mickey yelled from the lounge when I told him about the busking.

Mikey came back carrying the finest whisky, coffee, tea, wine and beer.

'What will you have to drink, Kiwi?' he asked.

'I just hope I don't throw up in your toilet.'

Did I say that out loud?

I sat with the same glass of whisky for the entire evening. We watched Celtic play on the telly and talked shit till six in the morning. The Three Ms told me how different the atmosphere was in their local that night.

'First of all, we noticed *you* were in our seats. Second thing we noticed was the atmosphere. Normally when you walk in, you get guys who give you the "What the fuck are you looking at?" glare. Tonight was different, it was chilled, it had a good vibe. Everyone was happy. Then we saw why, bloody Kiwis, eh?'

I took this as a compliment.

Sitting, nursing my drink, trying desperately to keep everything down, I realised why it was I was feeling so bad. I was still suffering from the flu and in the time it took 1970s Elton to play a benefit concert, I'd injected my body with a conglomerate of colourful potions, namely, Sudafed, beer, whisky and wine. Meanwhile, Mickey kept asking Mikey to call him a taxi.

'No problem,' he'd say, making out he was going to get the phone. Instead he'd come out of the kitchen with another bottle of vino. The Three Ms were great mates and I loved them for that.

'One time I called Mikey,' said Mickey, 'and he asked me to lunch. I said sure, thinking he was down at the local. But he wasn't, was he? He was in bloody Dublin, staying in a swank hotel and about to see The Eagles that night. I told him I'd call back in five minutes. I then made a few calls, called work to say I'd be leaving early, got on a plane, rang back and said, "I won't be able to meet you for lunch but I'll see you for pre-dinner drinks."'

For the fifth time in as many minutes Mickey had asked Mikey to call a taxi.

'Soon, mate,' he said. 'It's still early.'

'It's twenty past five in the morning! I've got kids!' Mickey protested.

'Why don't you try busking to J. K. Rowling?' Mikey asked me, completely ignoring his poor mate.

'Does she live in Edinburgh?' I asked.

'She lives opposite the garden centre. I saw her a couple of weeks ago.'

'It *wasn't* a couple of weeks ago,' Mickey argued.

'Well, about a month.'

'More like six months ago, Mikey.'

'Yeah, well, anyway, I was talking to her at a party for two or three hours.'

'Two or three hours! More like ten minutes. Come on, Mikey, you don't know her that well. Have you called that taxi yet?'

'No, I haven't. Anyway,' he said, turning his attention to me again, 'I know where she lives and I think you should sing your Harry Potter song to her. For God's sake, this is the land of Harry Potter. This is where it all started!'

'Can you *please* call me a taxi?' Mickey begged.

'Yes, yes, all right,' he conceded. 'But first we'll have a quick beer.'

I WOKE AT 11.05 a.m. Mickey had very kindly paid for the taxi and dropped me off at the hostel. It was nearly light when I got in. Unfortunately, the mix of Sudafed, beer and whisky had made me lose my mind. This was confirmed when I lay in bed; when the room wasn't spinning I spied a sign on the wall: *Fire alarms will be tested every Tuesday.*

'Hear that, fire alarms? You'd better swot on Monday night and line up with all the other fire alarms on Tuesday, because you *will* be tested.'

Then the actual examination begins: 'Right, *are* you a fire alarm?'

'Yes.'

'What noise does a fire alarm make?'

'Woof?'

'No, no, no, you're fired. This is a process of elimination – all fire alarms must meet back here next Tuesday.'

Things were not looking good. I was still around £100 short, I was having bizarre thoughts about fire alarms and my nostrils would have cigarette smoke in them for weeks. I didn't care any more. I just wanted the misery to end. I wanted Mark to streak at Wimbledon. I was tired, exhausted, lonely and hung over. I couldn't take it any more. I just needed to finish.

Biting the bullet was not an easy thing to do considering what I really needed was bacon, eggs and coffee, but I had to. I was in Edinburgh, for God's sake, the home of Harry Potter. Hung over or not, I had to busk or attempt to busk to J. K. Rowling.

I found the house with relative ease; the Three Ms' instructions were spot on. I found her home. I saw the house. I saw her car. I chickened out. I was too nervous, I mean, what the hell was I going to say? She probably gets dickhead journos coming to her door all the time. I'd read that she gets at least three calls a week asking who she'd shagged lately and how she was spending her money. I didn't want to be one of those, so decided to hit other houses in the street first. My thinking being, maybe one of them will know her and I'll have an 'in'.

The busking was painless, just like Glasgow. People were open and friendly. Funny how most thought I'd just picked their street at random.

'You've picked the right street,' one lady said, excitedly. 'The author of *Harry Potter* lives right there!'

You don't say? Come on then, this is when you're supposed to say you're her best friend and you take me over to meet her. No such luck.

'Do you think she'll like my song?' I asked.

'No!' she laughed.

'You should go and see her,' said the little girl next to her mum. Dad also turned up on his bike with his son in tow. He had the look I received often: 'Who the hell is this weirdo at my front door?'

How cool must it be to be that little girl, knowing that when she lay in bed reading *Harry Potter*, the author was less than fifty metres away, typing his next adventure?

'Do you think she's home?' I asked the mum, hoping one last time she'd take me over herself.

'Well, her car's there,' she said.

Ten fresh pounds lay in my pocket. I had no excuse. Either I was to talk to J. K. Rowling or fall over in a heap. I didn't hold much hope talking via an intercom but it was now or never.

Buzz.

'Hello?'

Holy shit, that's J. K. Rowling!

'Hi I'm from New Zealand and I'm a door-to-door busker. Would you like to hear a song?'

'No, not just at the moment, thanks. Bye.'

'Bye.'

That was J. K. Rowling! It occurred to me as I walked off that what she said could mean any number of things.

It *could* mean come upstairs, I'm going to make you rich.

It *could* mean you have a voice like a robin on a spring morning.

It *could* mean I find Kiwi men the sexiest on the planet.

But it probably means, no, not just at the moment, thanks. Bye.

But, what did you expect? She would open the door to a strange man in a duffel coat? Is she obligated to open the door just because she's famous? She'd proved she's just like 80 per cent of us; she won't listen to a song from the door-to-door busker.

And I think that's kinda cool.

Liverpool

Earnings to date: £407, a port bottle, a banana skin, a kiwi fruit, a car, Christmas mince pies, some custard, a plastic teaspoon and a Frank the Painter pen

LIVERPOOL SCARED ME for some reason. Walking the street at night I watched my back more than normal. Bouncers stood outside clubs on a Monday night. A scraggly, unshaven man sat outside the YMCA smoking and drinking cider. 'Don't walk alone at night around Duke and Hanover Streets' is what my guidebook told me. I definitely didn't have the same confidence busking here that I had in Scotland.

Meantime, I was starving, having eaten nothing at all en route from Edinburgh. Rather unwisely, I opted for a dodgy chicken restaurant.

'Double chicken burger, please.'

'Only doing singles,' he said, wiping his nose with his sleeve, pointing to some crispy, dry old chicken pieces that sat behind him in the grill.

'Single then,' I sniffed.

It had pissed down all the way from Edinburgh. I had gotten lost and taken more wrong turns than I care to remember, let alone admit, and I still had the flu. I took my meal to the back of the restaurant where two middle-aged people sat. Maybe I can have a chat. Maybe they can cheer me up.

She sat there in silence, humming every now and again. He sat there as if he'd just been told he'd lost his home and family in a house fire. He was a continually frowning man with greasy grey hair, wearing old track pants with black dress shoes. The eczema around his lips and nose, bright red in parts, kind of put me off my already inedible meal. He stared into space with his chunky sausage-like fingers plummeting into his gravy to retrieve the odd chip. She continued humming. He continued to look depressed. Two teenage guys ate pizza next to me, scoffing it. The floor was disgusting, there were chicken bones on my table. I wanted the sunshine. This is Liverpool. What a change from the delight and surprise of Edinburgh.

MARIA WAS MY new friend; she ran the hotel just up the road from where I ate the bad chicken. She was sixty-odd, a heavy smoker and had a fantastic accent. She told me all the things I could do in Liverpool and, most importantly, which areas to stay away from. As I was eating my greasy eggs and bacon after a lie down in my extremely cramped room with no toilet or shower, she came up with a ripper of an idea: busk down Penny Lane.

'And do the Beatles tour,' she said. 'You've got to do the Beatles tour. They take you around Strawberry Fields and past John Lennon's house. You can't come to Liverpool and not do that.'

'Good point, Maria.'

'Just don't sing a Beatles song,' she said. 'That would be sacrilege.'

Busking on a street that has been immortalised through song and three decades of music filled me with apprehension and a fair amount of nerves. Although to be honest, the 'blue suburban skies' in the song were nowhere to be seen; a cold, wet, miserable day awaited me.

It came as a bit of a shock to see that an ordinary road called Croyden Ave should link up with one of the most famous roads ever. Imagine that, 'Croyden Ave, you're in my ears and in my eyes!'

Not quite the same, is it?

But all the places in the song are really there. There's the bank, bus stop and the barber (although now it's a hair and beauty salon with *Brand New Sunbeds* advertised in the front window – what would Lennon say about that?). There was also a DIY store, Washarama and Chinese takeaway; I don't remember those in the song. Dog shit wound its way down the road and rubbish was splayed all over Millennium Green, a park opposite the houses. Graffiti lined the brick walls along the grass.

To be honest, Penny Lane was a dog of a street, but it's famous and like the song says, it's in our ears and in our eyes so I kept going. And it's weird, you can't help but hum the song as you walk down it.

An old man who could barely make it to the door was my first client this morning. Poor old bugger, it took him a couple of minutes just to walk down the hallway. I thought he was gonna kark it before he even got there. 'No, I'm not very well and my wife's not very well,' he said.

I felt terrible, getting him to come to the door like that. He was struggling even to stand for long.

Another old man walked past, carrying *The Sun* and a carton of milk, just like on any other suburban street in any other town in the UK. Did he realise or even care how famous this piece of road was?

I could see a TV flickering in the next house but no one

answered; once again I knew they were watching me through the curtains, but weren't coming to the party. Things weren't going well in Penny Lane. I wondered to myself how well Paul McCartney would do as a door-to-door busker, although he's probably smart enough to keep his trap shut during rugby games.

The guy next door was young and thankfully not about to thump me, or die on me. I explained my bet from the tape recording in my head, with the biggest smile I could manage considering my flu. He looked interested; I smiled more, knowing I was making progress. Then I heard from the lounge, 'No!'

I looked at him as if to say, well, I can sing to you? He shrugged his shoulders.

'Are you sure you don't want a song?' I asked.

'Yes!' The scream came once again from the lounge.

'Bloody hell, she's got eyes in the back of her head and sonic hearing, your mum,' I said.

Give her a whack for me, I wanted to say.

He looked embarrassed, then said, 'It was nice to meet you, good luck.'

Yeah, well luck's not gonna pay for the flight, big boy. Go talk to your mum about manners.

I walked off, penny lame.

At least I saw someone else suffer misfortune further down the street. (Is this what my life had become?)

A woman strolling with a friend made a bad life choice by walking past a very deep puddle just as a boy racer was screaming down Penny Lane. This was not an opportunity he got often, so with both hands firmly on the wheel, he drove through at full speed, absolutely drenching the poor girl.

I tried not to laugh. I laughed.

'Oh, nice one!' she yelled as he drove off.

Then the sun came out on Penny Lane.

My next customer couldn't even get his front door open. It was jammed and the harder he tried to pull it, the more it seemed to stick. He was really starting to lose his rag.

'Oh shit! Bloody hell, this stupid thing!' came a muffled voice.

It still wouldn't come. This is normally my cue to panic a little. When he realises it's not actually someone delivering a large sum of money, just a Kiwi loser who lost a bet, he's gonna knock my bleeding head off. All of a sudden the guy from Sheffield jumped into my head: 'Does anyone ever thump you?'

Meanwhile, my (hopefully) first customer of the morning was still struggling with the door. I was now considering 'playing dead' or jumping into the bushes, pretending to … find my … car keys, that's it! I quickly skulked towards the letterbox.

'Can I help you there, mate?' I heard as I attempted to hide behind the fence.

Jammed doors may have pissed this man off but, I'm glad to report, door-to-door buskers didn't.

'Oh, that's a bit different,' he listened as his girlfriend watched, talking on the phone in the kitchen. She didn't think I could see her, peeked through the door and asked, 'Who is it, Carl?'

'It's a door-to-door busker,' he said, proudly.

I then heard her say on the phone, 'Um … a door-to-door busker, I think he said.'

I loved that, just wished I could hear the person on the other line, 'A door-to-door what?'

She hung up and came to the door handing me two quid.

'You're in a good mood,' I said.

'Yeah, well, I'm off snowboarding today, unlike my *boyfriend* who's going to fix this door, aren't you darling?' she said squeezing his cheek like your mum used to do.

'Yes, dear,' he grumbled.

My first £2 from Penny Lane; this gave me immense confidence.

I found a derelict old house that looked like fire had got the best of it. I was about to knock on the old door but, as it turned out, I didn't need to; there was a builder working upstairs with the radio on. I love it when you're walking down the street and builders have got the radio on. The songs always sound better, it signifies life in the street and makes you think there's a party somewhere you haven't been invited to. Just like music on someone else's stereo; it always sounds better. And you can always find cooler CDs at someone else's house.

'Go on then, sing us a song,' John the builder said to me from the second floor.

I sang 'Harry Potter', but he didn't turn the stereo down. This was a real Romeo and … well, Romeo moment. Him on the second floor holding a paintbrush, me on the ground floor strumming away. I'm over the fear of serenading guys now, it's only them who feel embarrassed. I just want their money. In this case he didn't give me any.

'Why are you doing this?' he asked.

'Lost a bet, have to make enough money to fly home,' I hinted.

'Oh,' he said. 'Well, you've picked the right place.'

'Yeah, why's that?'

'Heard of the Beatles?'

'Yes, sir.'

Give me your money, John.

'Well, this is Penny Lane!' he said, arms open wide as if he owned the street.

'Oh yeah? That's cool.'

I take Visa, John.

'The Beatles, Penny Lane, get it?' he exclaimed.

'Oh right, Penny Lane!'

Give us your wallet, Granddad.

'As in … "Penny Lane, you're in my ears and in my eyes, la de dah de dah!"'

You're just lucky this house is already burnt down, John.

I could still hear John singing when I arrived at another student's house. He listened attentively, as if he'd be questioned afterwards, then asked, 'What do you accept?'

A question you should never ask a door-to-door busker.

'Visa, American Express and automatic payment,' I said. 'So what's it like living on Penny Lane?'

'I don't know, something to tell your grandkids, I suppose.'

I walked past the world famous Penny Lane Wine Bar and Quarter Records and across the road saw Sergeant Pepper's Bistro, which is where the original bus stop in the song used to be. Was it just me or were people living in the past here?

It was now a pleasant day, the sun hitting suburban English streets just like those of the *Coronation Street* variety. This didn't stop punters coming up with new excuses for not wanting a bar of me, though. A man, who saw me from the front room of his house, surprised me by answering at all.

'Look,' he said, showing me his hands, which didn't have a mark on them.

'What?' I queried.

'I'm painting,' he said, again pointing to supposed paint stains.

'Would you like a song?' I asked.

'No, *look* at these hands.'

I loved the creative excuses people came up with. Something I noticed a lot was men's less-than-adequate decision-making abilities. Often a woman would answer the door, while the man would stand on the stairs a couple of feet behind her. The interesting thing was, the woman always seemed to make the decision about whether a song would be coming their way. Men never seemed committed to answering. They didn't like to say yes or no. Maybe they didn't want to be serenaded by another man, or maybe it's because the house really was the woman's domain; it was her nest and she was the boss.

After an hour of busking I wasn't exactly setting the world alight in Penny Lane. Just as I was about to retire for the day, a flat load of students who had been staring at me for God knows how long were pointing and sniggering. One last try.

I barely needed to knock, a girl had answered the door before I had the chance. Three girls, one from Swindon, one from Edinburgh and one from London, had just finished their exams the day before and were celebrating by wearing pyjamas and slippers and watching crappy morning TV. The only bloke in the room, an Asian from London, was not as relaxed; his exam was looming tomorrow.

'What is your exam on?' I asked.

'Orthoptics (eyes), I'm trying my best not to think about it,' he said, rubbing his own, which looked heavy and in need of a good sleep.

'Don't worry, mate, if everything else fails, you can always join me on the streets.'

'Yeah, right, I can't play a musical instrument.'

'Hey, neither can I!'

'Would you like a cuppa?' the girl from Swindon asked.

'I would *love* a cuppa,' I said, wiping my nose for the eighty-ninth time today.

'Have a seat, I'll get you one.'

This was all good. I was warm and I had a generous, slipper-loving crowd. I sang them a song and they rewarded me with the sound of eight hands clapping.

'Hey, you should see if you can get on one of these crappy TV shows, they're always looking for crazy people.'

I took this as a compliment. Swindon Girl came back with a cup of tea, £6 and a can of Red Bull.

'To keep you going,' she said.

'Magic.' I could have stayed there all afternoon. 'So, what's it really like to live on one of the world's most famous streets? What's it like to say to your mates you live on Penny Lane?'

'Well, we get the Magical Mystery Tour every afternoon.'

'I'm going to do that today,' I said, remembering Maria from the hotel had threatened I couldn't leave Liverpool without doing it. 'Have you guys ever been on it?'

'Never,' they said in unison.

'You're joking. You live on Penny Lane and you haven't done the Mystery Tour? You know what you should do? Next time the bus comes through with a bunch of tourists, you should jump on, pretend you're some crazy bastards and yell, "I don't care what I do," and throw a rock through your own flat window.'

'Yeah, OK.'

'Right,' they said.

Maybe that Sudafed was still having an effect on me.

JIM THE LOLLIPOP Man was helping kids cross the road as I ventured back to the car via the Chinese takeaway and Washarama. I stopped to have a chat.

'Oh, that's novel!' he said in a thick Liverpudlian accent.

Jim was a helluva nice man, would have been pushing 60 and obviously knew his history when it came to his hometown.

'This is Dovedale Primary School where Paul and George went to school,' he pointed to a school off Penny Lane. 'Hello, dear, how are you?' he asked a woman walking past with shopping bags. It seemed Jim knew everyone in the area. No surprise really as he'd been Chief Lollipop Man for 18 years.

'Often down at the pub I'll see guys I don't even recognise buying me drinks, all because I helped them cross the road when they were five.'

I'd noticed earlier that Penny Lane was actually painted onto the brick wall at the start of the road. Jim told me why: 'Do you know how many of those signs have been stolen over the years?'

Just like in York, I was to become a tourist in Liverpool for the afternoon. Penny Lane had donated £16 and a can of Red Bull, but now it was time to climb aboard the Magical Mystery Tour.

Our tour guide started by telling us we were about to pass the River Mersey.

'This is one of the oldest used rivers in the world, dating back to the fourteenth century. You may remember the infamous song by Gerry and the Pacemakers, or as he's known now, Gerry and *his* Pacemaker.'

I suppose what astounded me most as we slipped our way through where the Beatles grew up and where they penned their songs, was the ordinariness of it all. It was nothing special to look at, yet they'd created special, unforgettable songs. God knows what they could have done if they grew up in Paris.

We passed Strawberry Fields where John used to spend a

lot of time as a kid. Coming from a broken home, he could relate to a lot of the orphans who lived here.

We drove past Madryn Street, where Ringo was born, and only about 100 yards away from where he'd spend most of his life as a young adult. A hundred yards from where you were born! Not exactly big travellers these boys. As we know, old Ringo wasn't an original Beatle and if it hadn't been for the firing of Pete Best, he might never have gone on to bigger and better things like being the voice for *Thomas the Tank Engine*.

George Harrison's house, now owned by Beatles fans, bore signs reading, *God Bless You, George* and *Here Comes the Sun*, due to his recent death. One of the houses Paul grew up in now belonged to the National Trust and had been renovated inside and out, to look just like it did back in the sixties. I'm sure the old fella living opposite was keen when this decision was made. The National Trust desperately wanted old, cruddy authentic windows for the McCartneys' house. They did a deal with the old bloke, who was offered swanky, new, freshly installed aluminium ones if he handed over his.

'Go on then, twist my arm, you bastards.'

And then we drove down Penny Lane, where I waved to my flatmates who were still drinking tea and watching daytime telly. Jim waved at us as he helped kids cross the street; boys and girls who'd be shouting him drinks in just a few short years. It was so cool to think that those lyrics were written right here, on this very ordinary street, in the north-west of England.

A STARK, BLAND restaurant awaited me for dinner. All I wanted was a salad and a nice relaxing drink. I got neither. Unfortunately, the waiter, who had the interpersonal skills of a wet paper bag, saw it as an opportunity to brush up on his geography while preaching weird religious ramblings to an unsuspecting Kiwi.

'Where would you like to sit?' he asked.

'Over here,' I replied.

'Are you from Australia?'

'No, New Zealand.'

'And, are you, do you, what are you doing in England?'

'I'm here on business.'

'Where are you staying?'

'Up the road.'

'What sort of drink would you like?'

'I don't know, I haven't seen the menu yet.'

He passed me a menu. I'm not a violent man but he had a face you just wanted to punch.

'I'll have a beer, thanks,' I said.

'Oh yep, lager or bitter?'

'Bitter.'

'*Bitter*? That's an interesting choice. I never saw an Australian, I mean, when I was in Australia, no one ever drank bitter.'

'Really?'

Just get my fucking order. Ten minutes later a warm beer and cold pasta arrived.

'So where are you from again?' he asked.

'Auckland.'

'Oh Auckland, that's right.'

Then he stood there for a while wondering why I had ordered bitter.

'Ever heard of Trevor Yaxley?' he asked.

'No.'

'Trevor Yaxley? You've never heard of Trevor Yaxley? He's an evangelist. He's been to heaven and hell. My Christian teacher was telling me about him.'

'And how do you know he's been to heaven and hell?'

'If you read his stuff you'd know what I mean.'

'Does he get duty free?'

'Duty free?' he looked confused.

'Yeah, Trevor? When he goes to heaven and hell, does he get duty free?'

'No, no, I don't think he does.'

You gotta laugh sometimes, otherwise you'd cry.

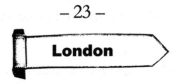

London

Earnings to date: £423, a port bottle, a banana skin, a kiwi fruit, a car, Christmas mince pies, some custard, a plastic spoon, a Frank the Painter pen and a can of Red Bull

www.doortodoorbusker.com

Hello Justin,
I've come across your quirky story on the net. We work for German public TV and would like to get in touch with you. It would be great if you could contact me on the below given number or drop me a line.
Hope to hear from you soon!
Good luck!
Mathias Marx
APM Media London

Hey sheep-shagger,
I hear you've got the flu and you're miserable. Excellent, I'll be thinking of you when we have a barby tonight. Just about to open a cold one.
Mark

Justin
Are you still here in the UK? If so, get in touch, I work on a show on Channel 4 called Richard & Judy, we're live Monday to Friday at 5 p.m. I'd be interested to hear from you. Perhaps we could do something on the show?
Good luck with your busking.

THESE THREE EMAILS greeted me as I gulped down coffee at a Liverpool Internet café. I was stunned, speechless, over the moon and nervous. What the hell was I going to do on nationwide TV? As for German TV, what was that about? This was starting to get out of control. BBC Radio Leeds had also tracked me down. Maria had knocked on my door at 8 a.m., saying there was an important phone call. They wanted to do a live interview. Somewhere on my website reports I must have said which hotel I was staying at. It's the only way anyone could have figured out where I was. I blagged my way through an interview, half-asleep with a fluey throat that made me sound like a cross between Barry White and Kermit the Frog.

The producer of the *Richard and Judy* show then phoned to say what time they wanted me in London the next morning, along with a time to meet at the studio.

I guess this meant I was going on the telly.

I didn't sleep a wink that night. Maria wished me well as I left the hotel the next morning at 8 a.m. I'd have to leave the car and my bags in Liverpool and come back that night to collect them. The producer of *Richard and Judy* had told me that I should pay for the ticket and she'd reimburse me once I got to London. No problem I said, until I found out the price. Waiting to see if £153 would melt my credit card was an anxious time. That's three weeks' busking, I wanted to tell the conductor.

True to form, the train was late.

'The horn on this train is buggered,' beamed the tinny speakers. 'For safety reasons this means we cannot travel at more than twenty miles an hour.'

This caused a carriage-full of suit-wearing execs to quietly panic, pick up mobiles and call prospective clients: 'Brian, I'm going to be late, you'll have to start without me.'

A few minutes later: 'We're pleased to inform you that the problem is not as bad as previously thought, hence we will arrive in London only half an hour late.'

'Thank God for that,' they all sighed. Again they phoned clients in unison: 'Brian, it's me again, I'm still going to be a little late but not as bad as first thought.'

Minutes later: 'Great news, folks, our technicians have completely eradicated the problem. We will now be arriving in London on time.'

Cue sixty executives redialling. Of course, what should have come over the tannoy now was 'These messages have been brought to you courtesy of British Telecom.'

Three hours later I arrived at Euston. I walked up the ramp and saw a man holding a Channel 4 sign with *Justin Brown* written on it. That must be me! I couldn't believe it. You mean I don't have to catch a bus? You mean I don't have to sing! I didn't know if custom meant you introduced yourself to your driver. I didn't care. He was just lucky not to get a bear hug. I loved him, my very own driver! I looked around, just checking to see if there were any other Justin Browns. No, must be for me.

'Justin Brown,' I said, shaking his hand for longer than necessary.

He looked uncomfortable. 'Yeah, well, come this way,' he said, getting the keys out of his pocket.

I skipped along behind him, like he was my dad taking me to the zoo for the first time.

'What level did you park on?' I asked, when after ten minutes of looking it became obvious we were lost.

'Five,' he said.

'Well, this is level three.'

'That'll be why then.'

Just like Dad, getting lost without admitting it. I wondered what kind of car we'd be riding to the studios in; probably a beat-up Nissan or an old Peugeot. We walked past rows and rows of cars in the concrete underbelly of Euston. Is it that one, I wondered. Is it *that* one? Then we hit the jackpot; he walked towards a brand new silver Mercedes. Fuck off. No, fuck off! I'm a busker, this was all too much. I opened the front door and eyed the plush black leather seats.

'Be better if you sat in the back,' he said.

'No worries.'

As we exited the car park he stopped at the booth where an old man sat with his arm out. I hope you've got three quid, mate, 'cos I'm skint I thought to myself. Once a busker, always a busker, I tell you. I rummaged around in my pocket thinking maybe, just maybe, I could cover him if it went completely pear shaped. Luckily he found some money.

'Bloody rip off,' he mumbled.

'Yeah,' I said, feeling guilty I hadn't chipped in. Maybe I could buy the first round?

'Channel 4 studios, driver.'

I could not help smiling sitting in the back of that Mercedes. I must have looked like a right idiot, grinning for no reason. Wow. I wanted to see someone that had closed the door in my face, someone from Reading or Canterbury or the village of New Zealand. Look at me now!

U2 came on as we drove through London over Waterloo Bridge. This is London, this is how rock stars felt.

Definitely a once in a lifetime, I lapped it up. George Benson was singing 'Give Me the Night' as we neared the TV studios. The leather seats melted into my back. I started playing with all the buttons. My reflection in the window showed a weary figure with a rooster head, bloodshot eyes and four-day-old socks.

Rock 'n' roll.

When I arrived at the TV studios a girl with a clipboard walked up to me and asked if I was hungry.

'No point trying to sell me lunch, I've been going without for eight weeks,' I should have said.

Then it clicked; not only had I scored a ride in a Merc, not only was I standing in the plush reception of the *Richard and Judy* show, not only was I about to go on nationwide TV, I was *also* being shouted lunch.

'A sandwich would be great,' I relented.

'Ham, chicken?'

'Ham and … salad would be great. I'll go and get it if you like?'

'No, I'll get it. White or brown bread?'

Holy shit, this was all too much.

She came back with a whopping sandwich while I tuned my guitar for the 453rd time.

'We need you for a sound check in fifteen minutes, Justin,' another girl told me.

'Have your sandwich and we'll give you a call.'

They were everywhere, spunky girls carrying clipboards and organising people.

'That's something else we need to talk about,' she said. 'Don't ever say "spunk" on TV. I've noticed you say it a lot, that and "take the piss". Never, ever, say either of those on this show.'

'It's in my mind now, I'll probably say it.'

'Don't,' she laughed.

Now if you're a Kiwi reading this, you'll think it's a bit harsh that I wasn't able to say someone's very good looking – spunky – on nationwide TV.

If you live in the UK, however, you'll realise this was probably for the best, because (and I didn't want to have to say this) spunky is mostly used in the context of 'There's spunk all over the bedsheets.'

Clipboard Girl then asked a question I never in my wildest dreams thought I'd hear on this trip. 'If Richard and Judy offered to fly you home to New Zealand tonight, would you go?'

She smiled. I stared into space. Bloody hell, a flight home, after two months of knocking on doors in the freezing cold and now someone was offering me a free flight home? I was floored, stunned, speechless, confused. Was this spunk taking the piss?

Just as the words, 'You'd better believe it,' were about to leave my lips, I remembered what my last week's plans in the UK entailed. For a start, collecting my bags from Liverpool, dropping the car off in Glasgow and most importantly, embarking on a long overdue, very large week in London with mates whom I hadn't given the time of day for the past eight weeks.

I owed them. Plus I needed sleep. Sure, a New Zealand summer was beckoning but I'd missed the best cricket anyway and barbecues and beer would still be there in a week's time. I couldn't just up and leave. I had people to thank and friendships to salvage.

'Because,' Clipboard Girl continued, 'we could do a thing at the airport sending you off.' Shit, what an offer.

'Has to be tonight?' I asked.

'Yes.'

'No, I don't think I can. I mean, I'd love to, it's a very kind offer but I can't.'

'No problem, it was just a thought,' she said.

Bugger.

It was a day of surprises and mild shocks. Within seconds of finishing my well-constructed and no doubt overpriced sandwich, I was escorted to the 'Green Room'. The only Green Rooms I'd seen the inside of were in dusty, smelly, beer-swilling pubs, not laden with funky furniture, bowls of fruit, beanbags and 28-inch TVs.

'The showers are this way,' Clipboard Girl said, maybe picking up on the fact that I smelt like a woolshed. Four-day-old socks combined with BO meant I really did smell. There was no point having a shower either; I had no clothes to change into. I had no clean clothes anywhere in the country. What you see is what you get, I'm afraid. Rock 'n' roll, a true busker doing it all for art.

'I'd prefer he didn't do it for art and just had a bloody shower,' I could hear Mum say.

On the way back to the Green Room we walked past two doors with *Enrique Iglesias* and *Enrique Iglesias's band* written on them.

'Is Enrique Iglesias on the show tonight?' I asked, expecting, 'Don't be stupid, he's on *Parkinson*.'

'Yeah, he'll be singing a few songs,' she smiled.

Bet he'll have clothes to change into, bastard.

The Green Room became my home for the afternoon. It was weird, it felt like your first day at school and you were only allowed in the library. I wanted to saunter down the corridors and play cricket with people, but I didn't know anyone. There was nothing on TV and I'd already played various games with fruit so I decided to call all the people I knew in London and say, 'Guess where I'm sitting.'

Another guest walked in just as I hung up from my last call. He was wearing a tracksuit but carrying a suit in a plastic bag. I was jealous. I wanted a suit. I wanted a shower. I wanted a band.

I wondered what tomorrow would be like if I really did go on *Richard & Judy* tonight. I guess the only difference would be having one of those *As Seen on TV* stickers on the guitar.

Another girl came in and informed me that a film crew was going to take me out on the streets of Kensington. The plan was to get some footage of me busking the streets near the studio. There was still four hours to go before the show was to start. I was knackered already. Two cameramen, another research girl and a director came door knocking with me, making it by far the easiest door-to-door busking I had ever done. I mean, the research girl even walked up to the door for me. Time after time she came back rejected, hurt and terrified.

'They're all saying no,' she grumbled.

'Tell me about it! It's crap, it's inhumane, welcome to the world of door-to-door busking!'

We visited Luke the school kid, Allan who was having an afternoon nap and Elizabeth, a 70-year-old fox who was in the middle of doing her accounts. All, I repeat, *all* let us in.

'Trust me, guys, this is not a true reflection of what it's like, not in London,' I told the group.

I sang 'Harry Potter' for what would be, I figured, about the one-thousandth time, and we headed back to the studio.

The *Richard & Judy* interview

'HELLO, AND THANKS for joining us, we're live for the next hour. Tonight a case of a man who got two young girls to expose themselves in front of him and despite making a full confession to the police, the law can't touch him. The girl's mother is here tonight and she is incandescent.'

Judy looked at camera one: 'He *was* Julio's little lad, now he's a pop god in his own right. Enrique Iglesias is here tonight.'

I was waiting in the wings, sweating and, fair to say, more

than a little terrified. I also had no idea what 'incandescent' meant. Richard then looked straight down the barrel of camera two: 'And the staggering fact that more British veterans in the Falklands have now taken their own lives than were killed by the Argentinians twenty years ago. What on earth is going on?'

Bloody hell. Men getting young girls to expose themselves, Falklands veterans and Julio's offspring. Was I on the right show?

'Now, if you're a man or woman of your word and you make a stupid bet, you have to pay up. Well, Justin Brown lost his bet, otherwise he wouldn't be sitting here now. He'd be sitting in the sun in New Zealand. You idiot.'

Richard looked at me on the couch. This was the first time I'd met them.

'I'm a complete idiot,' I said. 'Everyone is back home having barbecues and beer and I'm freezing my nads off door-to-door busking around the UK.'

I was dying to say 'spunk' or 'take the piss'. I could see Clipboard Girl from where I was sitting. Why did that flight have to be *tonight*?

'Tell us about the bet,' Richard said.

I was so nervous I missed out half the things I wanted to say.

'So you promptly got on a plane?' Judy said. 'I mean, I wouldn't have done. I would have just said I didn't mean it.'

'But I'm a man of my word, Judy. You have to do these things; he would have tracked me down.'

'His name's Mark, isn't it?' Richard asked.

'It is.'

'Well, he's on the line at the moment from Sydney.'

Bloody hell, what a glory seeker. What an actor, any whiff

of being on TV and he's there with bells on. I do all the hard work and he swans in at the end.

'Hi, Mark,' Richard said.

'Gidday, how ya doin'?'

'Mark, would you have kept your side of the bargain if you'd lost this bet?' Richard asked.

'Look, I know Justin would have made me. I can assure you it would have been an outside court.'

'You lot down there are nutters, you know that?' Richard said. 'You're not like the blokes here. You're mad.'

'I don't think Mark would have done it, he wouldn't have streaked at Wimbledon,' I said.

'Come on, course I would have!' he whined.

'Well, you might have streaked at Wimbledon because it's reasonably warm at Wimbledon,' Judy quite rightly pointed out, 'because it's summer, but I don't think you would have done what he's done.'

You go, Judy, we'll keep you on.

'Well, listen, New Zealand's got a cricket match tomorrow. Don't suppose you guys want to go double or quits?' Richard asked.

'All right, now we're talking!' I said.

I felt very confident about this seeing as New Zealand had beaten Australia three times in a row. This *was* the summer of cricket and I was missing it.

'What's your stake, Mark, what are you putting up for this?' Richard asked the man calling from Oz.

'Well, I was kinda thinking if Australia win, Justin has to wear a Wallaby jersey for a month, day and night.'

Richard and Judy laughed.

'That's ridiculous, no one does that!' I said.

'Do you accept it?' Richard asked me.

'I accept.'

'And I'll wear the All Black jersey for a month if New Zealand win,' Mark said.

Judy was laughing, quite uncontrollably. Richard had to ask what was going on.

'Sorry,' she gasped. 'I just got confused. I was just wondering why wallabies would wear jerseys at all!'

Richard laughed. Judy had seriously thought we meant thirty marsupials were feeding scrums, intercepting lineouts and kicking penalties.

'OK, thanks, Mark,' she said when she'd regained her composure. 'And now thanks to you he has to get home. And you've got how much money?'

'I've got to get to four hundred and ninety-seven pounds. I have four hundred and twenty-three pounds, a port bottle, a banana skin, a kiwi fruit, a car, Christmas mince pies, some custard, a plastic spoon, a Frank the Painter pen and a can of Red Bull.'

'And you've been really honest about this?' Richard asked.

'I have. I've been here since the fourth of December.'

'And you've done no other work in between? You've done it purely through busking?'

'Yes, sir.'

'Well, give us a busk then. Maybe you're not as embarrassing as you think you are. What's your best number?'

'This is a little song I do called "Grow up Harry Potter".'

'Go on then, just a couple of lines if you don't mind.'

I dropped my pick and quickly realised my guitar was out of tune. Was it cold in this studio? I had a terrible feeling I was going to forget the lyrics on nationwide TV. I sang the song.

'Ah, you're very good. So you belong to the Rex Harrison school of singing, sort of speak your way through songs?'

I smiled, nodding, thinking who the hell is Rex Harrison?

'Well, listen, we've got your mum on the line now because you missed Christmas. Good morning, Mrs Brown.'

'Good morning,' Mum said.

This was starting to feel like *This is Your Life.*

'Does all this make you feel affectionate and Mum-like?' Judy asked Mum.

'Oh dear, I still think he's a bit mad.'

This was too much, first Mark squawking out of the speakers, now my own mother.

'You thought he was joking, didn't you?' Richard asked Mum. 'When he told you he was doing this, you really thought he was winding you up, didn't you?'

'It wasn't until he went shopping for a duffel coat in a second-hand shop that we realised he was serious.'

Richard continued to take the piss out of how we said 'yes' and 'bet'.

'Look, you're seventy-four pounds short,' he said. 'If you made that money, when would you go home, tonight, tomorrow, next week?'

'Yep, I'd head off in the next week or so.'

'What Judy and I have decided to do is for you to go out and busk for us now –'

'It's cold,' I interrupted.

'Put a jumper on!' Judy said. 'Don't go out like that!'

'If you go and busk now,' Richard continued. 'Whatever you raise in the next half hour we will match.'

'You guys are coming with me, yeah?'

'No, we have to *stay* and do the show,' Judy said. 'But the deal is, we will be waiting and we will match whatever you make. If you make thirty pounds we will double it.'

'Rock 'n' roll,' I said.

'If you wouldn't mind leaving the set. You haven't got long.'

I left the set and watched the TV monitor in the corner of the room where Judy said, 'He's great. I bet his mother's going to mother him unbearably.'

Definitely keeping you on, Judy.

Enrique Iglesias then waltzed onto the set. I was proud to see someone in the world with bigger eyebrows than me. Mind you, he smelt good. And I bet those clothes were clean. I envied anyone with clean clothes.

Richard then asked questions about his latest video featuring Anna Kournikova.

'I heard,' he said, 'that the reason you didn't kiss Anna Kournikova in the video was because you had an outbreak of herpes?'

'Me, herpes? No, I'd be mad if I *didn't* want to kiss her, but I don't have herpes. I don't know where you get these stories.'

'That's just what we read, and we heard that you wanted to clear it up,' said Richard.

Enrique walked past me after the interview, probably back to the Green Room while Richard and Judy cut to a recorded shot of me on the streets of Kensington.

'And he's out there giving it all he's got, our New Zealand busker who lost the stupid bet that meant that he had to come to mid-winter Britain from hot summer New Zealand and earn his passage back by singing door to door.'

'He's a charmer,' said Judy.

You go, Judy, hope you've got the chequebook.

Another clipboard girl, a brunette, escorted me to the back of the set where she, along with three other girls, whispered and started counting coins. Their plan was simply to hand me £37 so that Richard and Judy could then match it with theirs. We were now right in the bowels of the studio, perched in-between two makeshift doorways and surrounded by unfinished walls and concrete. Funny how the main set can look like your parent's living room and behind the scenes can look like a timber yard.

I'd been told it was imperative to keep the noise down as 'sound travels in a TV studio'. I was too nervous to worry about talking. Meanwhile, the girls were still counting coins. I was just trying not to think about how noisy it would be if I dropped thirty-odd coins on a concrete floor backstage.

A look of panic descended on the brunette's face. She had obviously heard something through her earpiece. 'Quick, just give him the money. We're about to go live!'

She grabbed my hand, emptied the plastic bag of coins and ... I dropped them. Every single, last one of them. Thirty-seven gold coins clinked and clanked and rolled their way around the acoustically sound concrete floor. A brilliant cacophony of glorious metal wound its way under tables, around legs and into crevices.

Brown, you're an idiot.

'Right, back with us now, we hope, is busking Justin Brown. At the start of the show he was seventy-four pounds short and we promised to match anything that he could scrape up before six o'clock.

'So, how much did you make?' Judy asked me as I settled on the couch.

'I've got thirty-seven pounds in my sky rocket.' Well, I did have until I dropped half of it backstage. Didn't you hear the clatter?

'Honestly? Thirty-seven pounds?'

'Yep.'

'I think there's something terribly embarrassing about someone busking right in front of your face. At least if you're on the street you can walk past,' Judy said.

'Well, we said we'd match every pound you got. So you've got thirty-seven pounds?'

'Yep.'

'Well, we'll call it forty pounds. Can you see there are two twenties in there?' Richard asked, showing me an envelope with two fresh notes in it.

'That's New Zealand dollars, isn't it?' I asked, winding him up.

'No, that's pounds sterling, my dear man. There's also your open return,' he said, slapping another envelope in my hand, 'back to New Zealand!'

'Really? Wow!'

This was a complete surprise. I was floored, caught off guard big time, speechless. So it *didn't* have to be tonight? My God, the Clipboard Girls must have had a meeting and decided to give me the flight anyway. Shit, maybe they thought I *was* leaving tonight?

'So, when are you going back?' Richard asked.

'Well, when's it for?'

'It's open, anytime you like,' they said in unison.

'Really? Fantastic! Thank you very much.'

This was all too much. Who needs a shower and clean clothes when you've got £500 and a ticket home?

'So, when are you going back is the question!' Richard repeated.

'Um, next week. Yeah, next week. Why not?' I sat back on the comfy couch, unable to think.

Judy told me: 'You're very good at what you do. You've got a job in radio, haven't you?'

'I have, back in New Zealand.'

'Have we just been conned?' Richard asked.

'I think, probably!' Judy said.

I needed a lie down. I was buzzing yet exhausted. Nationwide TV and a return ticket had taken the fizz out of me. I still needed deodorant. I still needed clean socks.

Everyone else still smelt nice. I still smelt like a woolshed. At the end of the show there was an immense sense of relief, all the spunks with clipboards, who were now enjoying a glass of wine, looked like they'd just passed an exam. We went back to the Green Room and ate asparagus and ham hors d'oeuvres and a lovely lady kept filling my glass with dry white wine. I skulled three in no time at all. I was on cloud nine.

We crowded around the food and I chatted to Richard and Judy, who told me I was great. Top people.

Just as I was settling in for the night a girl asked, 'Justin, what time would you like your car to pick you up?'

I looked at my watch: six o' clock. I looked at the table of food. I looked at the bottle of wine.

''Bout eight, is that all right?'

'Well, most of us are gone by about seven. We don't stay that long.'

'Oh, not eight then, how 'bout half an hour?'

I hugged everyone goodbye.

Outside, the silver Mercs were all lined up. A big black man shook my hand.

'Have a good night, sir,' he said in a booming voice, which if he wasn't opening doors for a living, could easily have got him a voiceover gig at CNN. 'Here's your car. Let me put your bag in the boot.'

The gates were unlocked, security guards swarmed and we drove off.

Madonna sang 'Get into the Groove' and Jennifer Lopez 'If You Want My Love' as we drove over Waterloo Bridge. London was lit up. I was half pissed. What a turnaround; kicked out of the Savoy Hotel eight weeks ago, now riding around in the back of a Mercedes. What a moment, I wanted to bottle it.

'Here you go, sir,' the driver said, pulling into Euston

Railway Station.

'Bugger, over so soon? Can't we go around the block again? I was just starting to enjoy myself.'

On the way back to Liverpool I got talking to some lads on the train. One guy was from Preston and the other from Greece. Preston Boy talked about his kids while Greek Boy talked about having someone waiting for him back home. He also complained how expensive Britain was. I said I could relate to that, but not now, we were celebrating my airline ticket and £80 made in record time. For three hours we drank and laughed. I bought the beers. I splashed out. More beers, sure, I didn't care. I had a flight home and just over £500. I was a happy man. Every time the train passed residential areas, relief washed over me.

Two months of knocking on doors was over.

MARIA WAS CLEANING the bar when I arrived back at the hotel.

'Were you on *Richard & Judy*?' she asked, when I flopped on the nearest barstool.

'Sure was.'

'Oh, no, I missed it! I had to pop out for the afternoon.'

'I've got the video,' I said.

'Really? Let's watch it!'

This was like coming home. Maria poured me a gin. She then started going on about how many people in Liverpool were dying of lung cancer. 'Highest in Europe,' she reckoned, as she lit another cigarette. She then ran off to get the video remote. Bless her. When she returned I explained my washing dilemma.

'You tell your mum that the lady from Liverpool had no idea you had four-day-old socks on. I would have washed them for you.'

'Oh love, you're very natural,' she puffed when she saw me blabber my way through the interview.

She had now poured me three gin and tonics. I was absolutely knackered. Tonight would be my best sleep in eight weeks.

'You're all right, love,' Maria said when I offered to pay for the drinks. 'It's on the house.'

'Thanks, Maria. Goodnight.'

'Hey, where's the envelope they gave you?' she said as I picked up my guitar to leave.

'In my guitar case,' I said.

'When's the flight for?'

'Anytime, they said.'

'And you haven't opened it yet!'

'No, haven't had a chance.'

'Well, come on, open it! Let's have a look.'

Maria's excitement was contagious. She wanted to join me in this final moment. After eight weeks of traversing this eccentric and strangely beautiful country, I had achieved my goal of making £497 purely from door-to-door busking. Now I could look forward to a flight home.

Home, the word sounded good. With that I opened the envelope:

PASSENGER TICKET AND BAGGAGE CHECK
FINNAIR LTD   21 DECEMBER 2001

FROM LONDON TO KITTILA

BARLEY/GRAHAM

I looked at Maria.

She looked at me.

Together we said, 'Who the fuck is Graham Barley?'

★

OTHER TRAVEL BOOKS FROM SUMMERSDALE

Off The Rails
Moscow to Beijing on Recumbent Bikes
Tim Cope, Chris Hatherly

The Worst Journey In The Midlands
One Man, His Boat and the Weather
Sam Llewellyn

The Backpacker
John Harris

Blue Road
Windy Baboulene

Full catalogue and **free sample chapters**
available at: www.summersdale.com

OTHER TRAVEL BOOKS FROM SUMMERSDALE

Don't Lean Out Of The Window!
A European Misadventure
Stewart Ferris, Paul Bassett

The Gringo Trail
Mark Mann

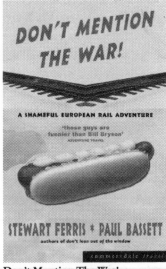

Don't Mention The War!
A shameful European rail adventure
Stewart Ferris, Paul Bassett

The Hotel on the Roof of the World
Five Years in Tibet
Alec le Sueur

Full catalogue and **free sample chapters**
available at: www.summersdale.com